MAKER
GROW A GARDEN!
COMICS

GROW A GARDEN!

Alexis Frederick-Frost

:01

First Second
New York

Gardening isn't without some risks. Don't let sunburn, bugbites, or other injuries spoil your fun.

You can get sunburned even if it's overcast, so apply sunscreen with SPF 15 or higher before going outside. A hat with a wide brim can help keep the sun off your face and neck.

Protect yourself from bugbites by using bug repellent.

Invest in a good pair of gardening gloves to help avoid skin irritation, cuts, and blisters! Wash your hands after gardening whether you wear gloves or not. Dirt can be pretty dirty!

When using garden tools, make sure to point them away from other people and keep the digging ends close to the ground.

Always be cautious when using power tools! Ask for help from an adult when using a hand drill or other devices. Wear safety goggles and sturdy closed-toe shoes when operating power tools.

Lift heavy objects (like bags of soil) with a two-stage lift:

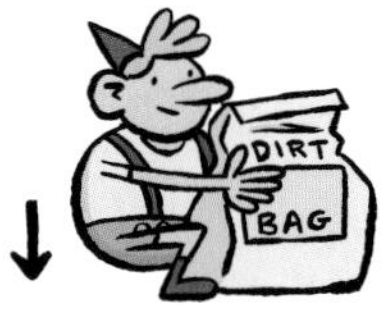
DIRT
BAG

1) Bend your knees and grab the heavy object, holding it close to your body.

2) Keep your back straight and push up with your legs.

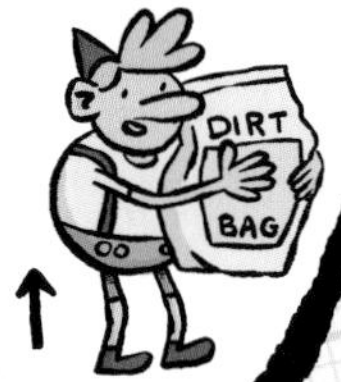
DIRT
BAG

If the object is too heavy, see if someone else can help you carry it. Use a wheelbarrow to move heavy loads from place to place.

If you plan on spending most of the day outside in hot weather, make sure you stay hydrated. Drink plenty of water and avoid sugary beverages.

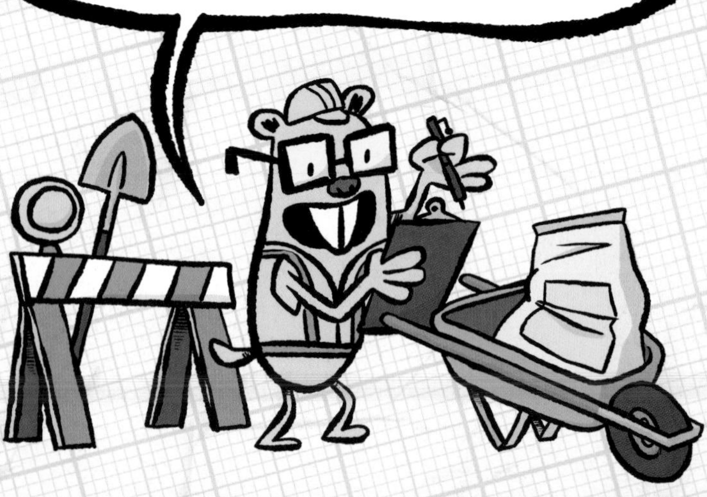

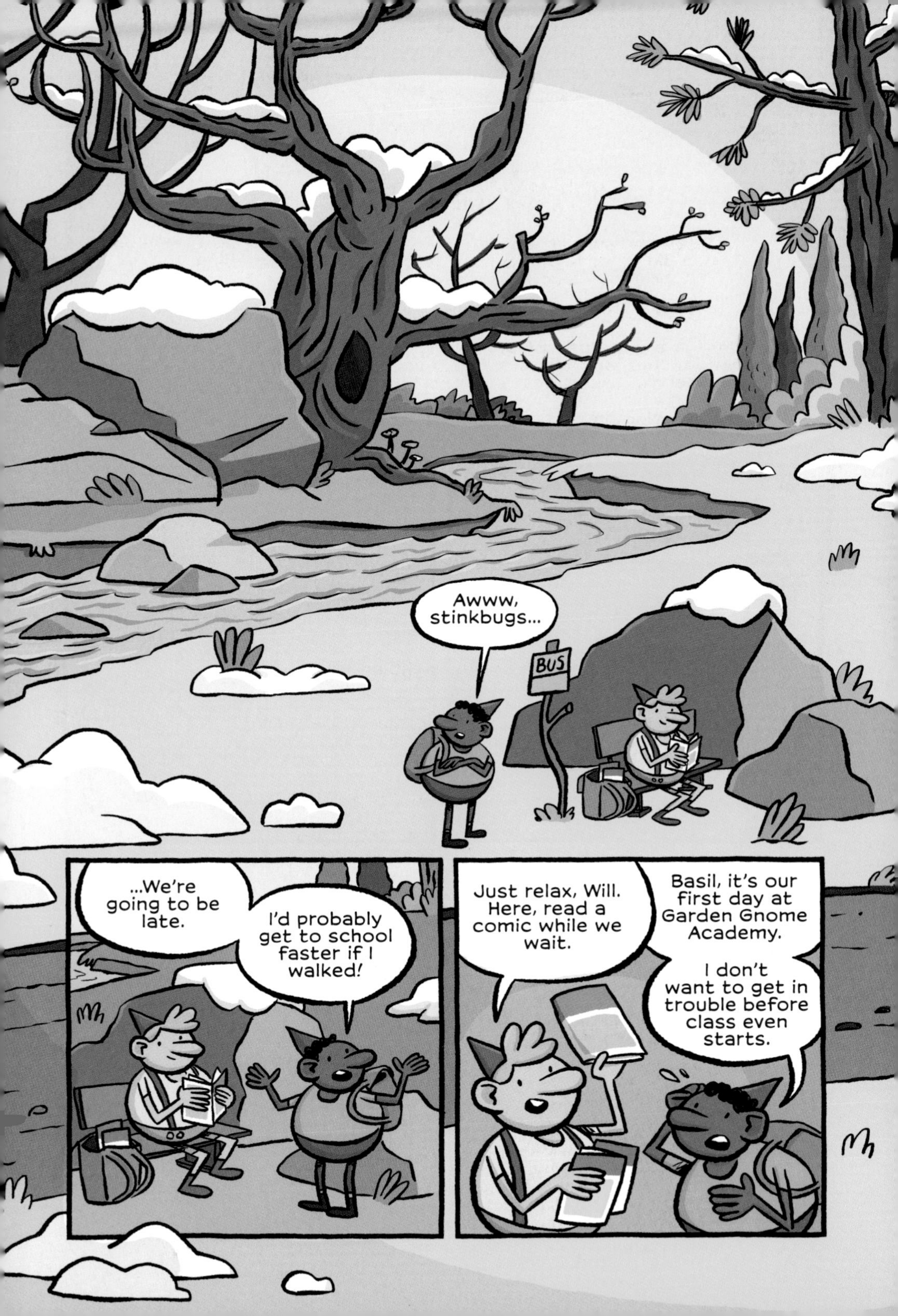
Awww, stinkbugs...
BUS
...We're going to be late.
I'd probably get to school faster if I walked!
Just relax, Will. Here, read a comic while we wait.
Basil, it's our first day at Garden Gnome Academy.
I don't want to get in trouble before class even starts.

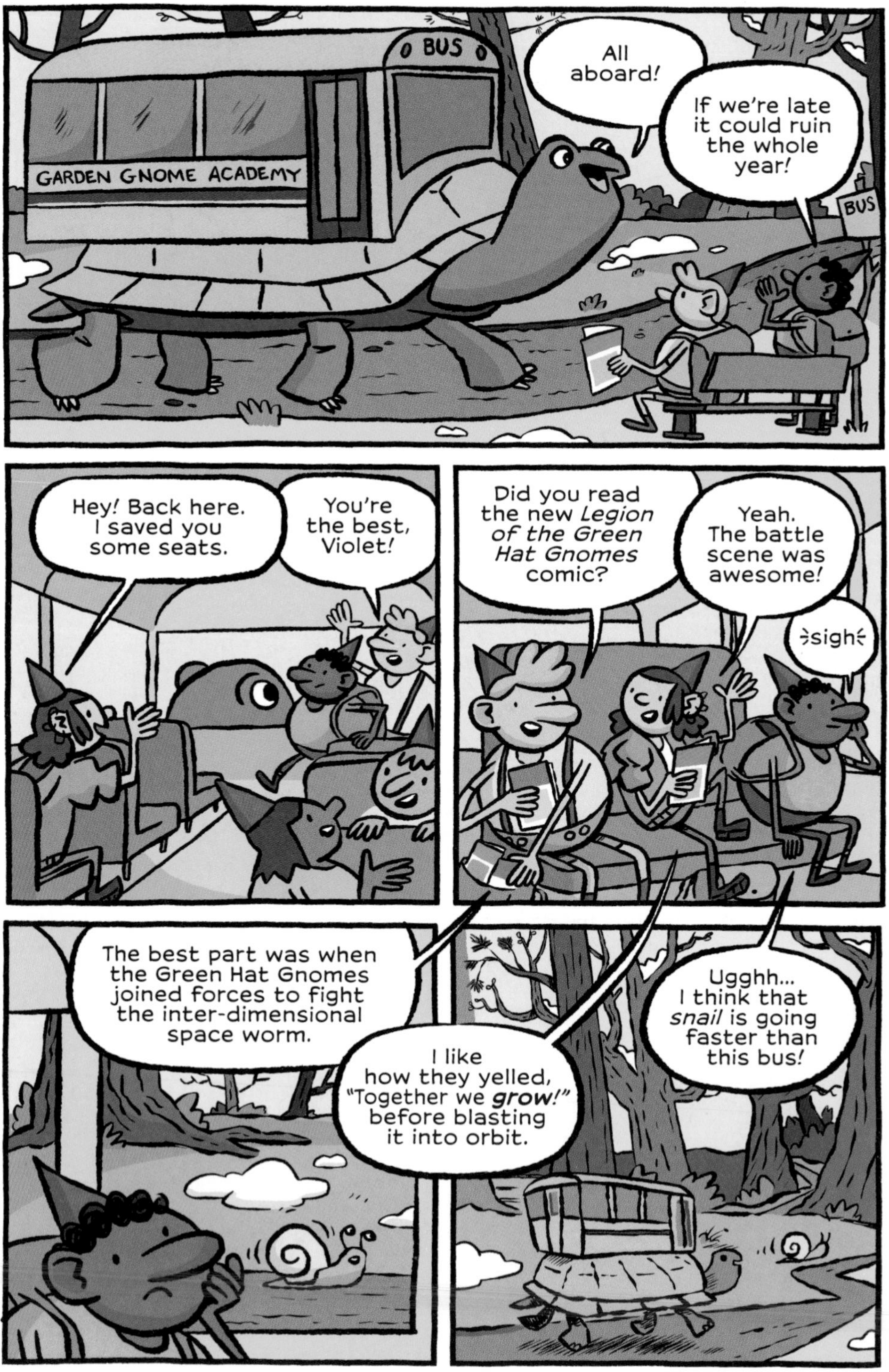
BUS
GARDEN GNOME ACADEMY
All aboard!
If we're late it could ruin the whole year!
BUS
Hey! Back here. I saved you some seats.
You're the best, Violet!
Did you read the new *Legion of the Green Hat Gnomes* comic?
Yeah. The battle scene was awesome!
sigh
The best part was when the Green Hat Gnomes joined forces to fight the inter-dimensional space worm.
I like how they yelled, "Together we ***grow!***" before blasting it into orbit.
Ugghh... I think that *snail* is going faster than this bus!

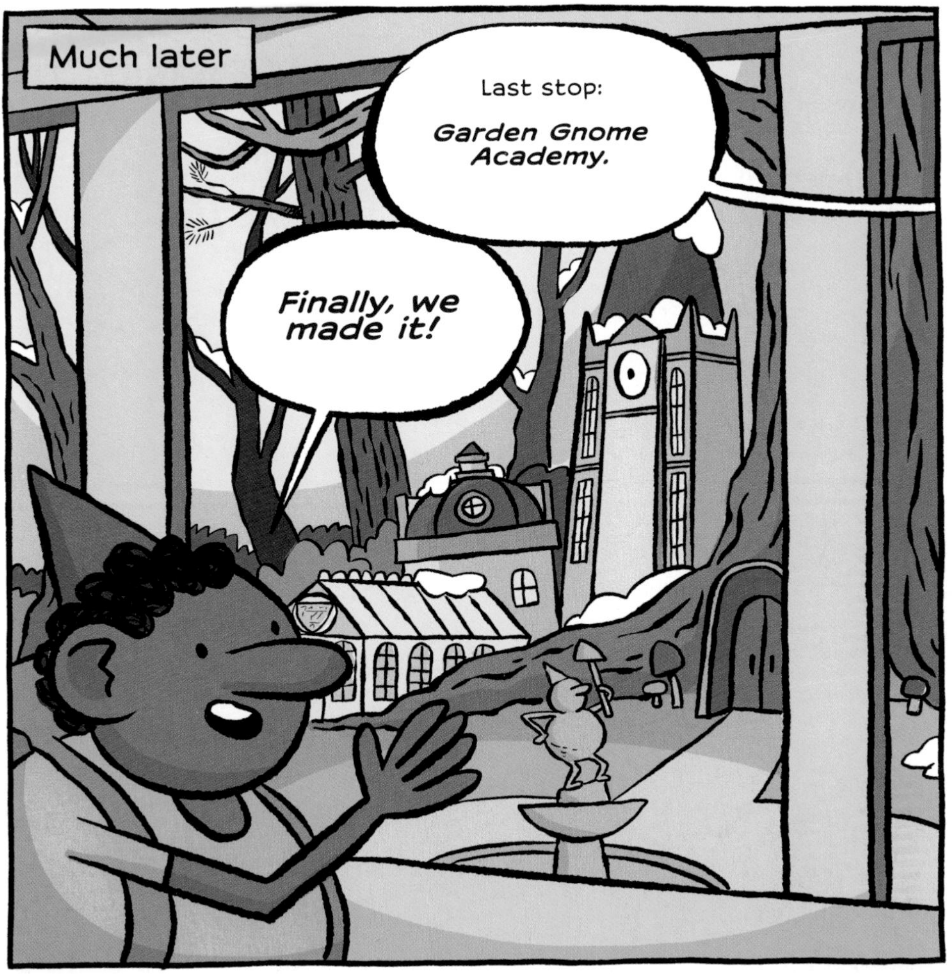
Much later
Last stop:
Garden Gnome Academy.
Finally, we made it!

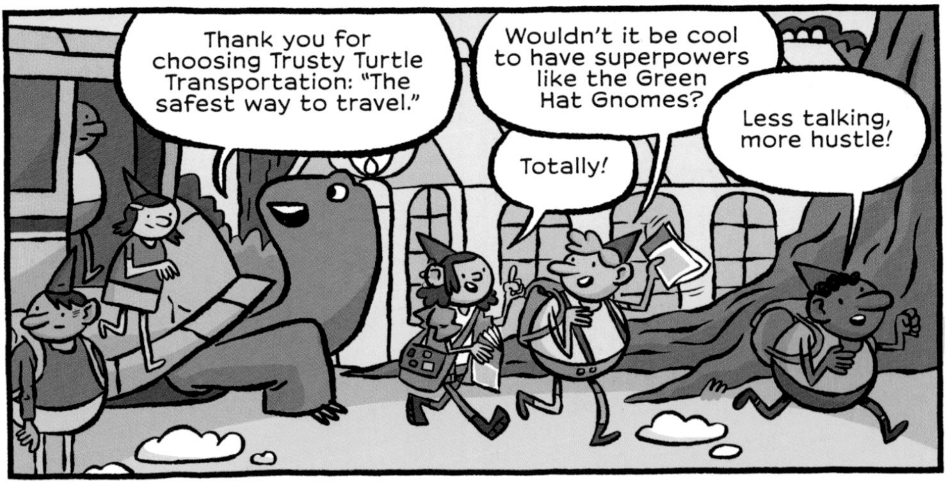
Thank you for choosing Trusty Turtle Transportation: "The safest way to travel."
Wouldn't it be cool to have superpowers like the Green Hat Gnomes?
Totally!
Less talking, more hustle!

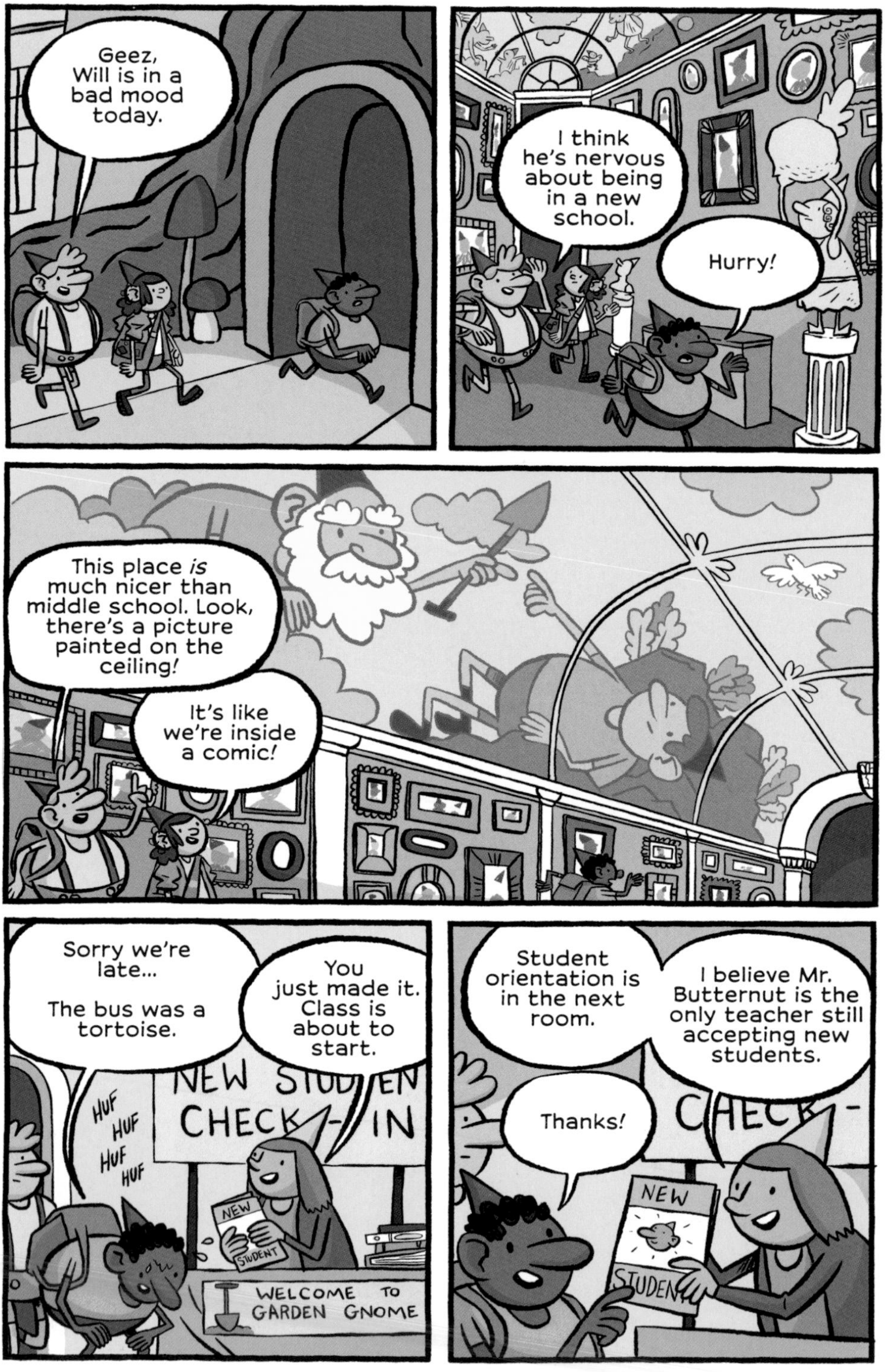
Geez, Will is in a bad mood today.
I think he's nervous about being in a new school.
Hurry!
This place *is* much nicer than middle school. Look, there's a picture painted on the ceiling!
It's like we're inside a comic!
Sorry we're late... The bus was a tortoise.
HUF HUF HUF HUF
You just made it. Class is about to start.
NEW STUDEN
CHECK-IN
NEW
STUDENT
WELCOME TO GARDEN GNOME
Student orientation is in the next room.
I believe Mr. Butternut is the only teacher still accepting new students.
CHECK-
Thanks!
NEW
STUDEN

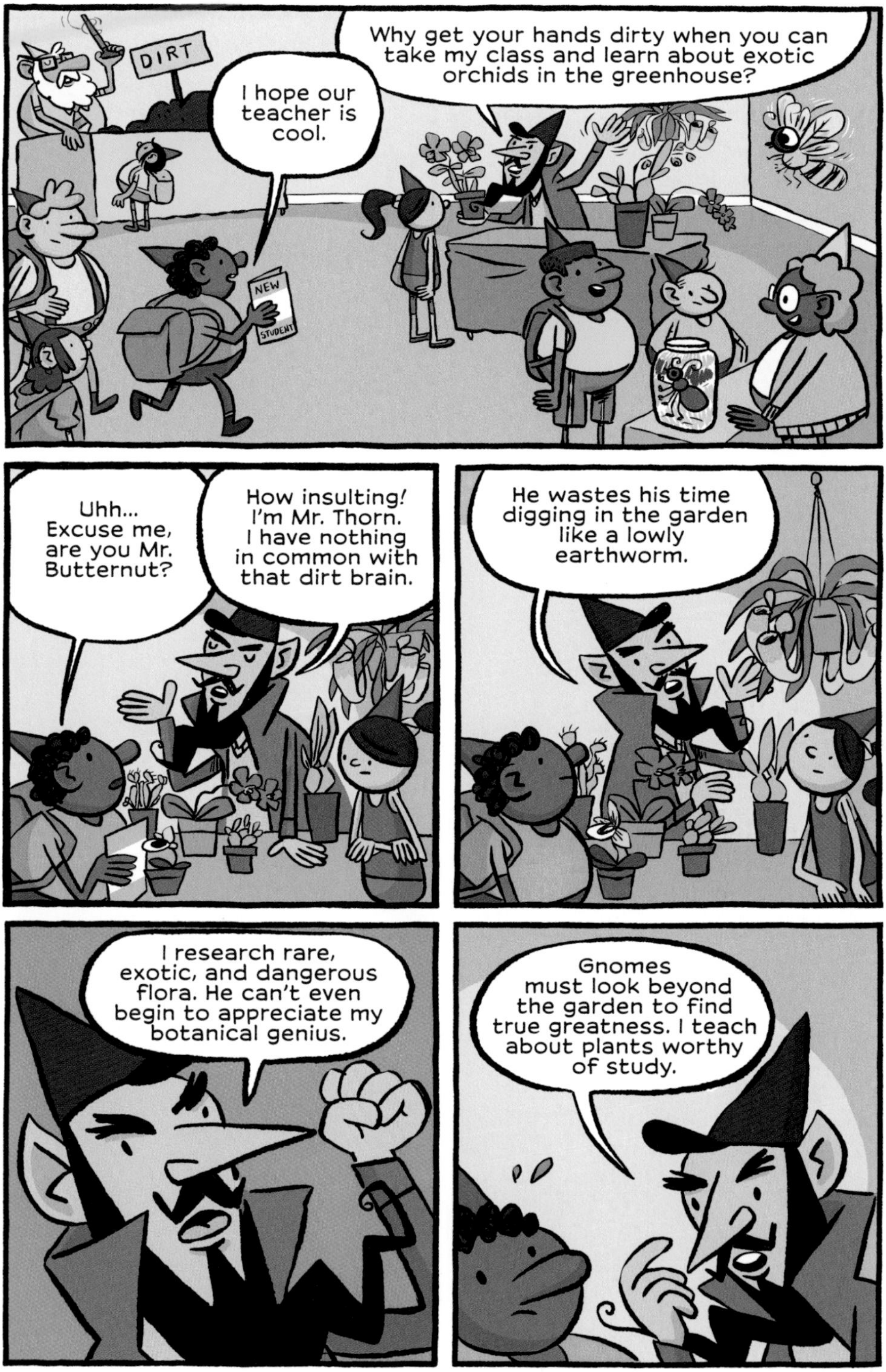
DIRT
I hope our teacher is cool.
Why get your hands dirty when you can take my class and learn about exotic orchids in the greenhouse?
NEW STUDENT
Uhh... Excuse me, are you Mr. Butternut?
How insulting! I'm Mr. Thorn. I have nothing in common with that dirt brain.
He wastes his time digging in the garden like a lowly earthworm.
I research rare, exotic, and dangerous flora. He can't even begin to appreciate my botanical genius.
Gnomes must look beyond the garden to find true greatness. I teach about plants worthy of study.

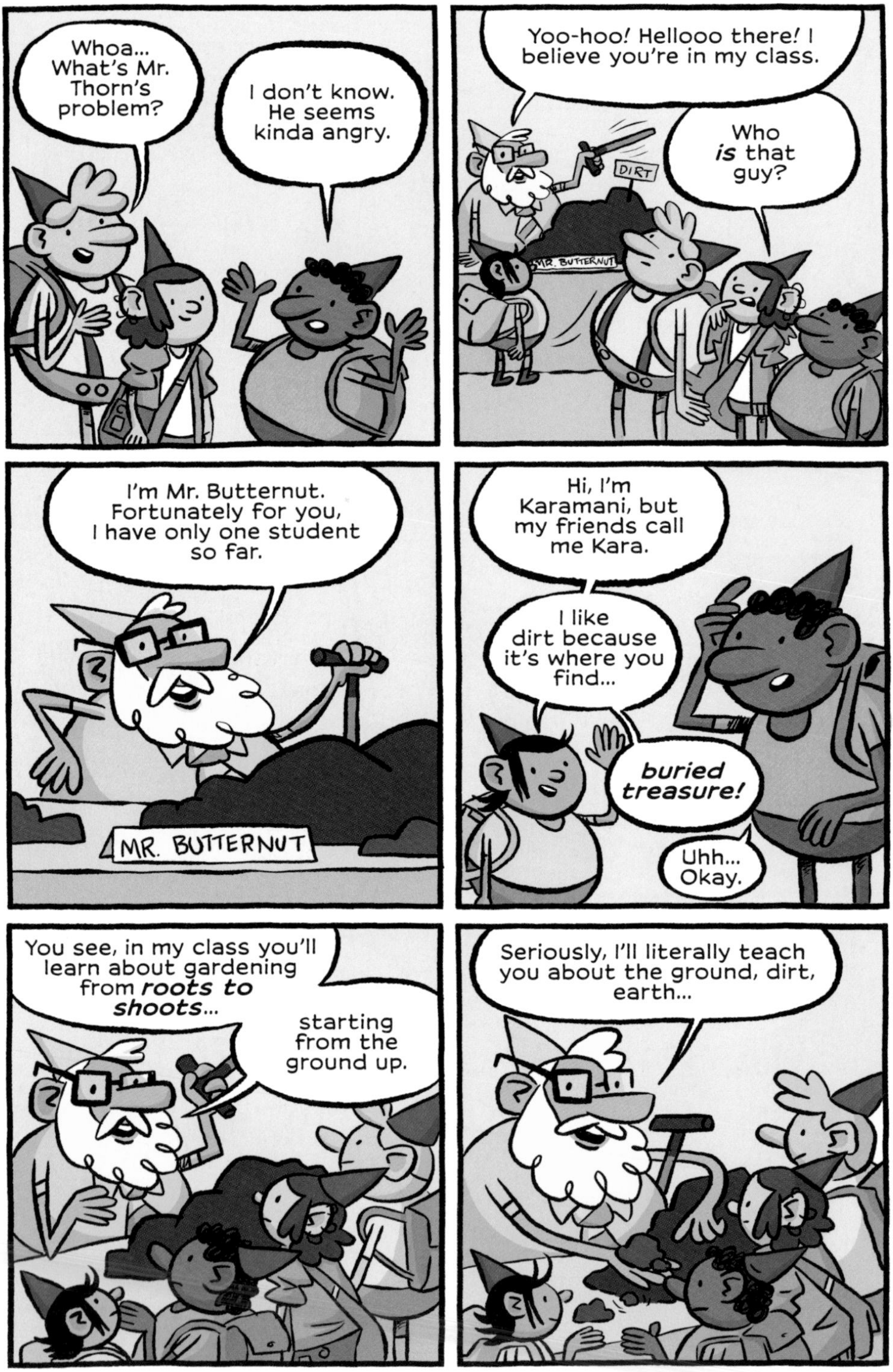
Whoa... What's Mr. Thorn's problem?
I don't know. He seems kinda angry.
Yoo-hoo! Hellooo there! I believe you're in my class.
DIRT
Who *is* that guy?
MR. BUTTERNUT
I'm Mr. Butternut. Fortunately for you, I have only one student so far.
MR. BUTTERNUT
Hi, I'm Karamani, but my friends call me Kara.
I like dirt because it's where you find...
buried treasure!
Uhh... Okay.
You see, in my class you'll learn about gardening from ***roots to shoots***...
starting from the ground up.
Seriously, I'll literally teach you about the ground, dirt, earth...

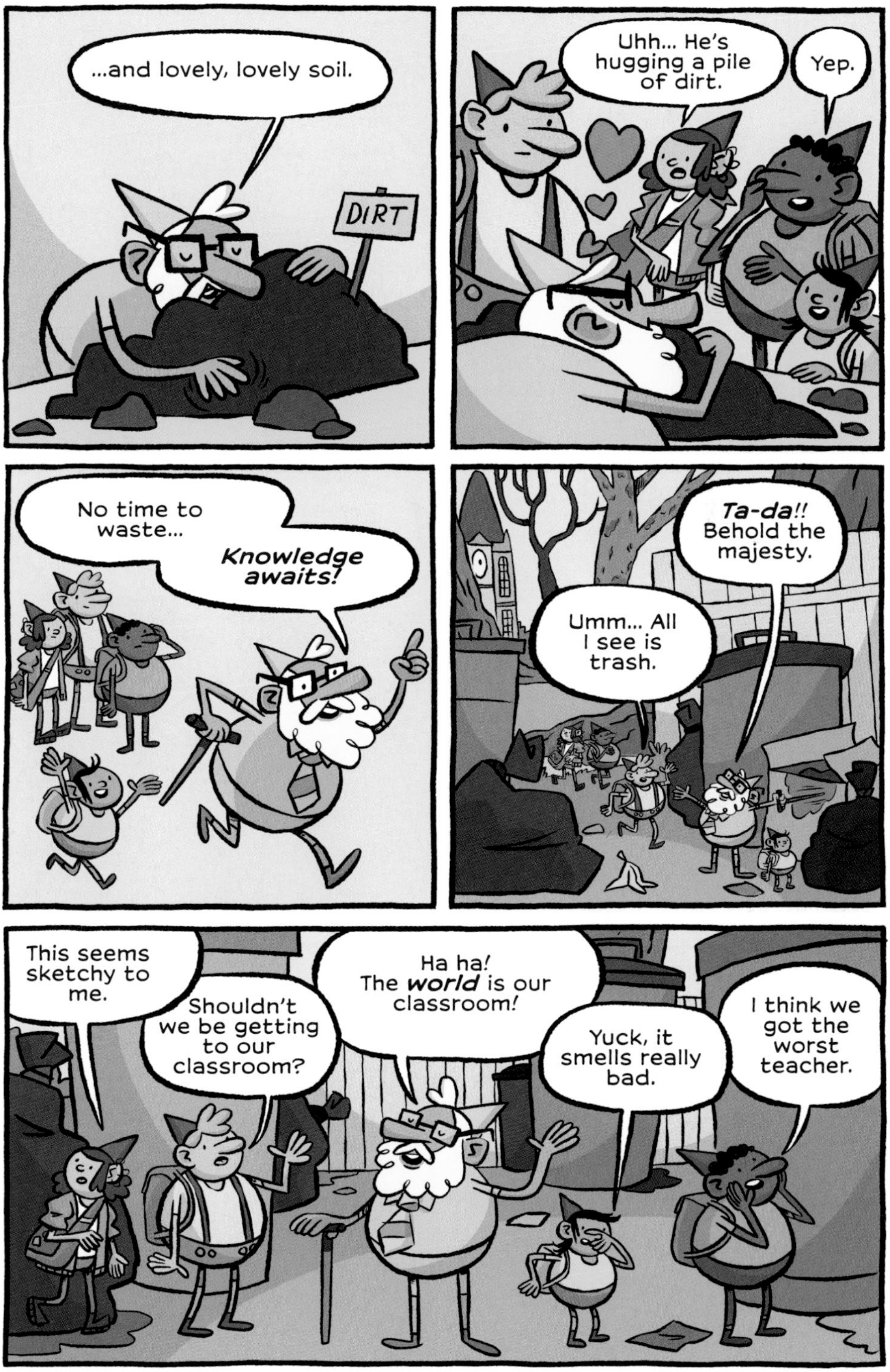
...and lovely, lovely soil.
DIRT
Uhh... He's hugging a pile of dirt.
Yep.
No time to waste...
Knowledge awaits!
Ta-da!! Behold the majesty.
Umm... All I see is trash.
This seems sketchy to me.
Shouldn't we be getting to our classroom?
Ha ha! The *world* is our classroom!
Yuck, it smells really bad.
I think we got the worst teacher.

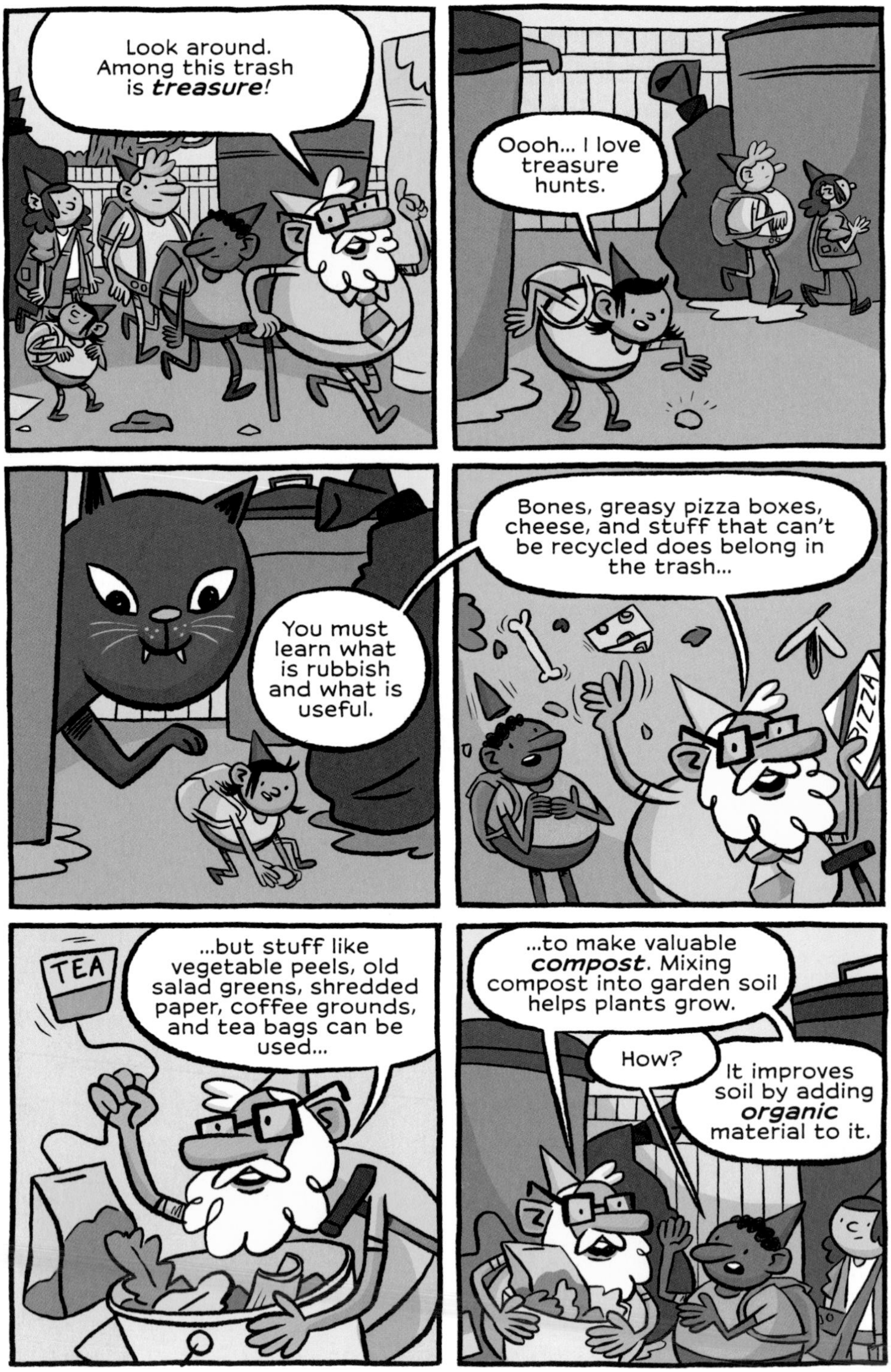
Look around. Among this trash is ***treasure***!
Oooh... I love treasure hunts.
You must learn what is rubbish and what is useful.
Bones, greasy pizza boxes, cheese, and stuff that can't be recycled does belong in the trash...
PIZZA
TEA
...but stuff like vegetable peels, old salad greens, shredded paper, coffee grounds, and tea bags can be used...
...to make valuable ***compost***. Mixing compost into garden soil helps plants grow.
How?
It improves soil by adding ***organic*** material to it.

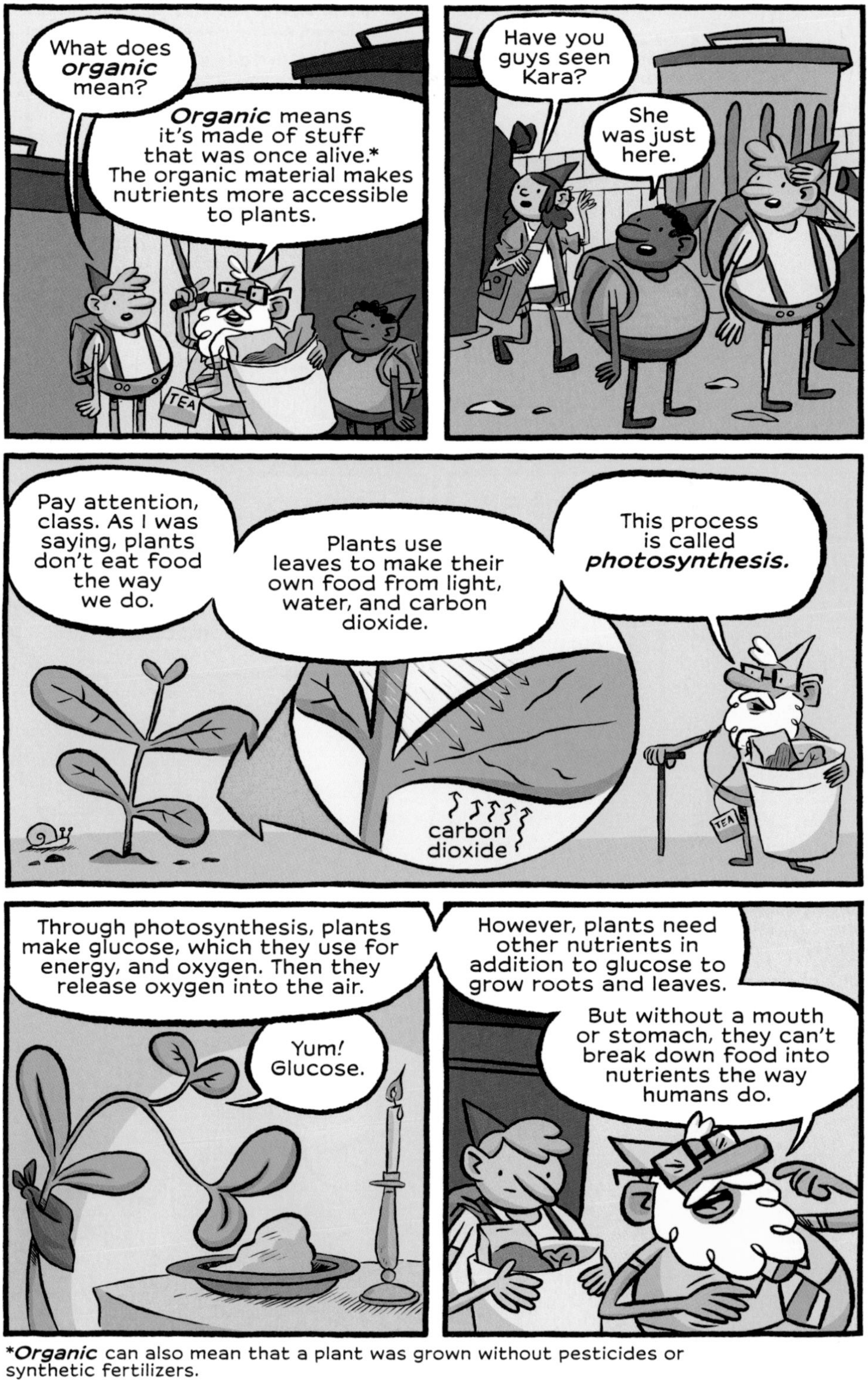
What does *organic* mean?
Organic means it's made of stuff that was once alive.* The organic material makes nutrients more accessible to plants.
TEA
Have you guys seen Kara?
She was just here.
Pay attention, class. As I was saying, plants don't eat food the way we do.
Plants use leaves to make their own food from light, water, and carbon dioxide.
This process is called ***photosynthesis.***
carbon dioxide
TEA
Through photosynthesis, plants make glucose, which they use for energy, and oxygen. Then they release oxygen into the air.
Yum! Glucose.
However, plants need other nutrients in addition to glucose to grow roots and leaves.
But without a mouth or stomach, they can't break down food into nutrients the way humans do.

****Organic*** can also mean that a plant was grown without pesticides or synthetic fertilizers.

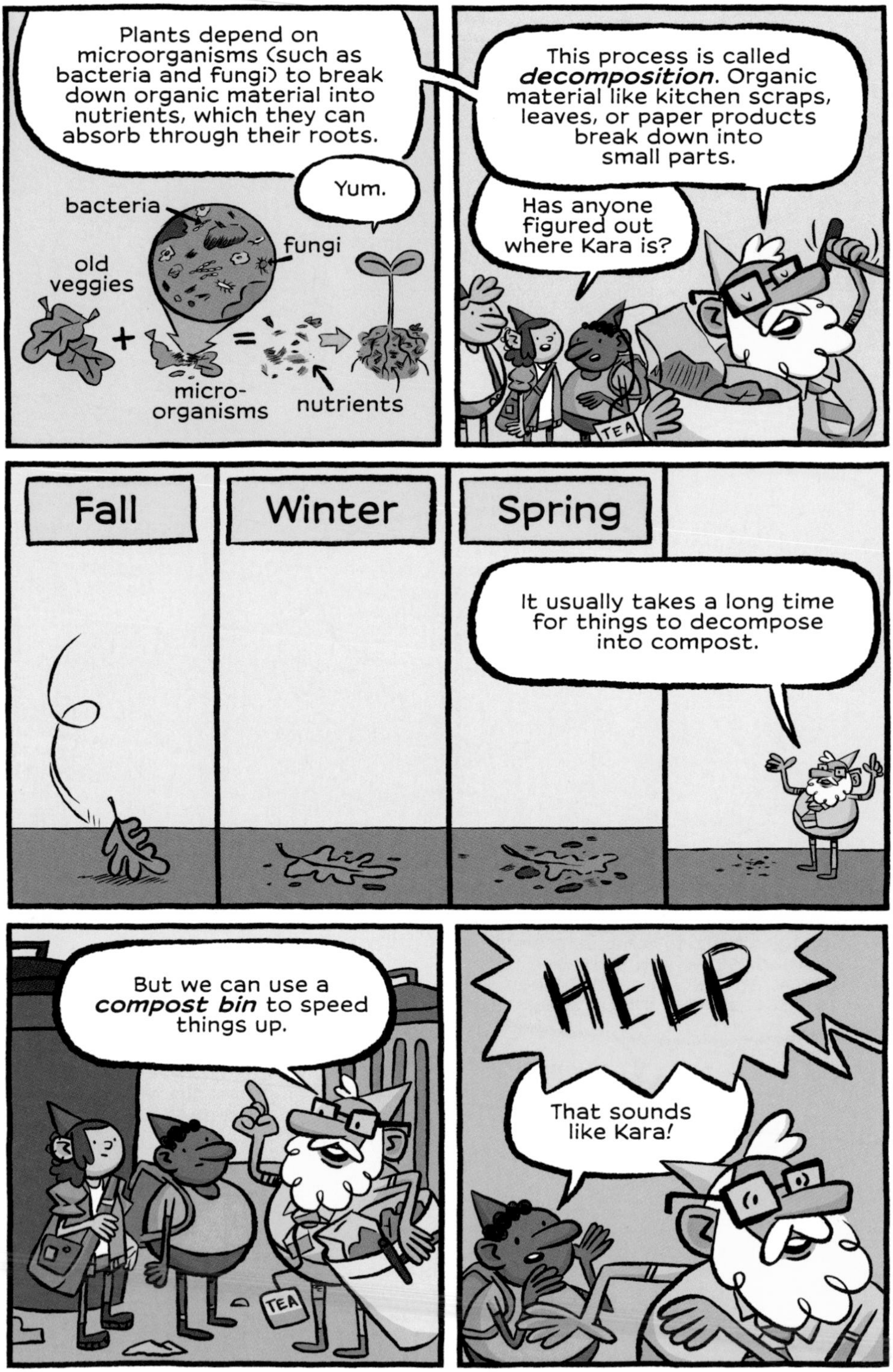
Plants depend on microorganisms (such as bacteria and fungi) to break down organic material into nutrients, which they can absorb through their roots.
Yum.
bacteria
fungi
old veggies
micro-organisms
nutrients
This process is called ***decomposition***. Organic material like kitchen scraps, leaves, or paper products break down into small parts.
Has anyone figured out where Kara is?
TEA
Fall
Winter
Spring
It usually takes a long time for things to decompose into compost.
But we can use a ***compost bin*** to speed things up.
TEA
HELP
That sounds like Kara!

Excuse me for a moment, students. It looks like someone has let the cat out of the bag.

It's tea-time!

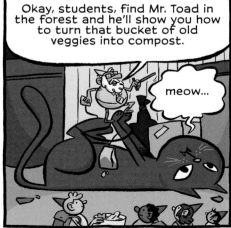

Okay, students, find Mr. Toad in the forest and he'll show you how to turn that bucket of old veggies into compost.

meow...

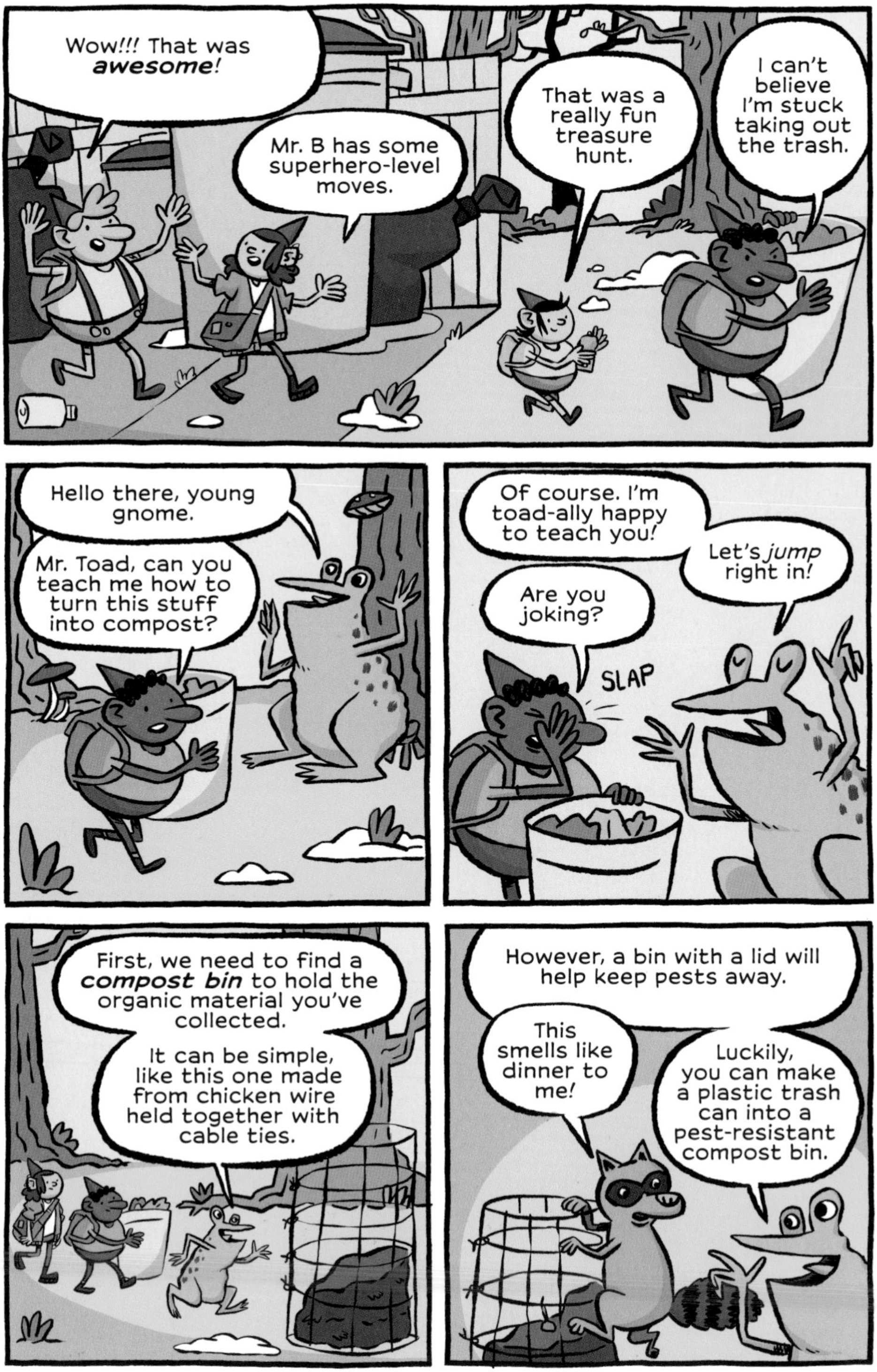
Wow!!! That was *awesome*!
Mr. B has some superhero-level moves.
That was a really fun treasure hunt.
I can't believe I'm stuck taking out the trash.
Hello there, young gnome.
Mr. Toad, can you teach me how to turn this stuff into compost?
Of course. I'm toad-ally happy to teach you!
Let's *jump* right in!
Are you joking?
SLAP
First, we need to find a **compost bin** to hold the organic material you've collected.
It can be simple, like this one made from chicken wire held together with cable ties.
However, a bin with a lid will help keep pests away.
This smells like dinner to me!
Luckily, you can make a plastic trash can into a pest-resistant compost bin.

MAKE YOUR OWN COMPOST BIN

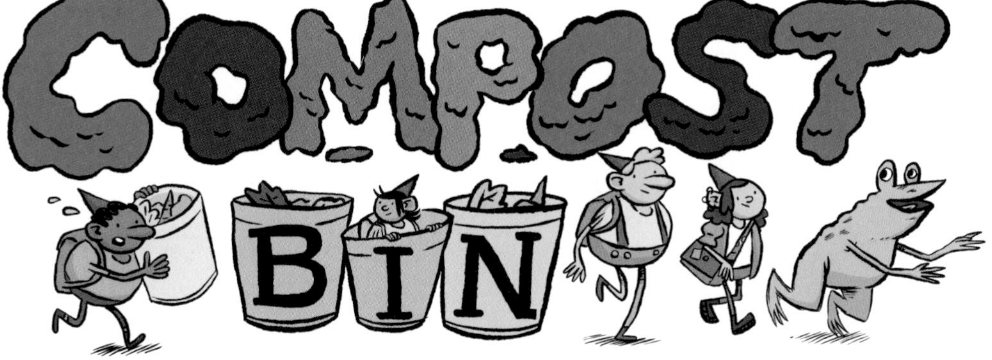

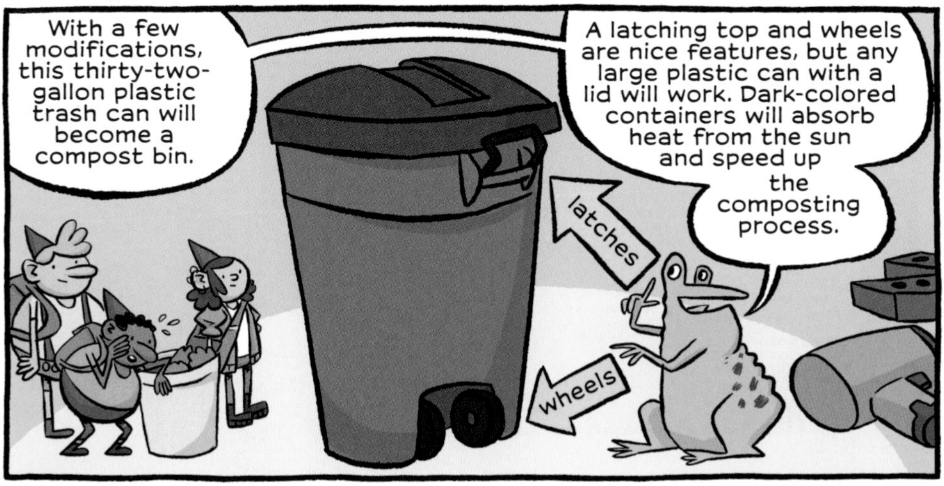
With a few modifications, this thirty-two-gallon plastic trash can will become a compost bin.
A latching top and wheels are nice features, but any large plastic can with a lid will work. Dark-colored containers will absorb heat from the sun and speed up the composting process.
latches
wheels

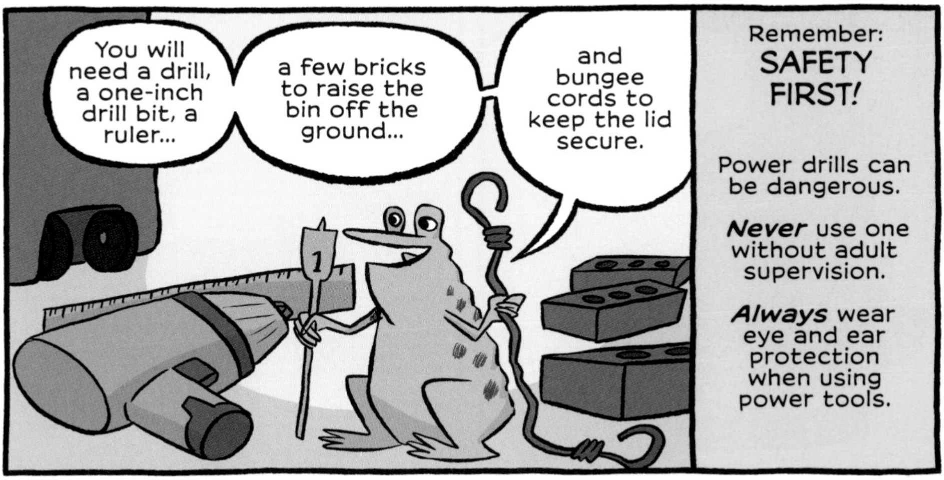
You will need a drill, a one-inch drill bit, a ruler...
a few bricks to raise the bin off the ground...
and bungee cords to keep the lid secure.
Remember: SAFETY FIRST!
Power drills can be dangerous.
Never use one without adult supervision.
Always wear eye and ear protection when using power tools.

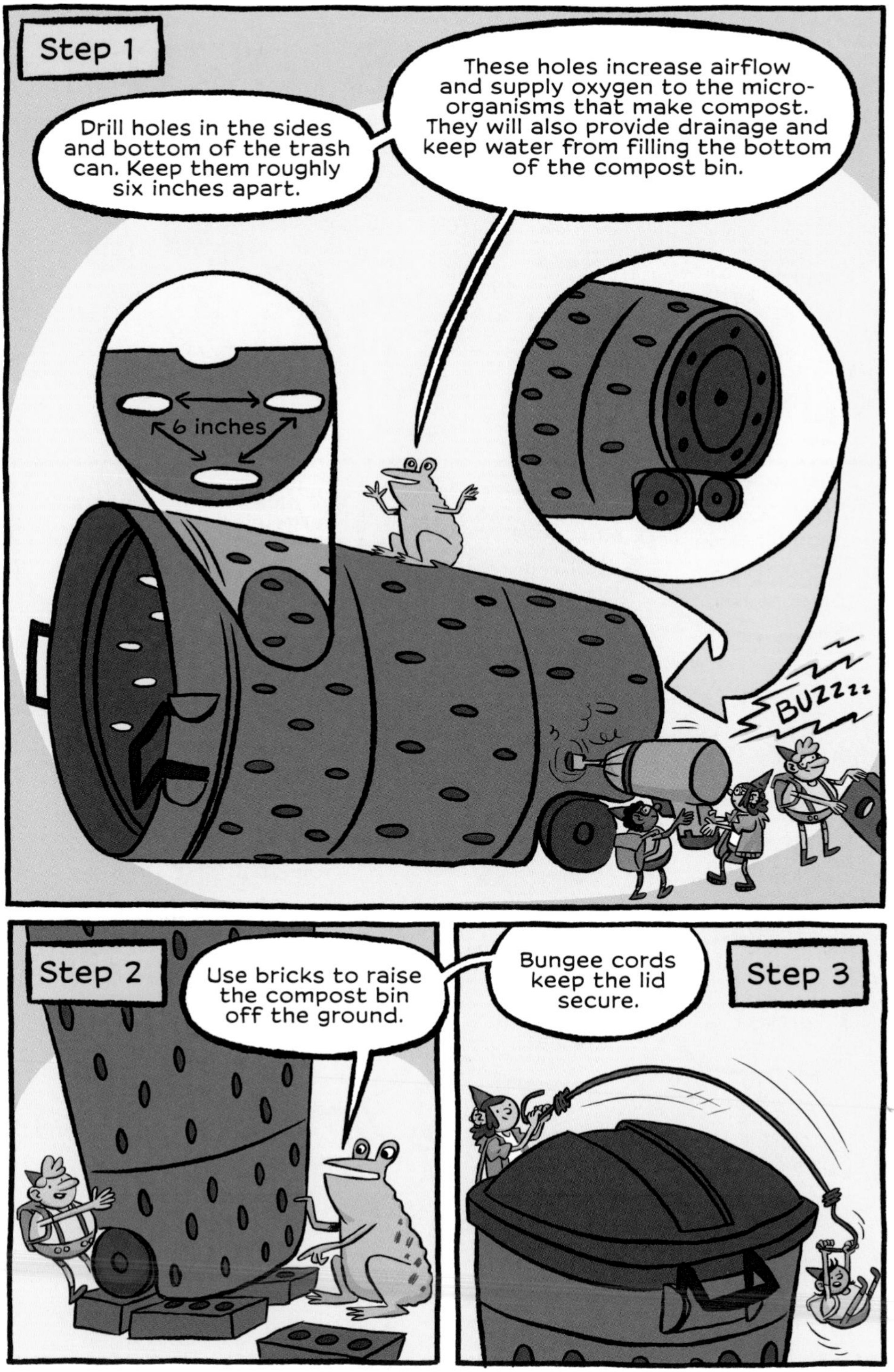
Step 1
Drill holes in the sides and bottom of the trash can. Keep them roughly six inches apart.
These holes increase airflow and supply oxygen to the micro-organisms that make compost. They will also provide drainage and keep water from filling the bottom of the compost bin.
6 inches
BUZZzz
Step 2
Use bricks to raise the compost bin off the ground.
Bungee cords keep the lid secure.
Step 3

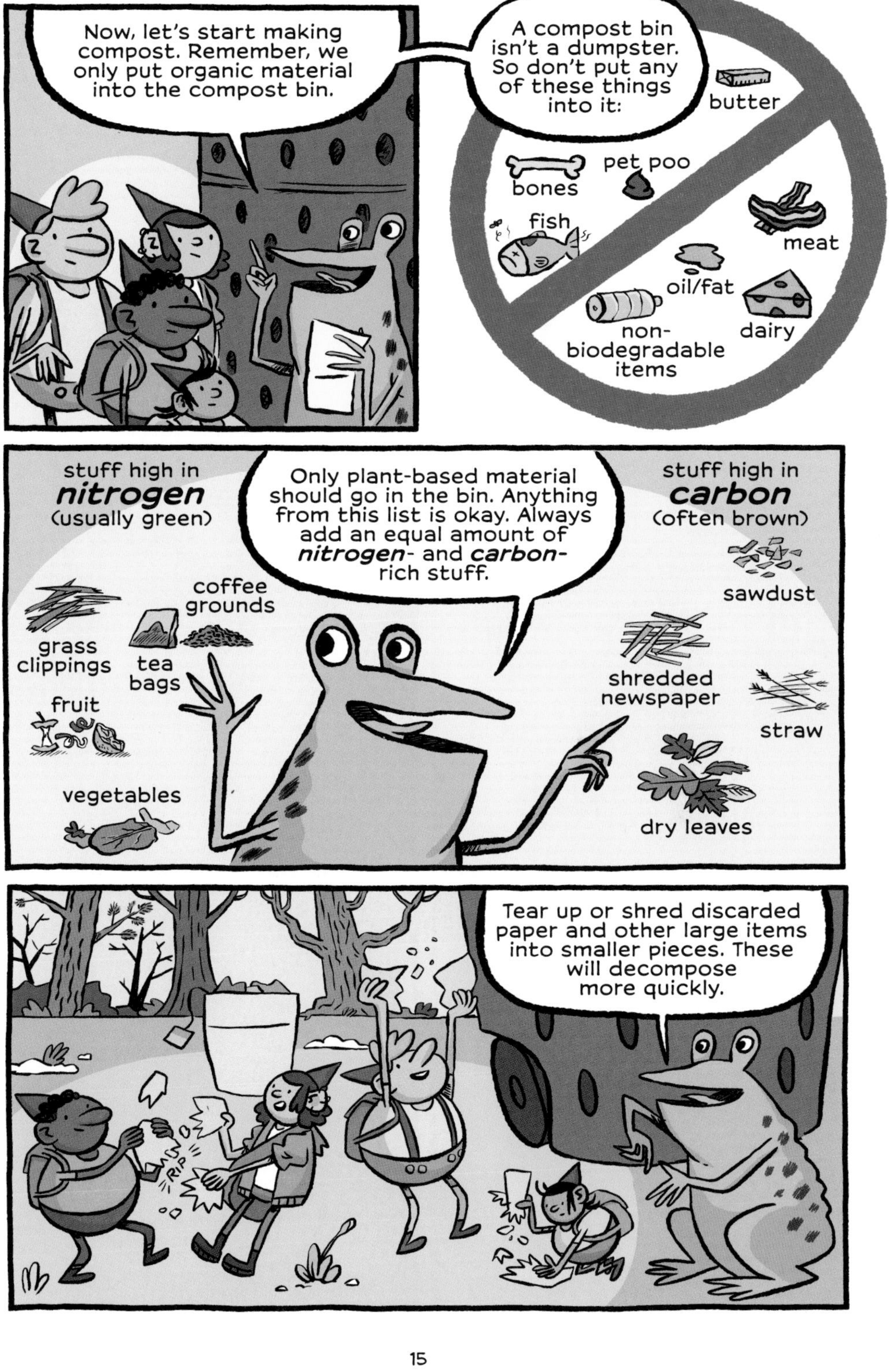
Now, let's start making compost. Remember, we only put organic material into the compost bin.
A compost bin isn't a dumpster. So don't put any of these things into it:
butter
pet poo
bones
fish
meat
oil/fat
dairy
non-biodegradable items
stuff high in *nitrogen* (usually green)
Only plant-based material should go in the bin. Anything from this list is okay. Always add an equal amount of *nitrogen*- and *carbon*-rich stuff.
stuff high in *carbon* (often brown)
coffee grounds
grass clippings
tea bags
fruit
vegetables
sawdust
shredded newspaper
straw
dry leaves
Tear up or shred discarded paper and other large items into smaller pieces. These will decompose more quickly.
RIP

Start with a three-inch base layer of carbon-rich material like dry leaves, shredded newspaper, or straw. Then add a three-inch layer of nitrogen-rich stuff.

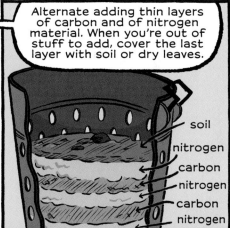

Alternate adding thin layers of carbon and of nitrogen material. When you're out of stuff to add, cover the last layer with soil or dry leaves.

soil

nitrogen

carbon

nitrogen

carbon

nitrogen

Spray the pile with a little water. It should be slightly damp, not soaked.

Not too wet!

Aaaaahh...

I'm decomposing!

It takes many months for things to decompose. But still, gnomes are not on the list of things to put in a compost bin!

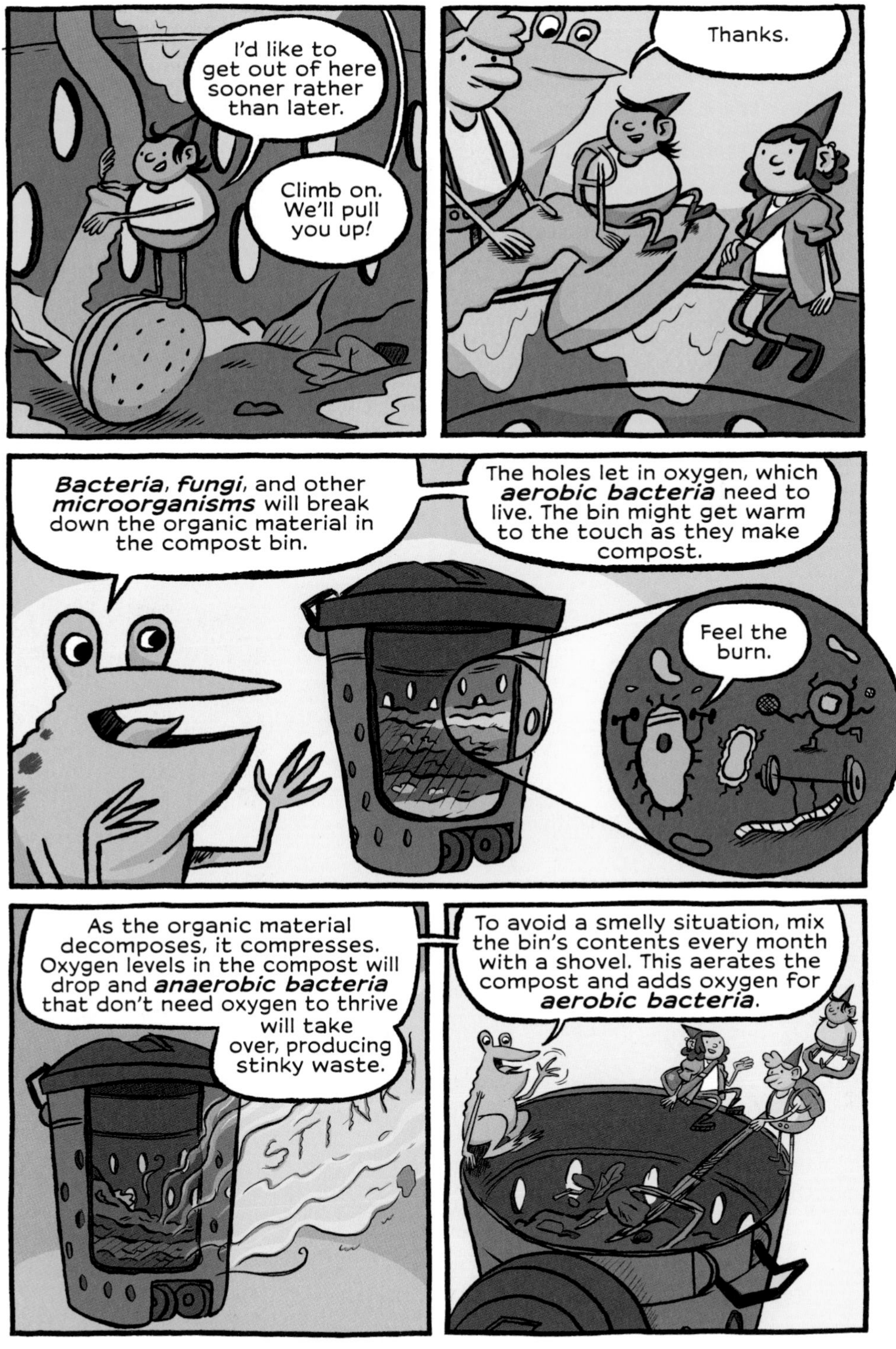

I'd like to get out of here sooner rather than later.
Climb on. We'll pull you up!
Thanks.
Bacteria, ***fungi***, and other ***microorganisms*** will break down the organic material in the compost bin.
The holes let in oxygen, which ***aerobic bacteria*** need to live. The bin might get warm to the touch as they make compost.
Feel the burn.
As the organic material decomposes, it compresses. Oxygen levels in the compost will drop and ***anaerobic bacteria*** that don't need oxygen to thrive will take over, producing stinky waste.
STINK
To avoid a smelly situation, mix the bin's contents every month with a shovel. This aerates the compost and adds oxygen for ***aerobic bacteria***.

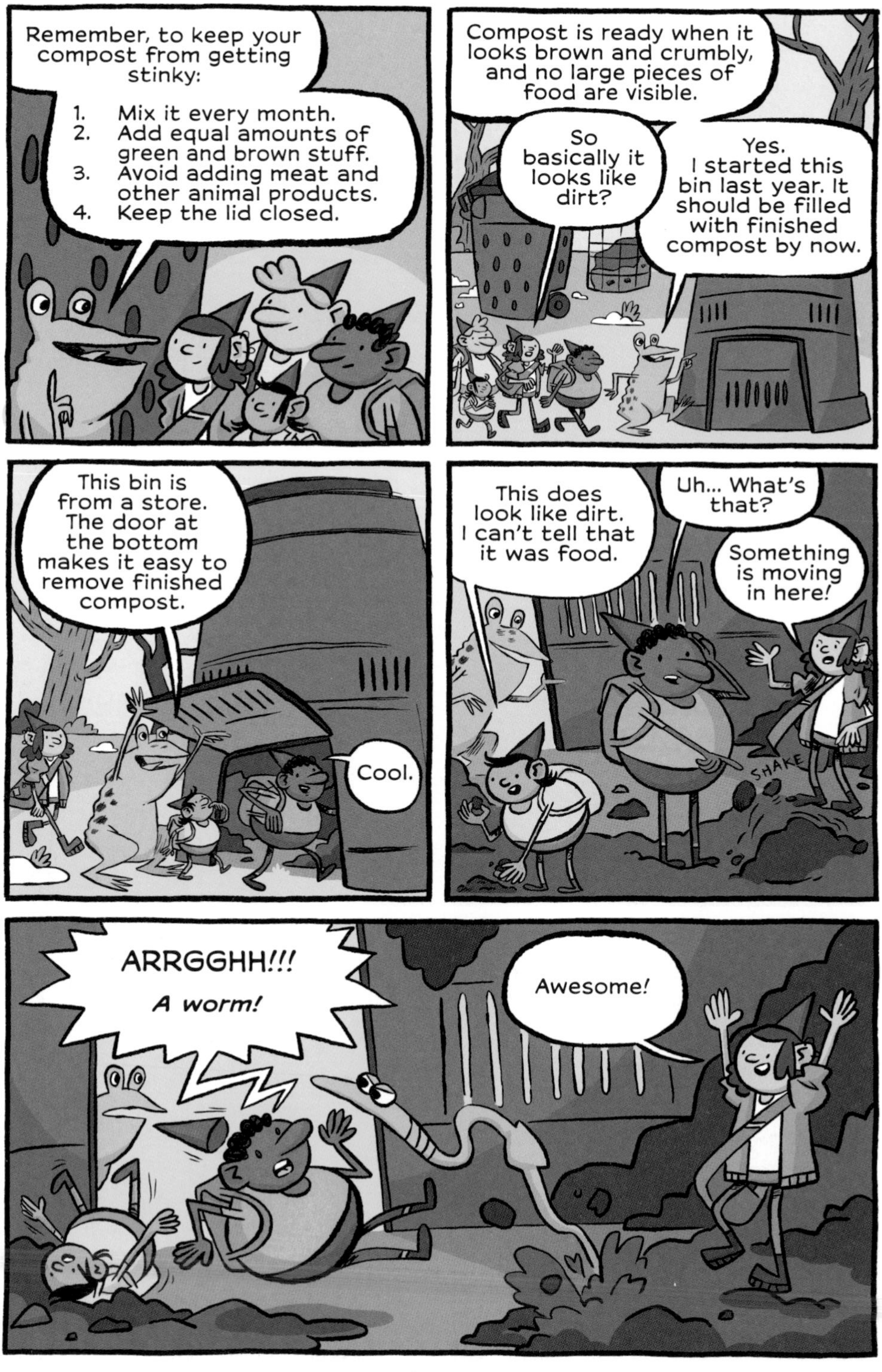

Remember, to keep your compost from getting stinky:
1. Mix it every month.
2. Add equal amounts of green and brown stuff.
3. Avoid adding meat and other animal products.
4. Keep the lid closed.
Compost is ready when it looks brown and crumbly, and no large pieces of food are visible.
So basically it looks like dirt?
Yes. I started this bin last year. It should be filled with finished compost by now.
This bin is from a store. The door at the bottom makes it easy to remove finished compost.
Cool.
This does look like dirt. I can't tell that it was food.
Uh... What's that?
Something is moving in here!
SHAKE
ARRGGHH!!!
A worm!
Awesome!

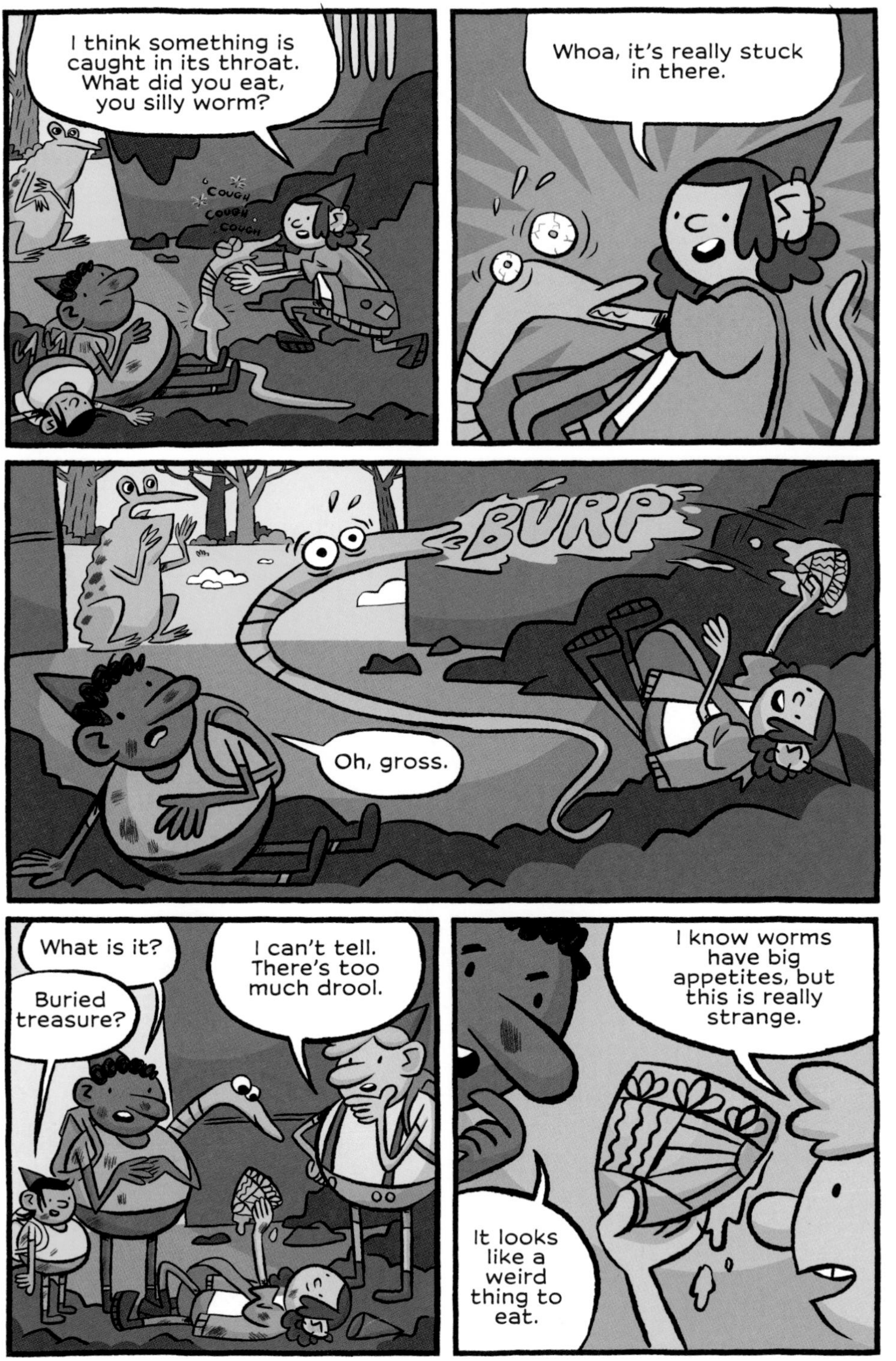

I think something is caught in its throat. What did you eat, you silly worm?
COUGH
COUGH
COUGH
Whoa, it's really stuck in there.
BURP
Oh, gross.
What is it?
Buried treasure?
I can't tell. There's too much drool.
I know worms have big appetites, but this is really strange.
It looks like a weird thing to eat.

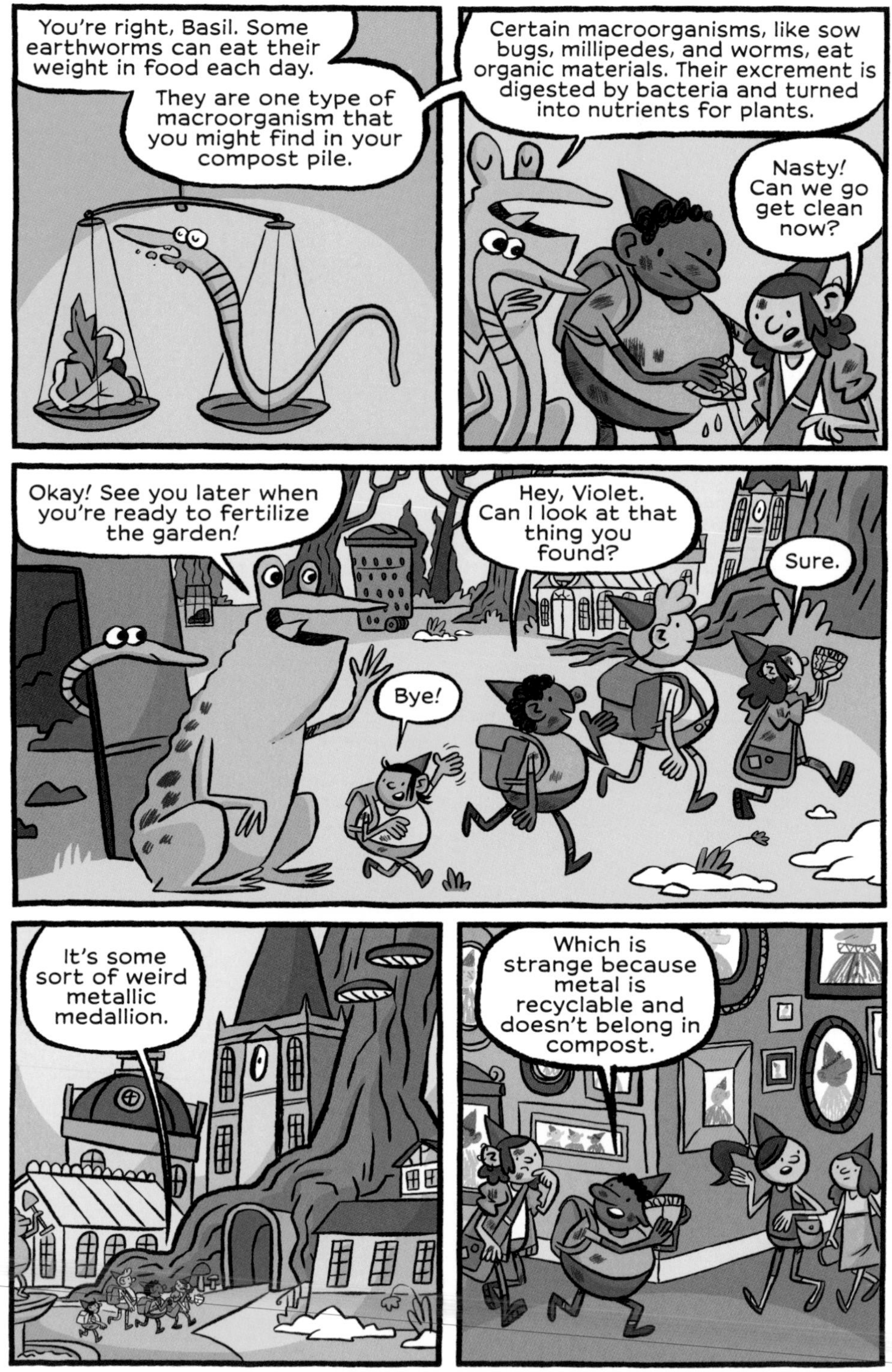
You're right, Basil. Some earthworms can eat their weight in food each day.
They are one type of macroorganism that you might find in your compost pile.
Certain macroorganisms, like sow bugs, millipedes, and worms, eat organic materials. Their excrement is digested by bacteria and turned into nutrients for plants.
Nasty! Can we go get clean now?
Okay! See you later when you're ready to fertilize the garden!
Bye!
Hey, Violet. Can I look at that thing you found?
Sure.
It's some sort of weird metallic medallion.
Which is strange because metal is recyclable and doesn't belong in compost.

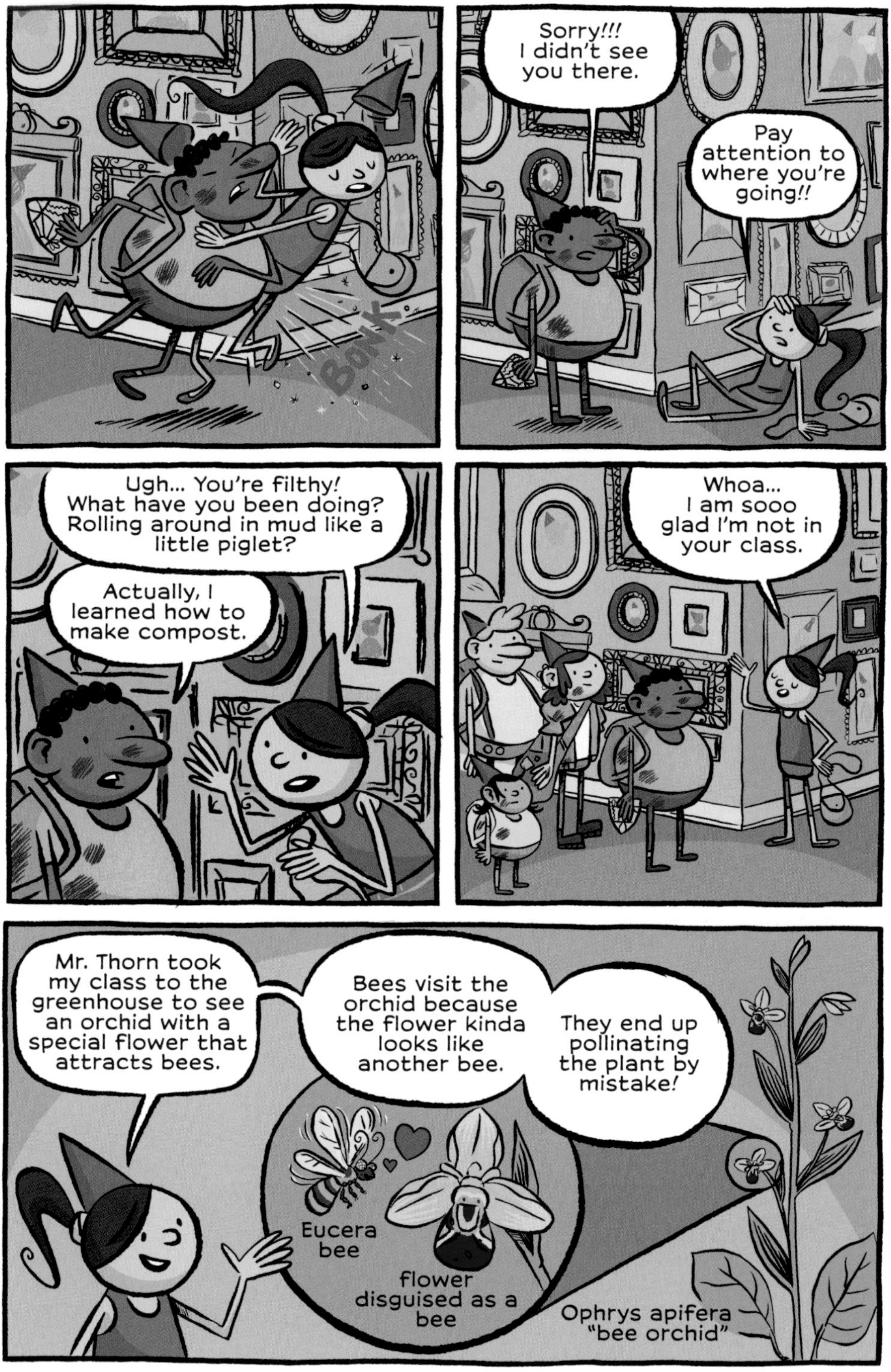
BONK
Sorry!!! I didn't see you there.
Pay attention to where you're going!!
Ugh... You're filthy! What have you been doing? Rolling around in mud like a little piglet?
Actually, I learned how to make compost.
Whoa... I am sooo glad I'm not in your class.
Mr. Thorn took my class to the greenhouse to see an orchid with a special flower that attracts bees.
Bees visit the orchid because the flower kinda looks like another bee.
They end up pollinating the plant by mistake!
Eucera bee
flower disguised as a bee
Ophrys apifera "bee orchid"

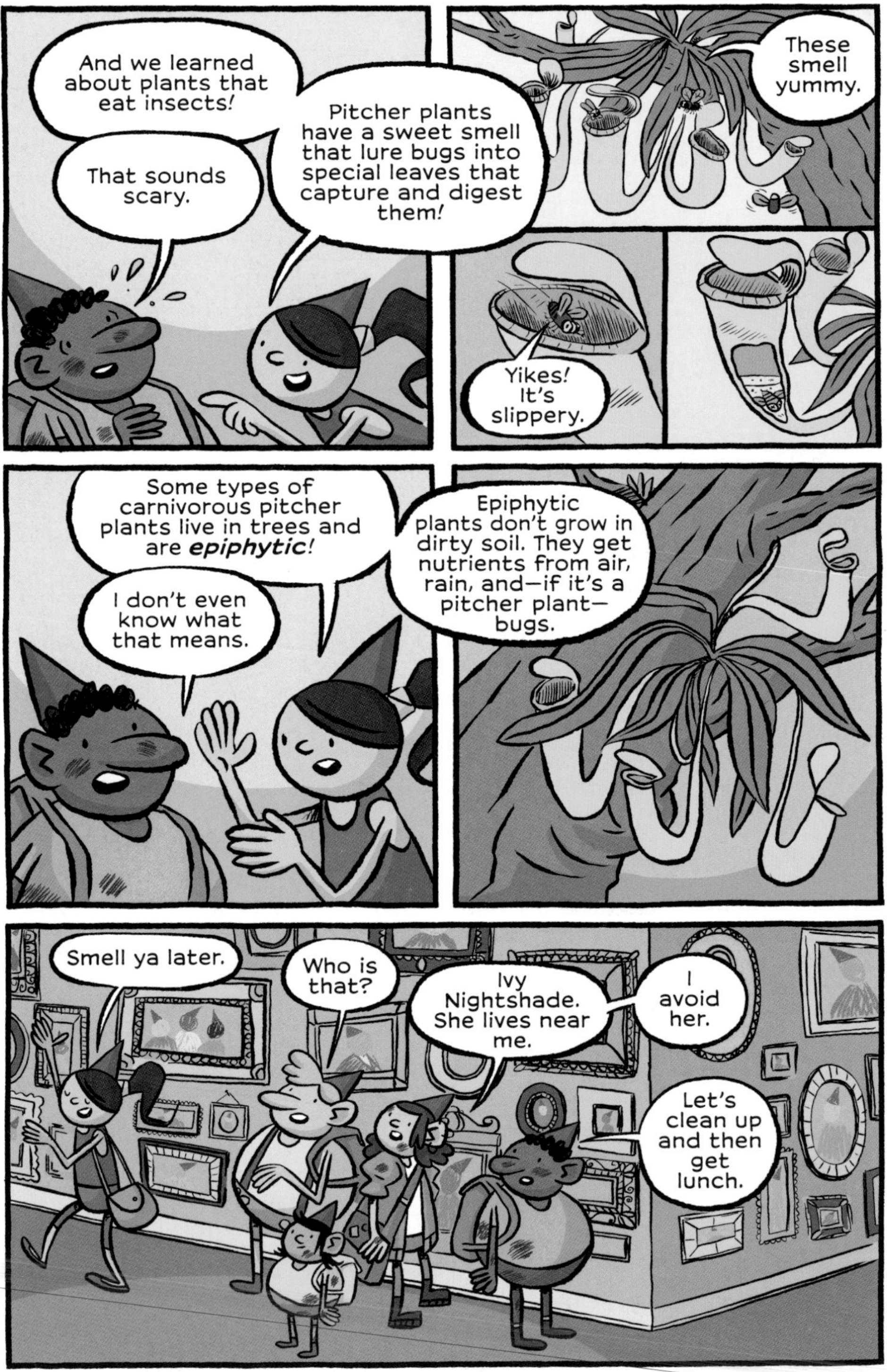

And we learned about plants that eat insects!
That sounds scary.
Pitcher plants have a sweet smell that lure bugs into special leaves that capture and digest them!
These smell yummy.
Yikes! It's slippery.
Some types of carnivorous pitcher plants live in trees and are ***epiphytic***!
I don't even know what that means.
Epiphytic plants don't grow in dirty soil. They get nutrients from air, rain, and—if it's a pitcher plant—bugs.
Smell ya later.
Who is that?
Ivy Nightshade. She lives near me.
I avoid her.
Let's clean up and then get lunch.

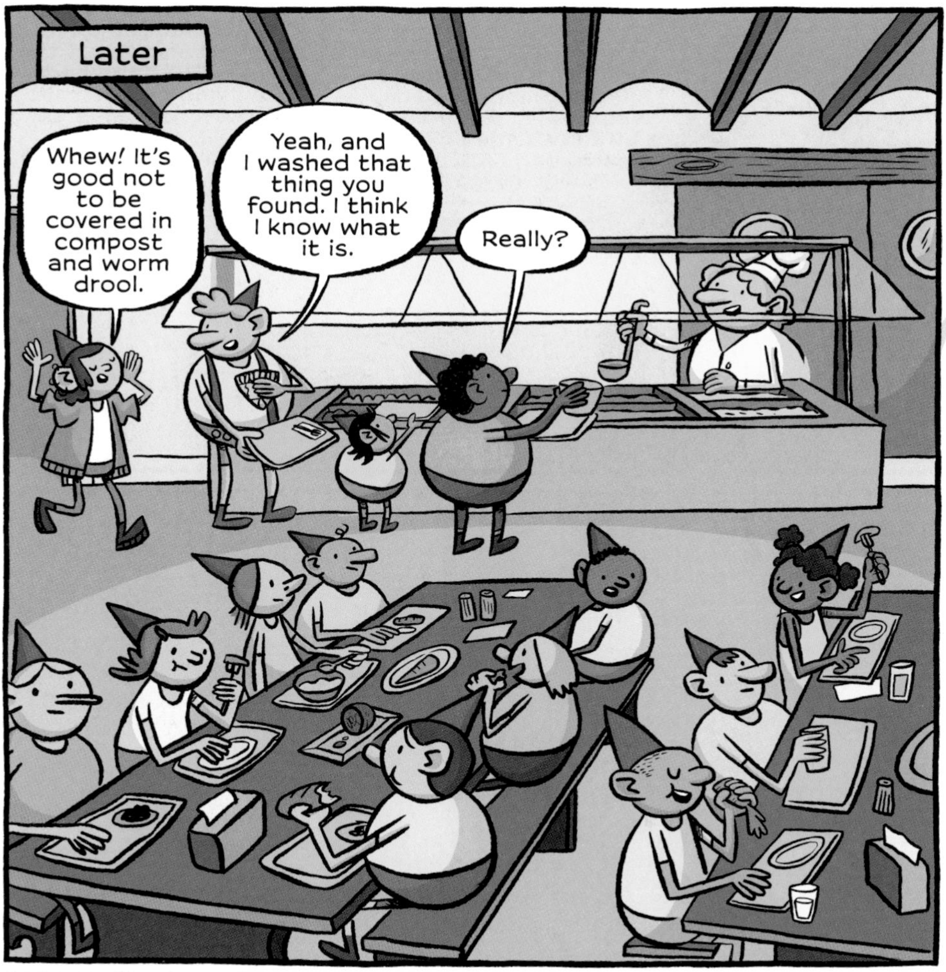
Later
Whew! It's good not to be covered in compost and worm drool.
Yeah, and I washed that thing you found. I think I know what it is.
Really?

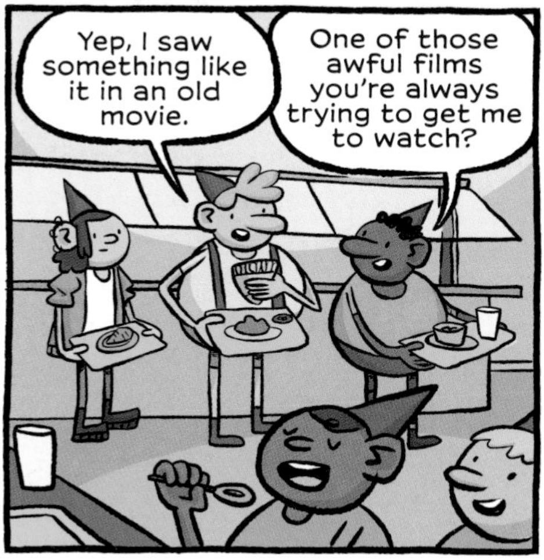
Yep, I saw something like it in an old movie.
One of those awful films you're always trying to get me to watch?

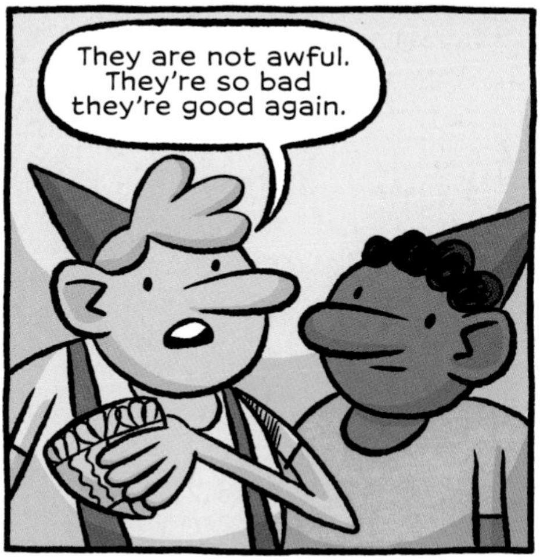
They are not awful. They're so bad they're good again.

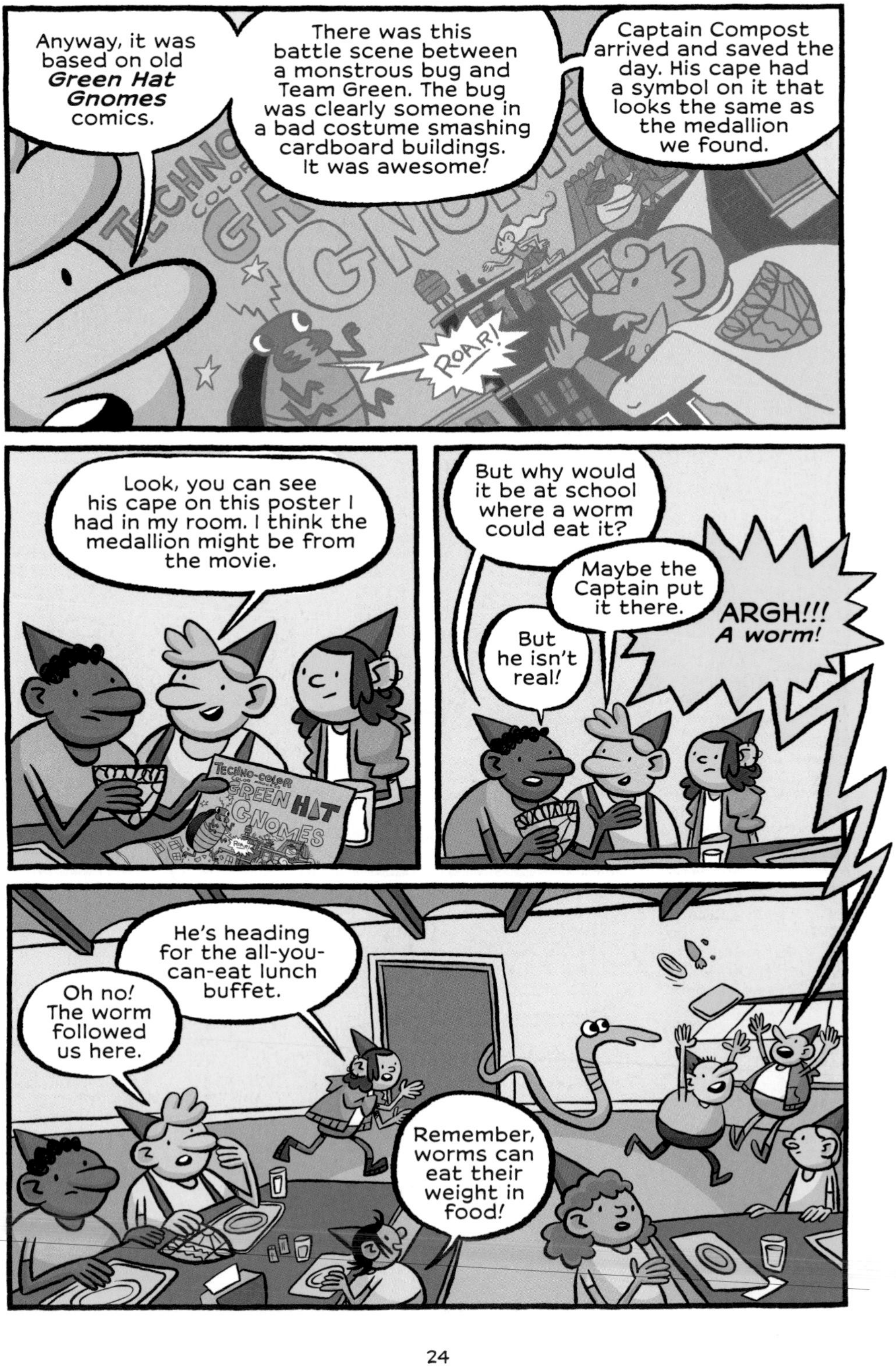
Anyway, it was based on old ***Green Hat Gnomes*** comics.
There was this battle scene between a monstrous bug and Team Green. The bug was clearly someone in a bad costume smashing cardboard buildings. It was awesome!
Captain Compost arrived and saved the day. His cape had a symbol on it that looks the same as the medallion we found.
ROAR!
Look, you can see his cape on this poster I had in my room. I think the medallion might be from the movie.
TECHNO-COLOR GREEN HAT GNOMES
But why would it be at school where a worm could eat it?
Maybe the Captain put it there.
But he isn't real!
ARGH!!! *A worm!*
Oh no! The worm followed us here.
He's heading for the all-you-can-eat lunch buffet.
Remember, worms can eat their weight in food!

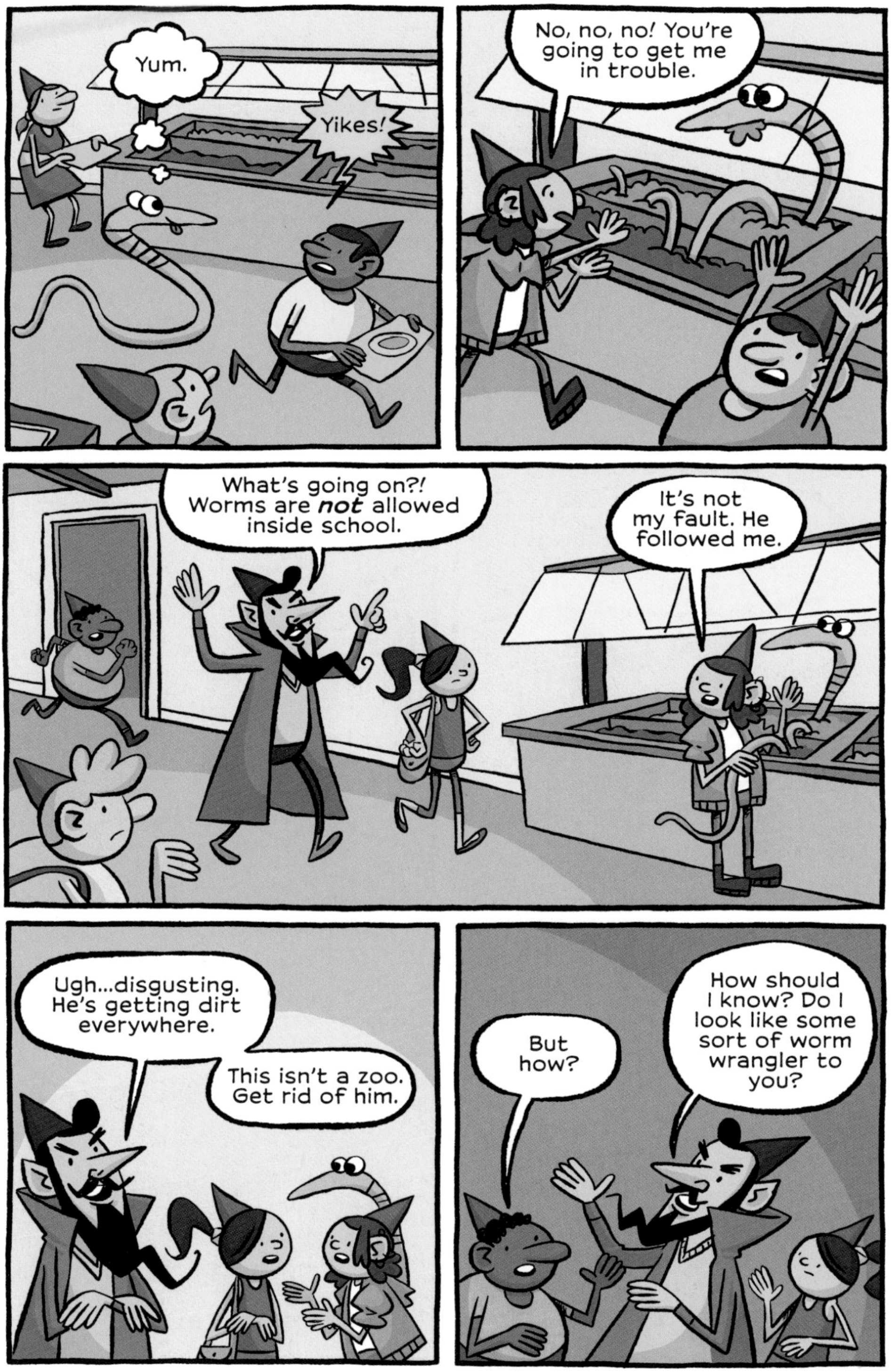
Yum.
Yikes!
No, no, no! You're going to get me in trouble.
What's going on?! Worms are ***not*** allowed inside school.
It's not my fault. He followed me.
Ugh...disgusting. He's getting dirt everywhere.
This isn't a zoo. Get rid of him.
But how?
How should I know? Do I look like some sort of worm wrangler to you?

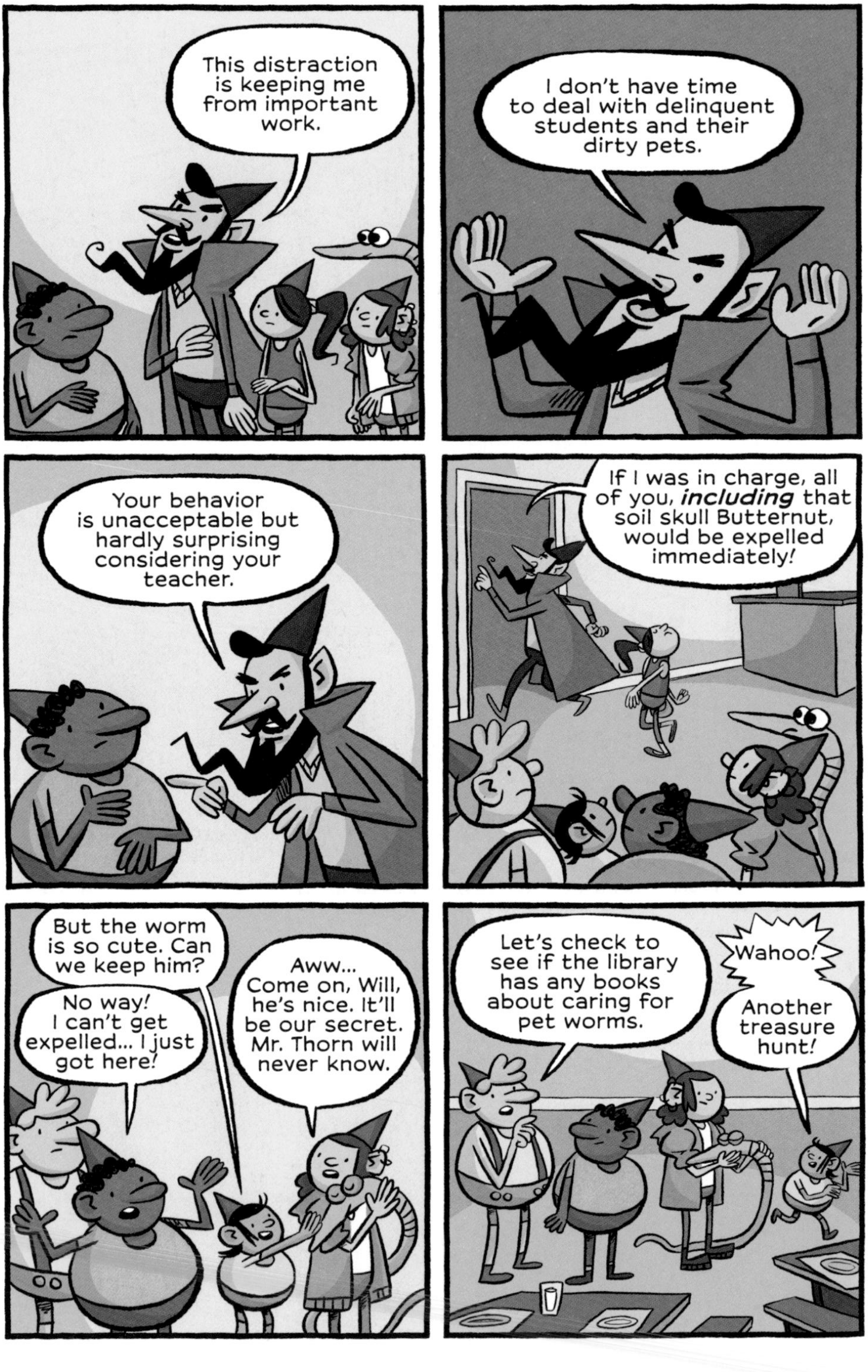

This distraction is keeping me from important work.
I don't have time to deal with delinquent students and their dirty pets.
Your behavior is unacceptable but hardly surprising considering your teacher.
If I was in charge, all of you, *including* that soil skull Butternut, would be expelled immediately!
But the worm is so cute. Can we keep him?
No way! I can't get expelled... I just got here!
Aww... Come on, Will, he's nice. It'll be our secret. Mr. Thorn will never know.
Let's check to see if the library has any books about caring for pet worms.
Wahoo!
Another treasure hunt!

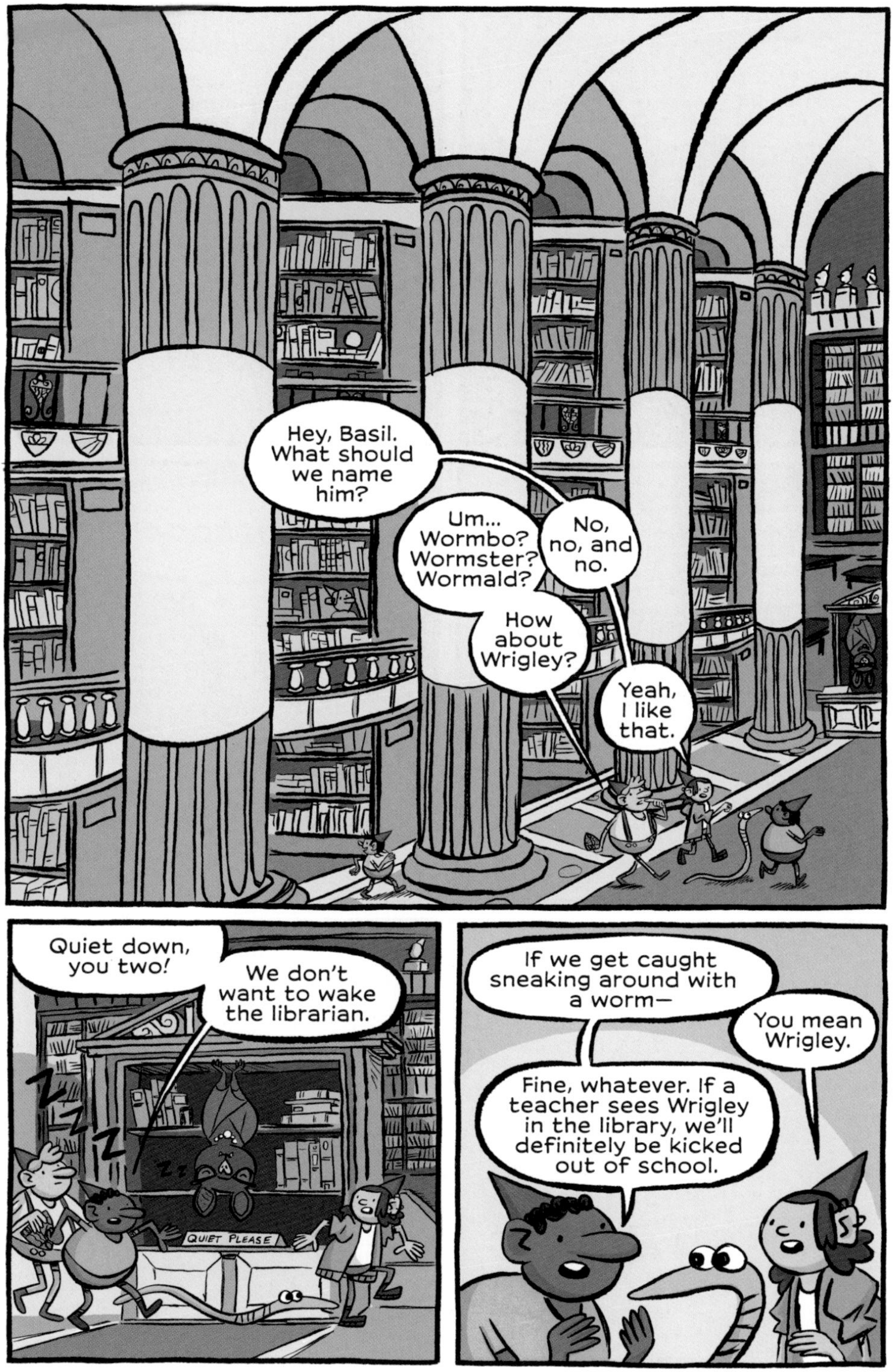
Hey, Basil. What should we name him?
Um... Wormbo? Wormster? Wormald?
No, no, and no.
How about Wrigley?
Yeah, I like that.
Quiet down, you two!
We don't want to wake the librarian.
QUIET PLEASE
If we get caught sneaking around with a worm—
You mean Wrigley.
Fine, whatever. If a teacher sees Wrigley in the library, we'll definitely be kicked out of school.

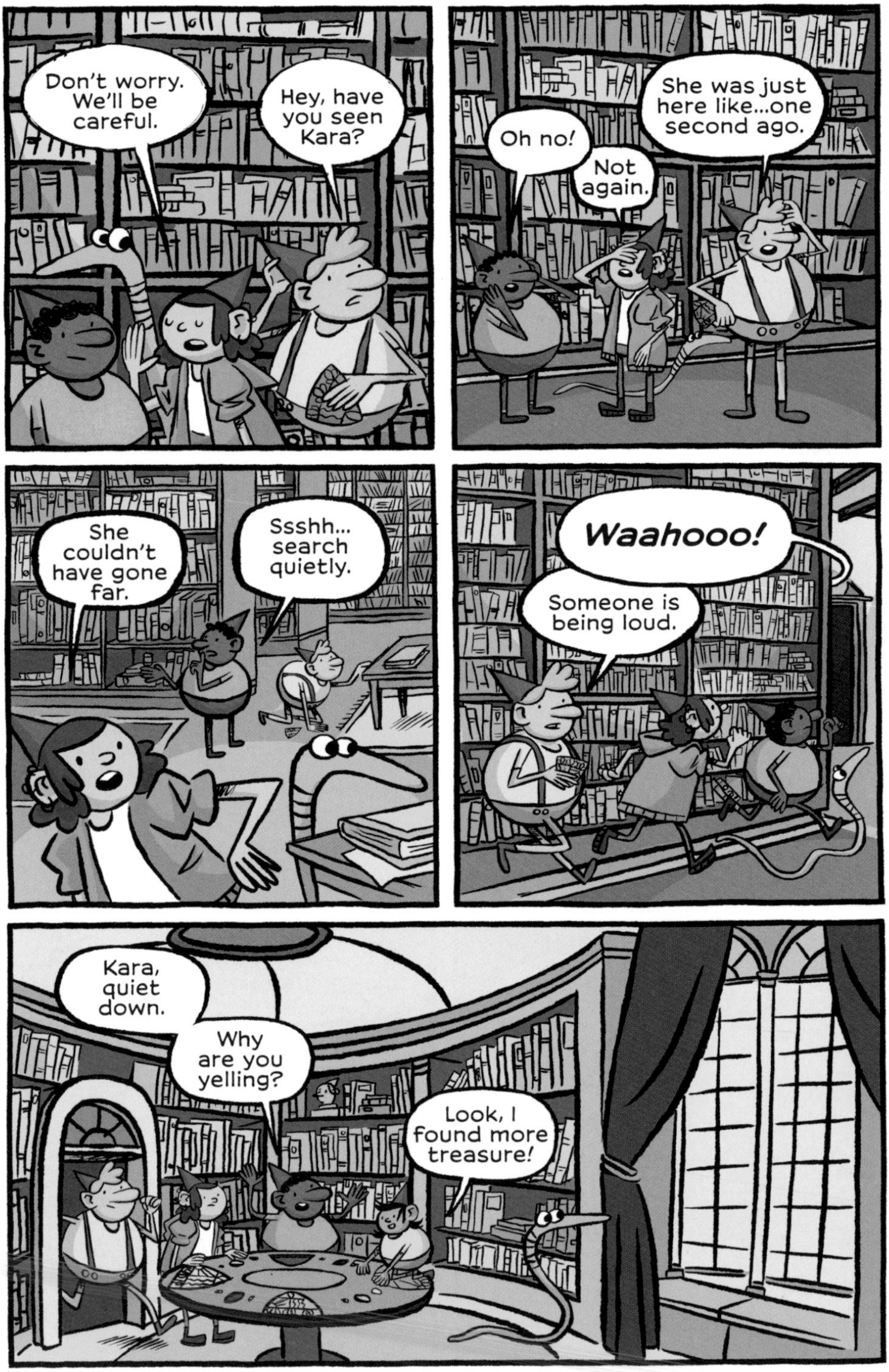

Don't worry. We'll be careful.
Hey, have you seen Kara?
Oh no!
Not again.
She was just here like...one second ago.
She couldn't have gone far.
Ssshh... search quietly.
Waahooo!
Someone is being loud.
Kara, quiet down.
Why are you yelling?
Look, I found more treasure!

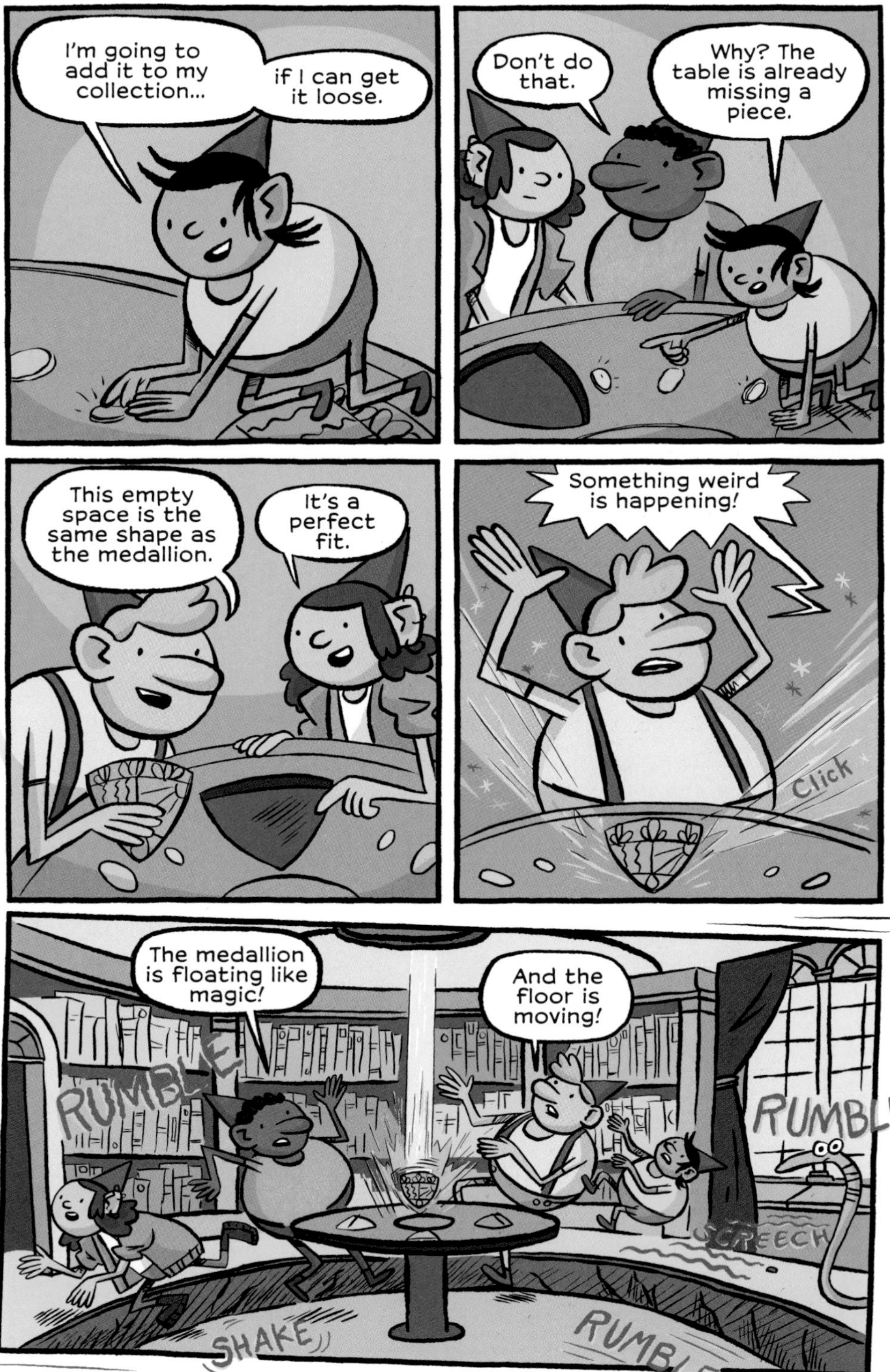

I'm going to add it to my collection...
if I can get it loose.
Don't do that.
Why? The table is already missing a piece.
This empty space is the same shape as the medallion.
It's a perfect fit.
Something weird is happening!
Click
The medallion is floating like magic!
And the floor is moving!
RUMBLE
RUMBLE
SCREECH
SHAKE
RUMBLE

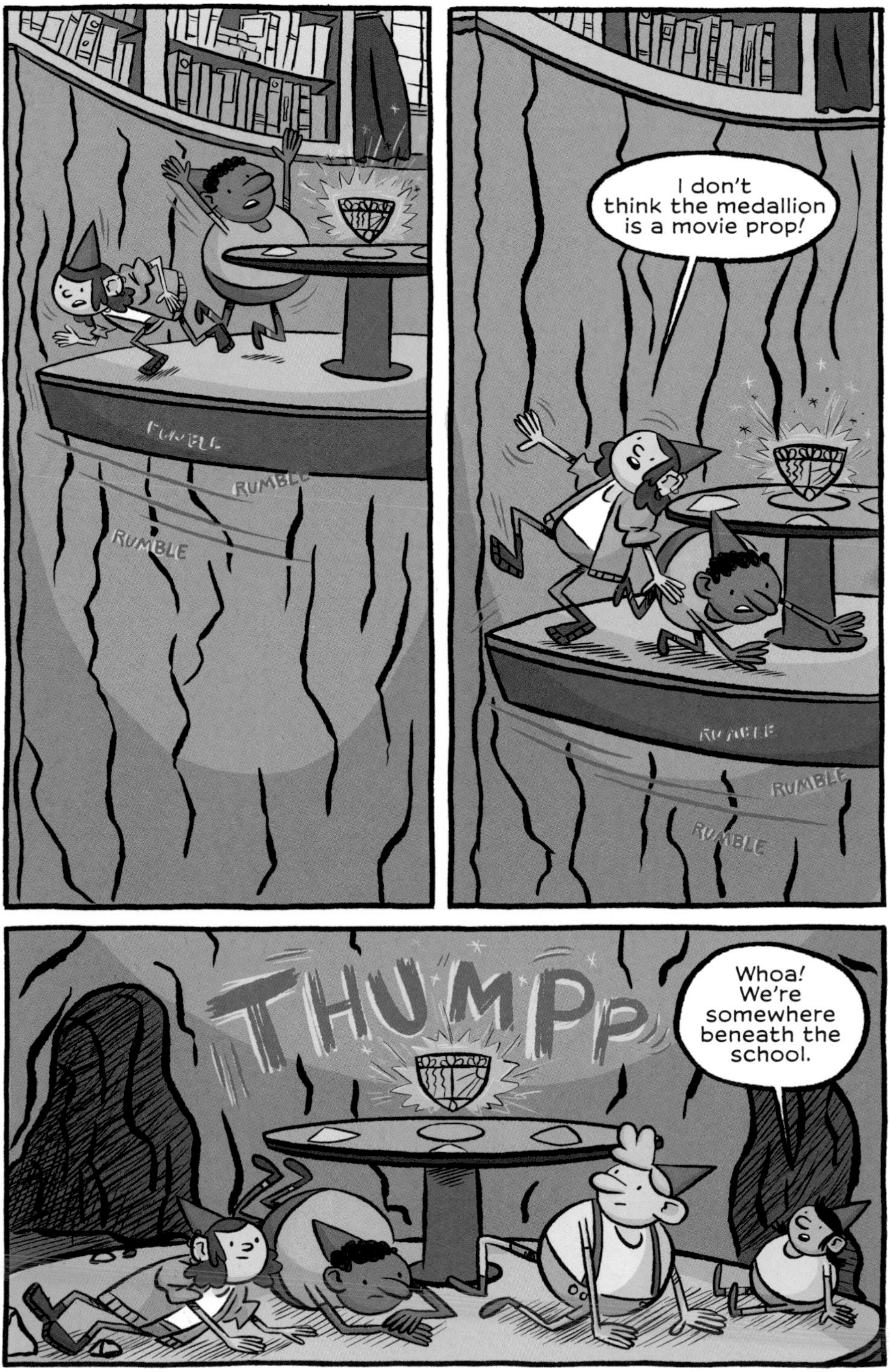
RUMBLE
RUMBLE
I don't think the medallion is a movie prop!
RUMBLE
RUMBLE
THUMPP
Whoa! We're somewhere beneath the school.

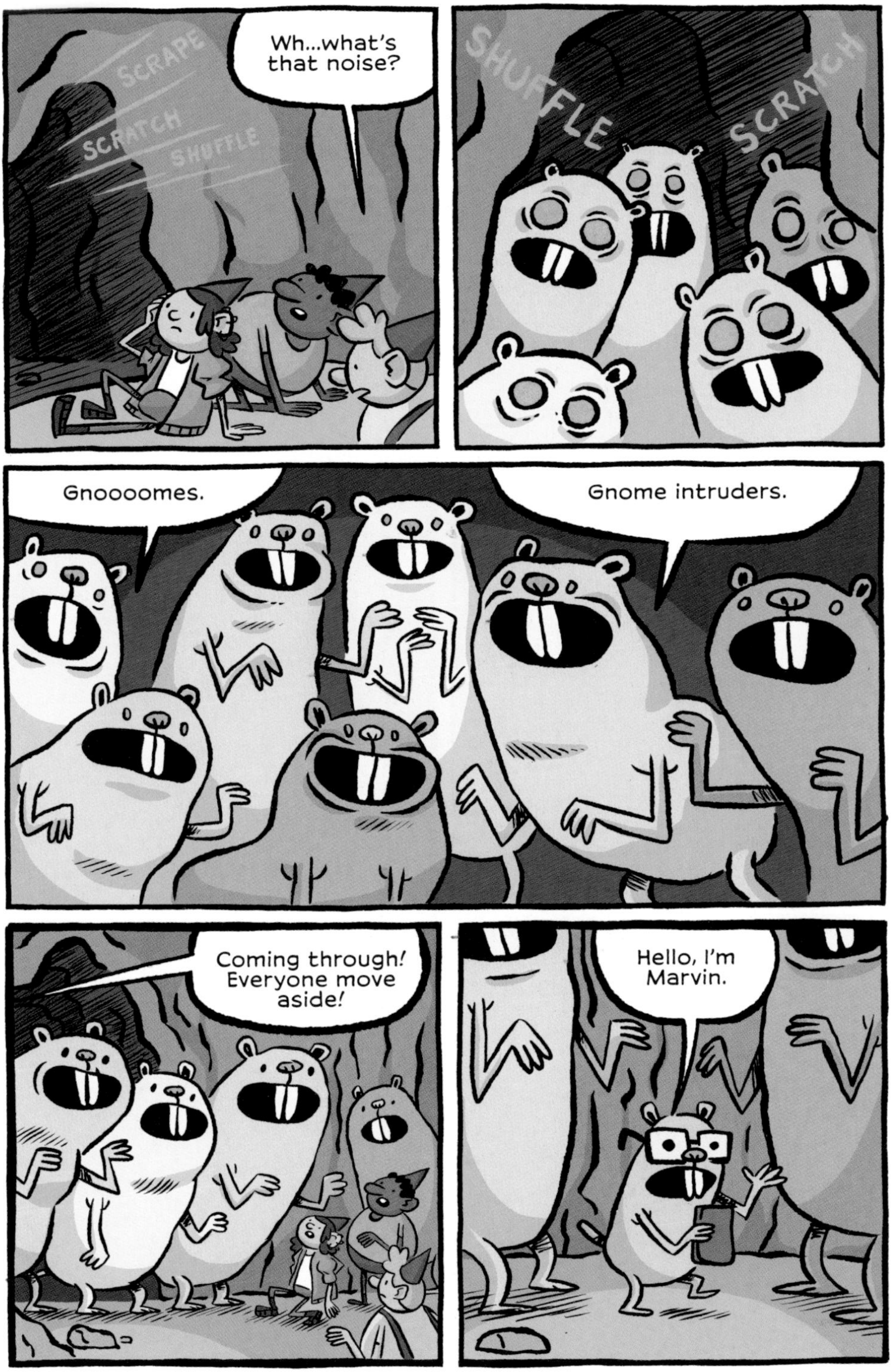
SCRAPE
SCRATCH
SHUFFLE
Wh...what's that noise?
SHUFFLE
SCRATCH
Gnoooomes.
Gnome intruders.
Coming through! Everyone move aside!
Hello, I'm Marvin.

Students aren't supposed to be in the library access tunnel.

Please don't expel us. We don't know what happened.

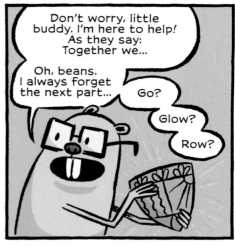

Don't worry, little buddy. I'm here to help! As they say: Together we...

Oh, beans. I always forget the next part...

Go?

Glow?

Row?

Together we *grow*? The Green Hat Gnomes' catch-phrase?

That's right.

I *never* remember the whole thing.

I guess that's why I'm stuck down here while those gnomes are planting gardens and saving the world.

Wait, wait, wait. Hold on just one second. The Green Hat Gnomes are real?

Of course they are. I work for them.

A bit of advice: Not everything is what it seems. Come on, I'll show you what I mean.

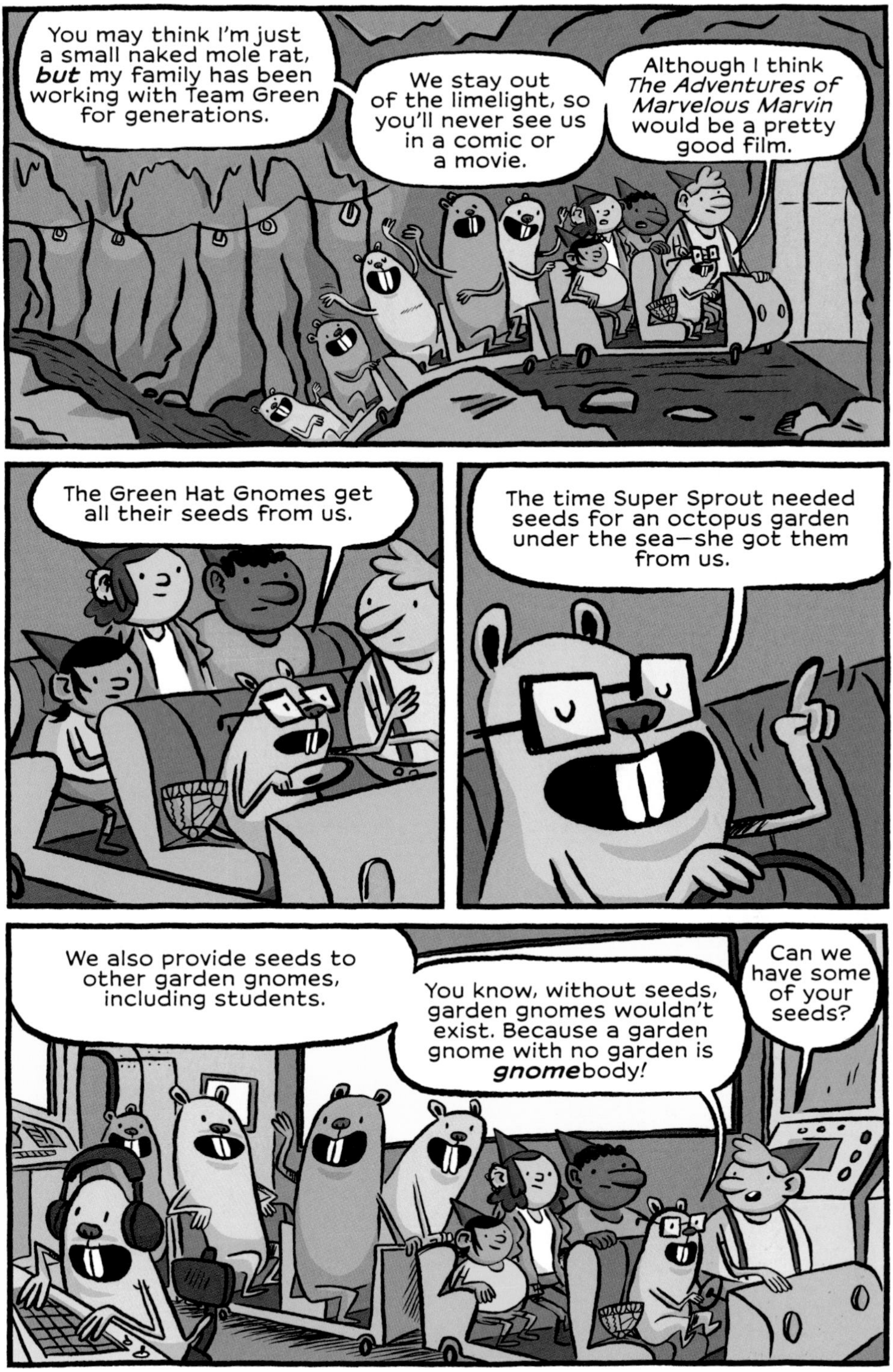
You may think I'm just a small naked mole rat, ***but*** my family has been working with Team Green for generations.
We stay out of the limelight, so you'll never see us in a comic or a movie.
Although I think *The Adventures of Marvelous Marvin* would be a pretty good film.
The Green Hat Gnomes get all their seeds from us.
The time Super Sprout needed seeds for an octopus garden under the sea—she got them from us.
We also provide seeds to other garden gnomes, including students.
You know, without seeds, garden gnomes wouldn't exist. Because a garden gnome with no garden is ***gnome***body!
Can we have some of your seeds?

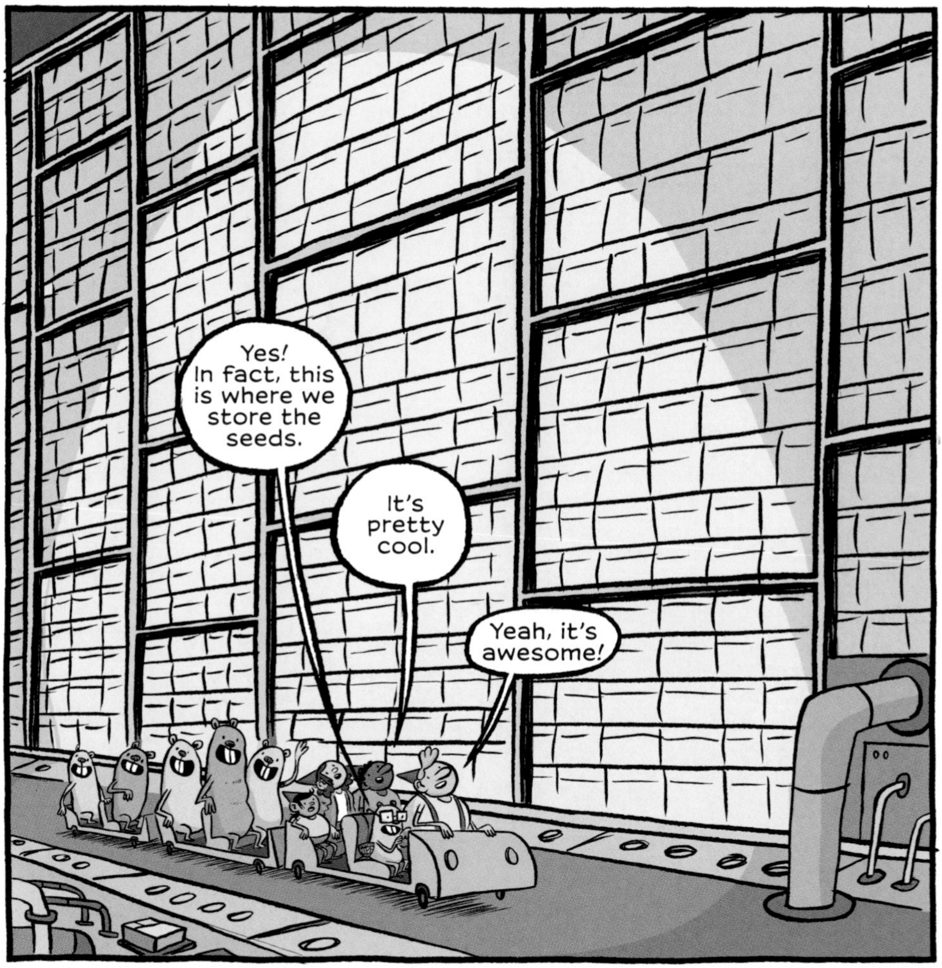
Yes! In fact, this is where we store the seeds.
It's pretty cool.
Yeah, it's awesome!

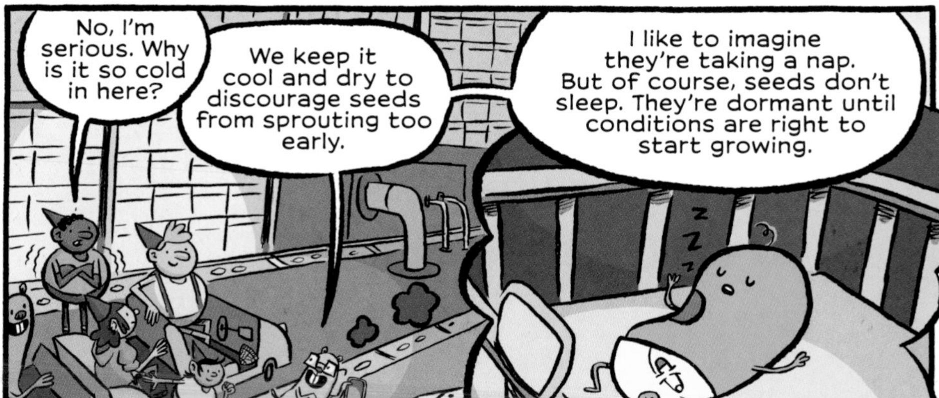
No, I'm serious. Why is it so cold in here?
We keep it cool and dry to discourage seeds from sprouting too early.
I like to imagine they're taking a nap. But of course, seeds don't sleep. They're dormant until conditions are right to start growing.
Z
Z
Z

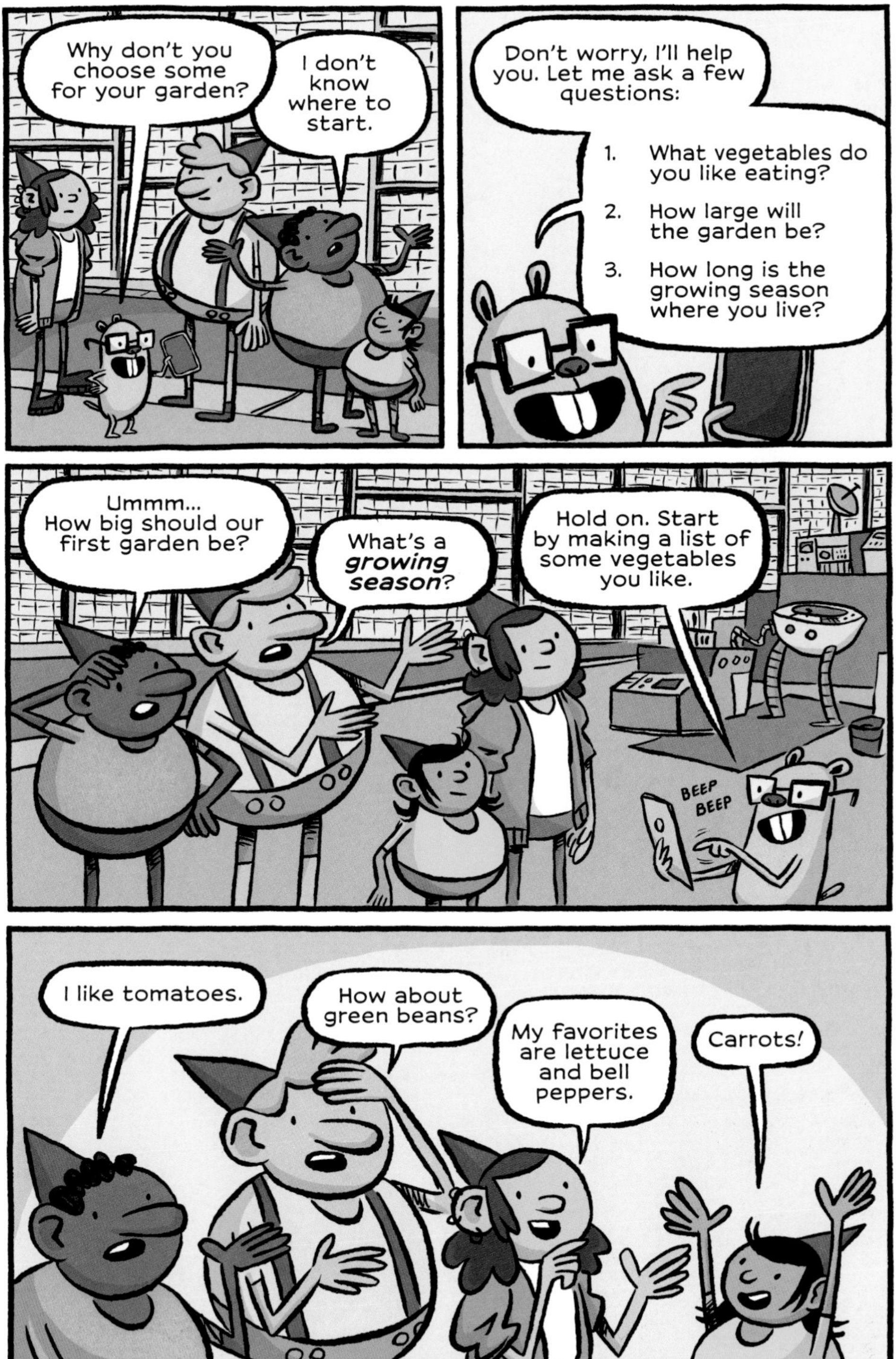
Why don't you choose some for your garden?
I don't know where to start.
Don't worry, I'll help you. Let me ask a few questions:
1. What vegetables do you like eating?
2. How large will the garden be?
3. How long is the growing season where you live?
Ummm... How big should our first garden be?
What's a ***growing season***?
Hold on. Start by making a list of some vegetables you like.
BEEP BEEP
I like tomatoes.
How about green beans?
My favorites are lettuce and bell peppers.
Carrots!

Your first garden should be relatively small. Start by cultivating one or two plants of each vegetable variety per gardener.

You will probably want to grow more carrots and lettuce, since each plant will only produce one vegetable.

2 tomato plants
2 bell pepper plants
2 bean plants
5 or more lettuce plants
10 or more carrot plants

Compact plants, which don't grow large, are best for small spaces.

CLICK
Clack

For example, determinate* tomato plants and bush beans are good choices because they stop growing when they reach a certain size.

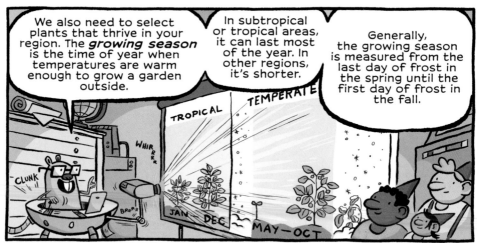

We also need to select plants that thrive in your region. The **growing season** is the time of year when temperatures are warm enough to grow a garden outside.

In subtropical or tropical areas, it can last most of the year. In other regions, it's shorter.

Generally, the growing season is measured from the last day of frost in the spring until the first day of frost in the fall.

WHIRRRR
CLUNK
BRRRR

TROPICAL
TEMPERATE
JAN DEC
MAY—OCT

*Tomato plants can either be **determinate** or **indeterminate**. **Determinate** plants stop growing when they reach a certain height while **indeterminate** varieties will grow until they are killed by frost.

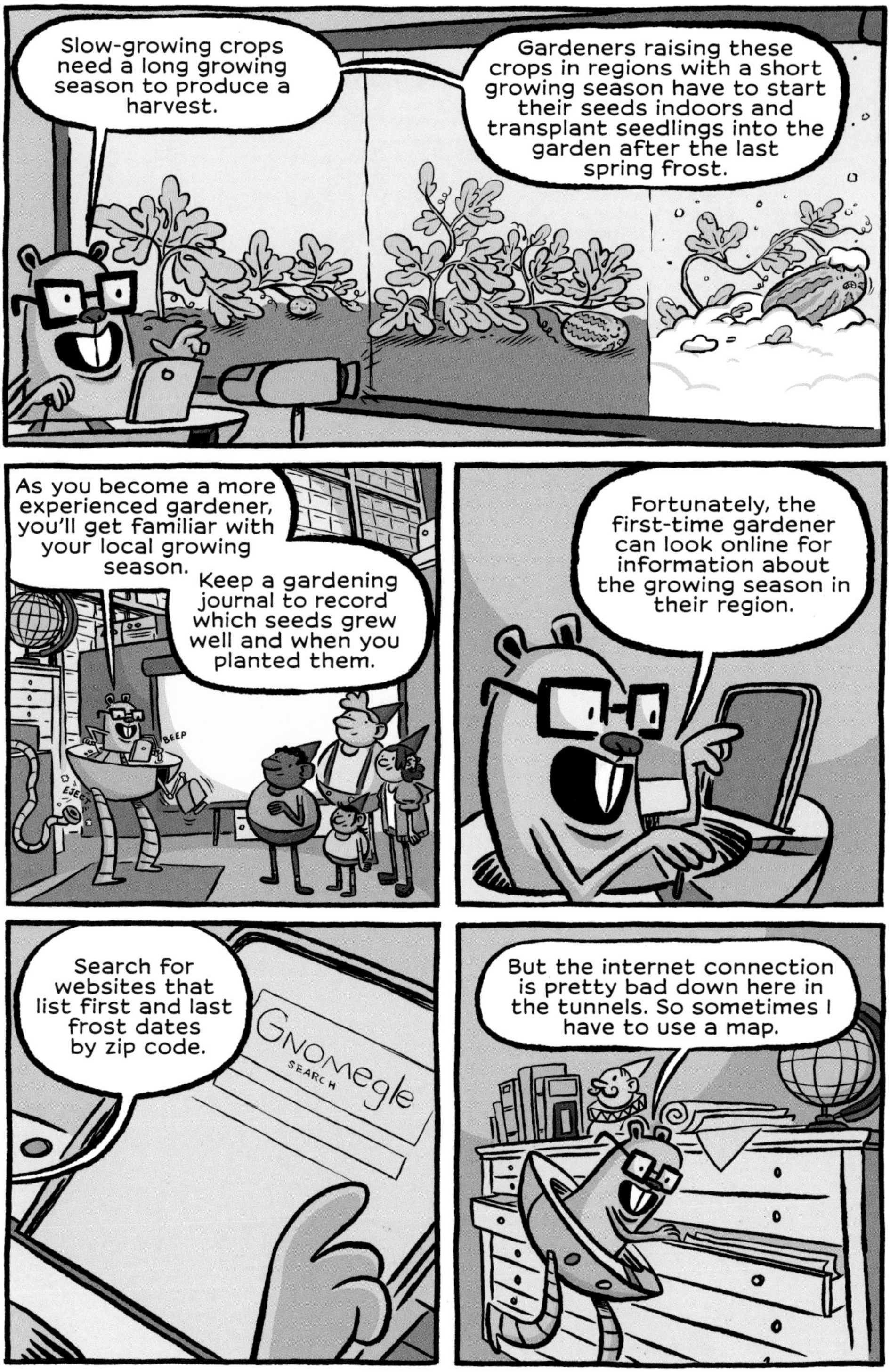
Slow-growing crops need a long growing season to produce a harvest.
Gardeners raising these crops in regions with a short growing season have to start their seeds indoors and transplant seedlings into the garden after the last spring frost.
As you become a more experienced gardener, you'll get familiar with your local growing season.
Keep a gardening journal to record which seeds grew well and when you planted them.
BEEP
EJECT
Fortunately, the first-time gardener can look online for information about the growing season in their region.
Search for websites that list first and last frost dates by zip code.
Gnomegle
SEARCH
But the internet connection is pretty bad down here in the tunnels. So sometimes I have to use a map.

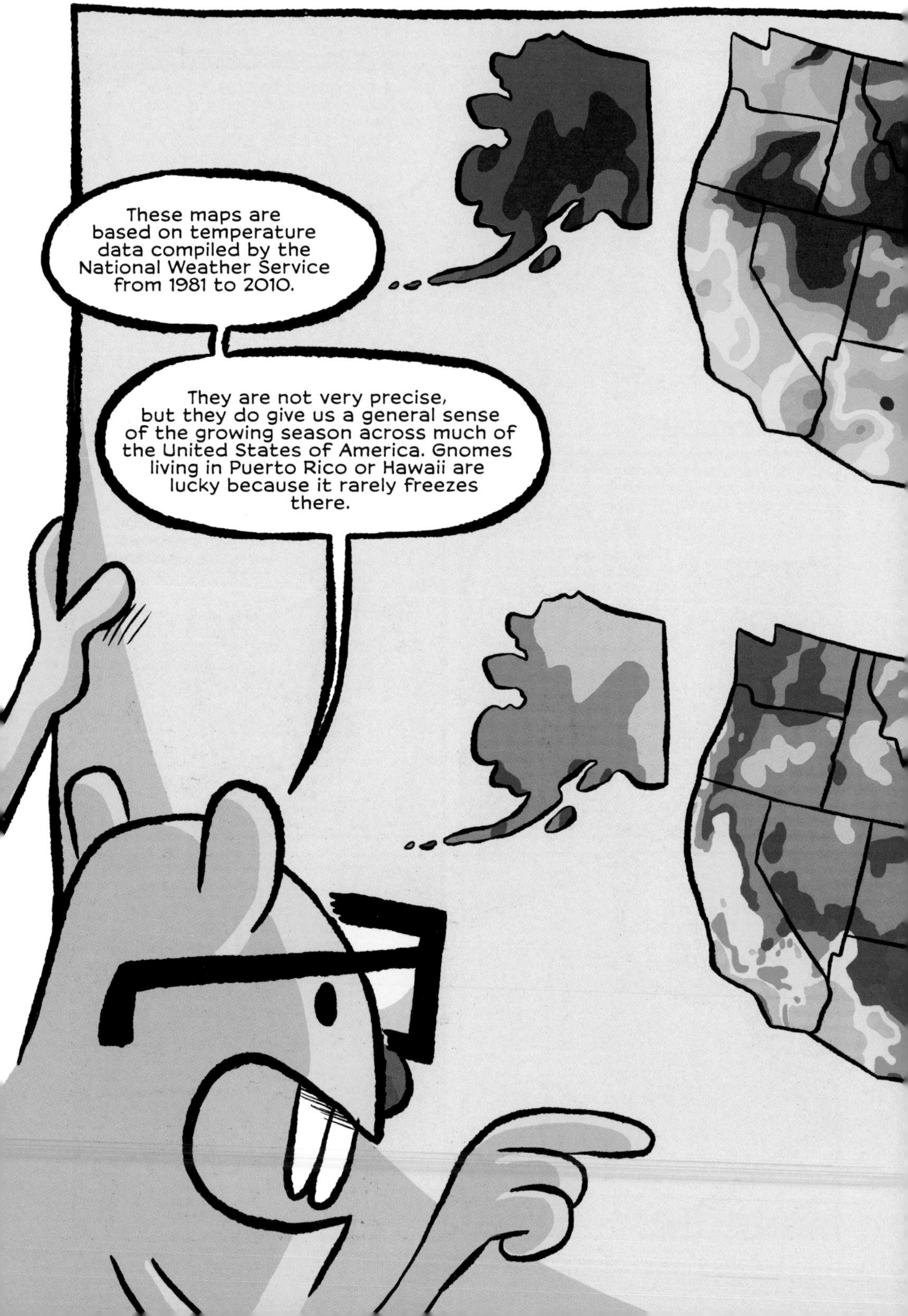
These maps are based on temperature data compiled by the National Weather Service from 1981 to 2010.
They are not very precise, but they do give us a general sense of the growing season across much of the United States of America. Gnomes living in Puerto Rico or Hawaii are lucky because it rarely freezes there.

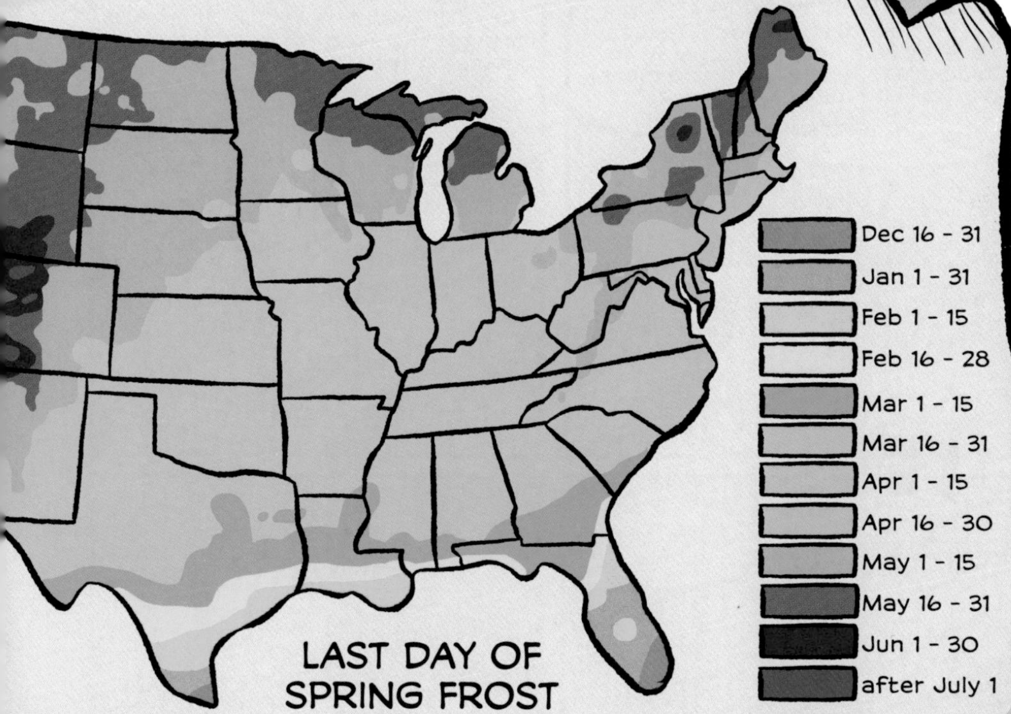
Dec 16 - 31
Jan 1 - 31
Feb 1 - 15
Feb 16 - 28
Mar 1 - 15
Mar 16 - 31
Apr 1 - 15
Apr 16 - 30
May 1 - 15
May 16 - 31
Jun 1 - 30
after July 1
LAST DAY OF
SPRING FROST

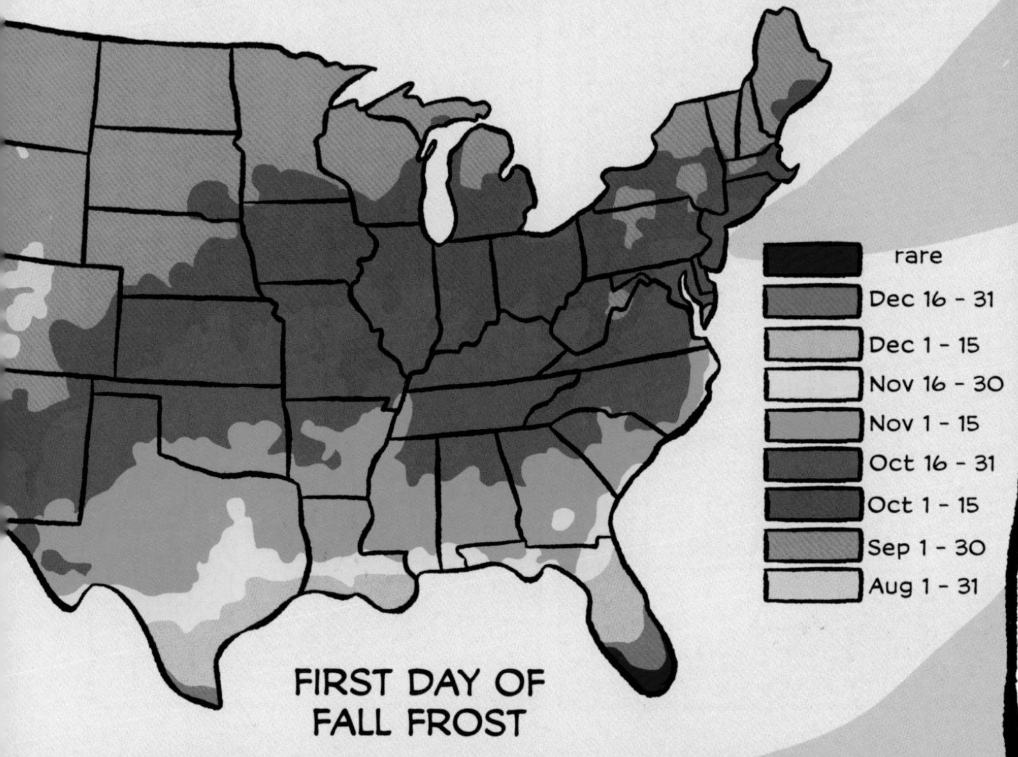
rare
Dec 16 - 31
Dec 1 - 15
Nov 16 - 30
Nov 1 - 15
Oct 16 - 31
Oct 1 - 15
Sep 1 - 30
Aug 1 - 31
FIRST DAY OF
FALL FROST

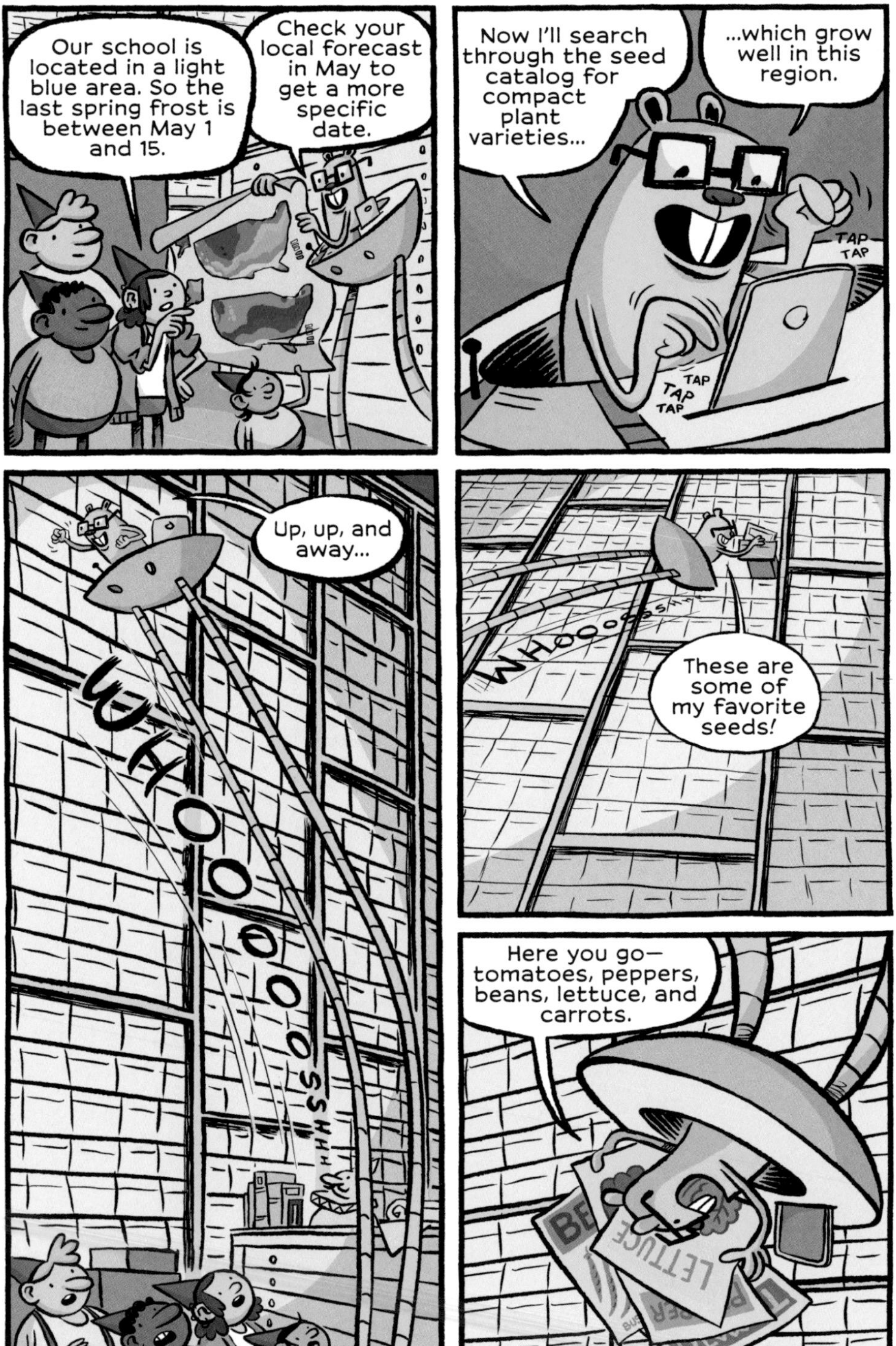
Our school is located in a light blue area. So the last spring frost is between May 1 and 15.
Check your local forecast in May to get a more specific date.
Now I'll search through the seed catalog for compact plant varieties...
...which grow well in this region.
TAP TAP
TAP TAP TAP
Up, up, and away...
WHOOOOOOOSSHHH
WHOOOSSHH
These are some of my favorite seeds!
Here you go—tomatoes, peppers, beans, lettuce, and carrots.
LETTUCE

These seeds will get you started.

WHOOOT WHOOT ALERT INTRUDER ALERT WHOOT

That's the security *alarm!*

ALERT INTRUDER ALERT

Monster! Intruder.

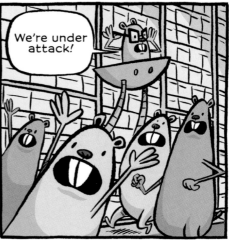

We're under attack!

CRUNCH

Something is attacking us from the greenhouse.

TOMAT BEAN

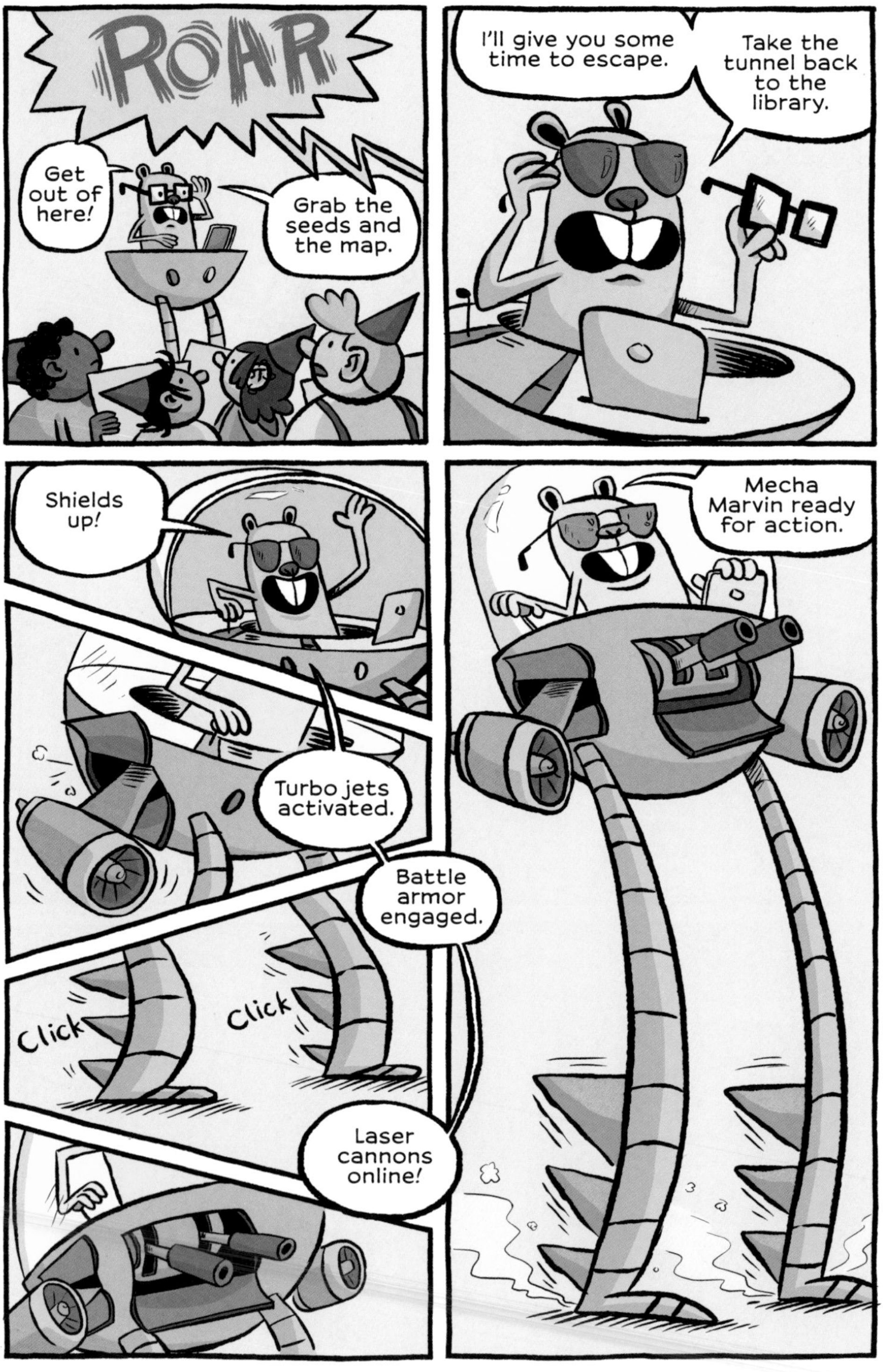
ROAR
Get out of here!
Grab the seeds and the map.
I'll give you some time to escape.
Take the tunnel back to the library.
Shields up!
Turbo jets activated.
Battle armor engaged.
Click
Click
Laser cannons online!
Mecha Marvin ready for action.

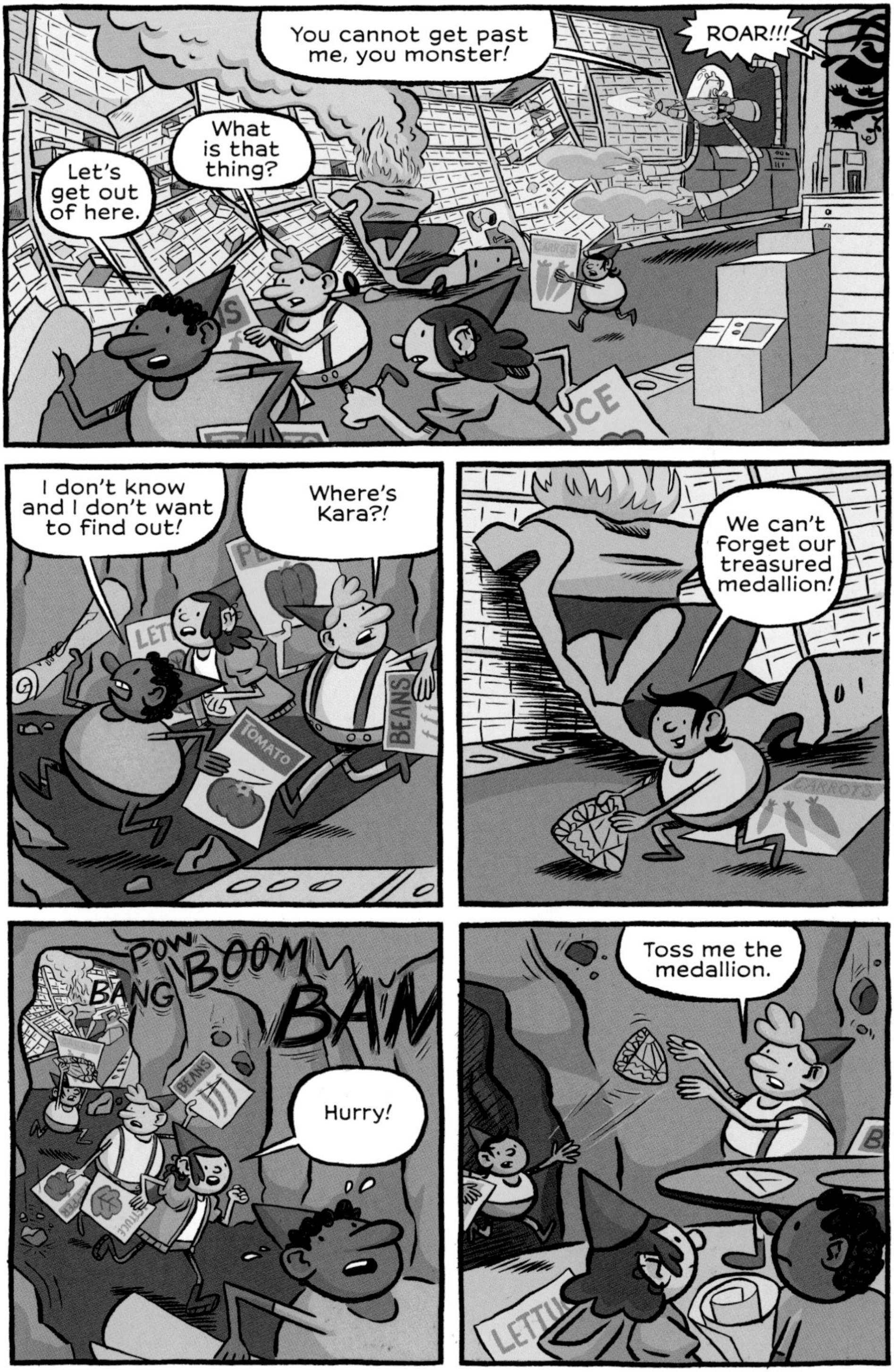
You cannot get past me, you monster!
ROAR!!!
What is that thing?
Let's get out of here.
I don't know and I don't want to find out!
Where's Kara?!
We can't forget our treasured medallion!
POW
BANG
BOOM
BAM
Hurry!
Toss me the medallion.

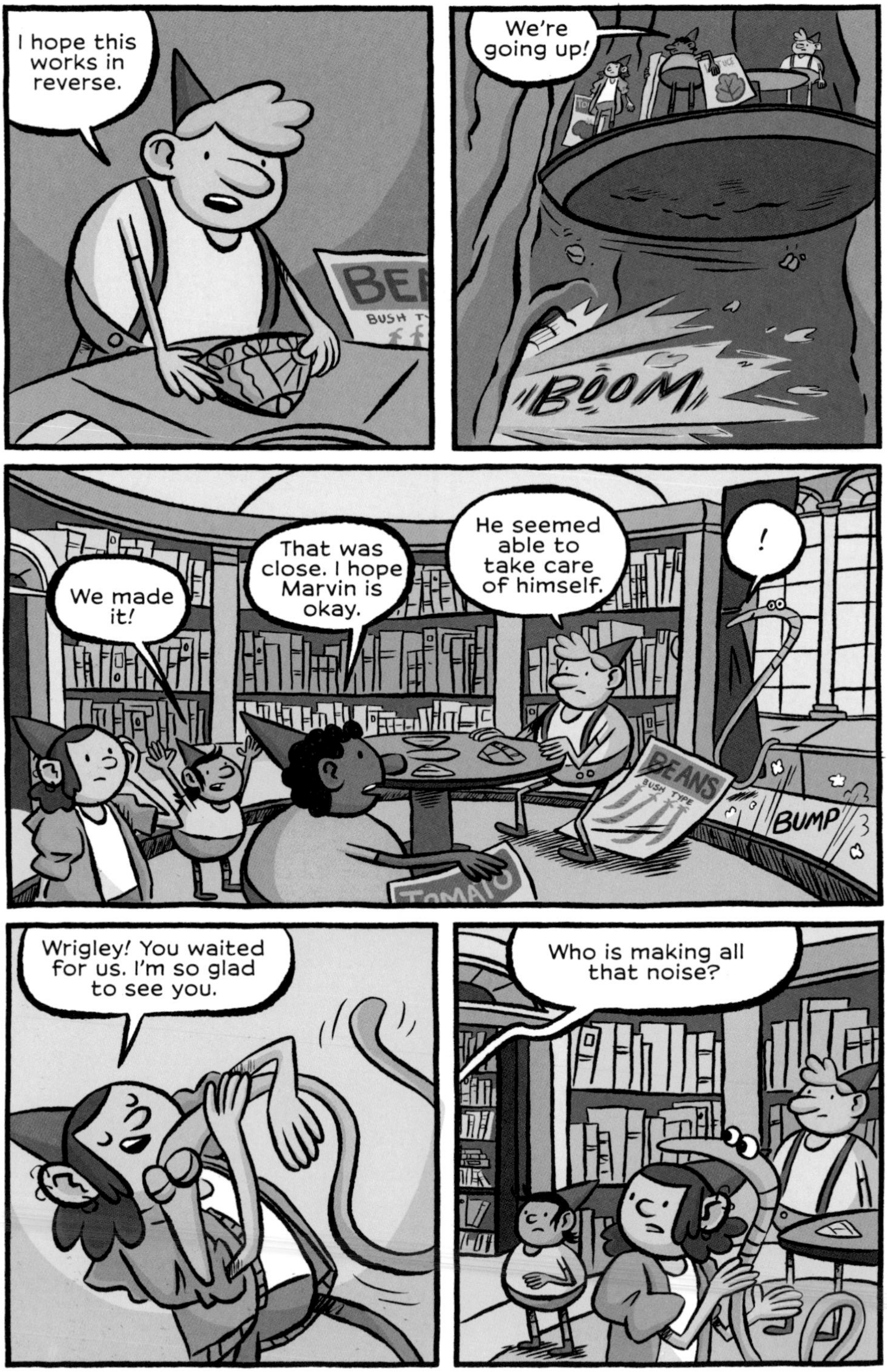
I hope this works in reverse.
We're going up!
BOOM
We made it!
That was close. I hope Marvin is okay.
He seemed able to take care of himself.
!
BEANS
BUSH TYPE
BUMP
Wrigley! You waited for us. I'm so glad to see you.
Who is making all that noise?

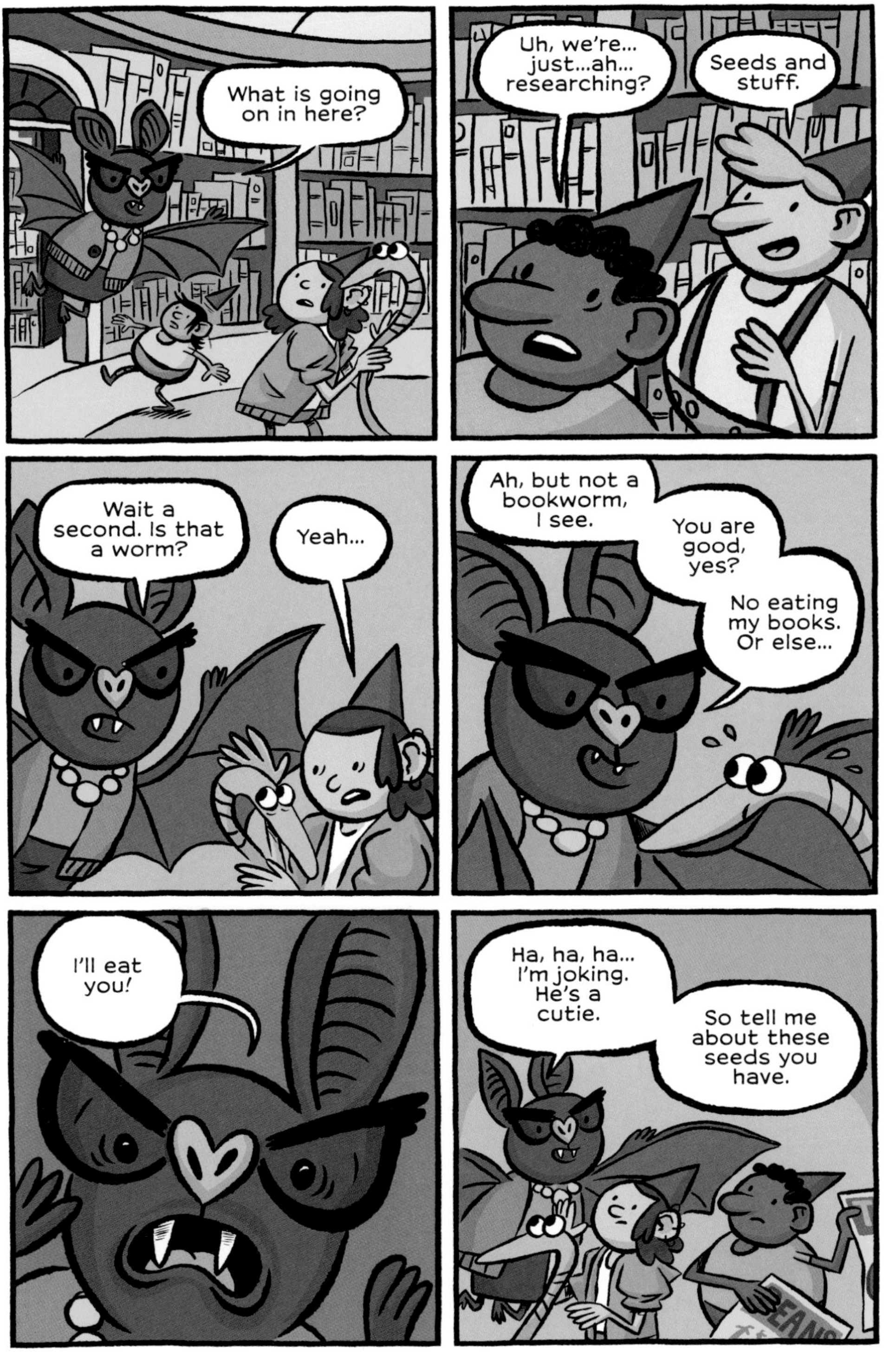
What is going on in here?
Uh, we're... just...ah... researching?
Seeds and stuff.
Wait a second. Is that a worm?
Yeah...
Ah, but not a bookworm, I see.
You are good, yes?
No eating my books. Or else...
I'll eat you!
Ha, ha, ha... I'm joking. He's a cutie.
So tell me about these seeds you have.

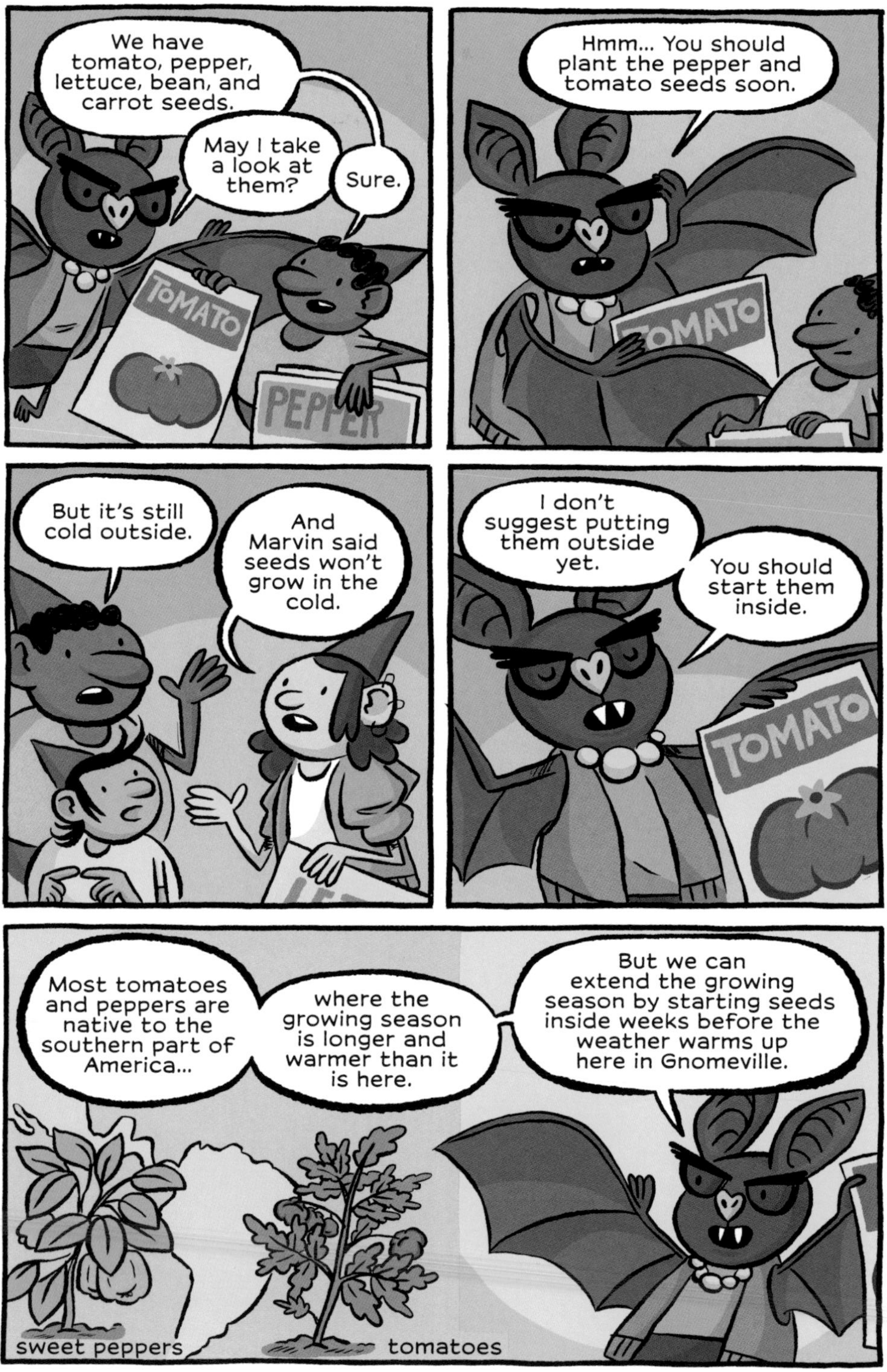
We have tomato, pepper, lettuce, bean, and carrot seeds.
May I take a look at them?
Sure.
TOMATO
PEPPER
Hmm... You should plant the pepper and tomato seeds soon.
TOMATO
But it's still cold outside.
And Marvin said seeds won't grow in the cold.
I don't suggest putting them outside yet.
You should start them inside.
TOMATO
Most tomatoes and peppers are native to the southern part of America...
where the growing season is longer and warmer than it is here.
But we can extend the growing season by starting seeds inside weeks before the weather warms up here in Gnomeville.
sweet peppers
tomatoes

How do you know which seeds need to be started indoors?

I *am* a very smart bat.

And more importantly, I read instructions.

Seed packages provide growing instructions, which explain if the seeds should be started indoors or sown directly in the garden.

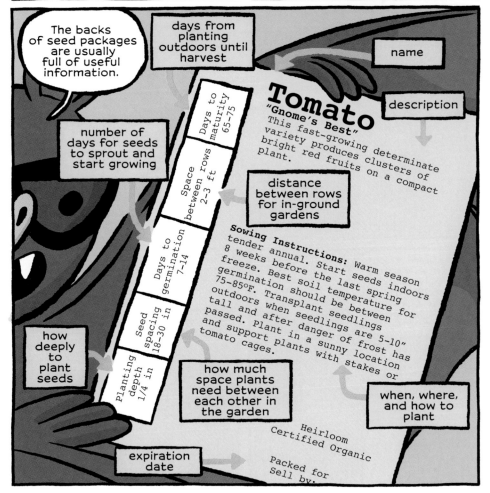

The backs of seed packages are usually full of useful information.

days from planting outdoors until harvest

name

number of days for seeds to sprout and start growing

Days to maturity 65-75

Space between rows 2-3 ft

distance between rows for in-ground gardens

Days to germination 7-14

Seed spacing 18-30 in

Planting depth 1/4 in

how deeply to plant seeds

Tomato
"Gnome's Best"
This fast-growing determinate variety produces clusters of bright red fruits on a compact plant.

description

Sowing Instructions: Warm season tender annual. Start seeds indoors 8 weeks before the last spring freeze. Best soil temperature for germination should be between 75-85°F. Transplant seedlings outdoors when seedlings are 5-10" tall and after danger of frost has passed. Plant in a sunny location and support plants with stakes or tomato cages.

how much space plants need between each other in the garden

when, where, and how to plant

Heirloom Certified Organic

expiration date

Packed for Sell by.

Some seeds, like lettuce seeds, can be started indoors or planted outside in the spring.

Lettuce

Sowing Instructions:
Direct sow or transplant in early spring as soon as the soil is workable.
Direct Seeding: Plant seeds 1/8 inch deep, in rows 10 to 12 inches apart. When plants develop true leaves, thin to 6 to 10 inches between sprouts.
Transplants: Sow inside 3 to 4 weeks...

Root vegetables, like carrots, don't like being moved and should be sown directly in the garden.

CARROTS

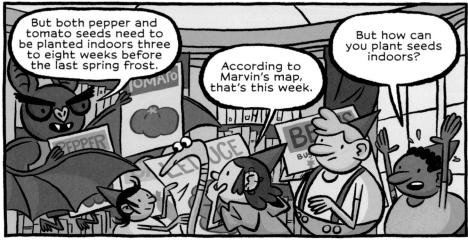

But both pepper and tomato seeds need to be planted indoors three to eight weeks before the last spring frost.

According to Marvin's map, that's this week.

But how can you plant seeds indoors?

You plant them in pots. Garden supply stores sell peat pots or plastic trays for starting seeds indoors.

But you can also plant seeds in recycled containers.

RECYCLE

I'm sure you can find something in the recycling bins outside.

Could you take these newspapers with you?

RECYCLE

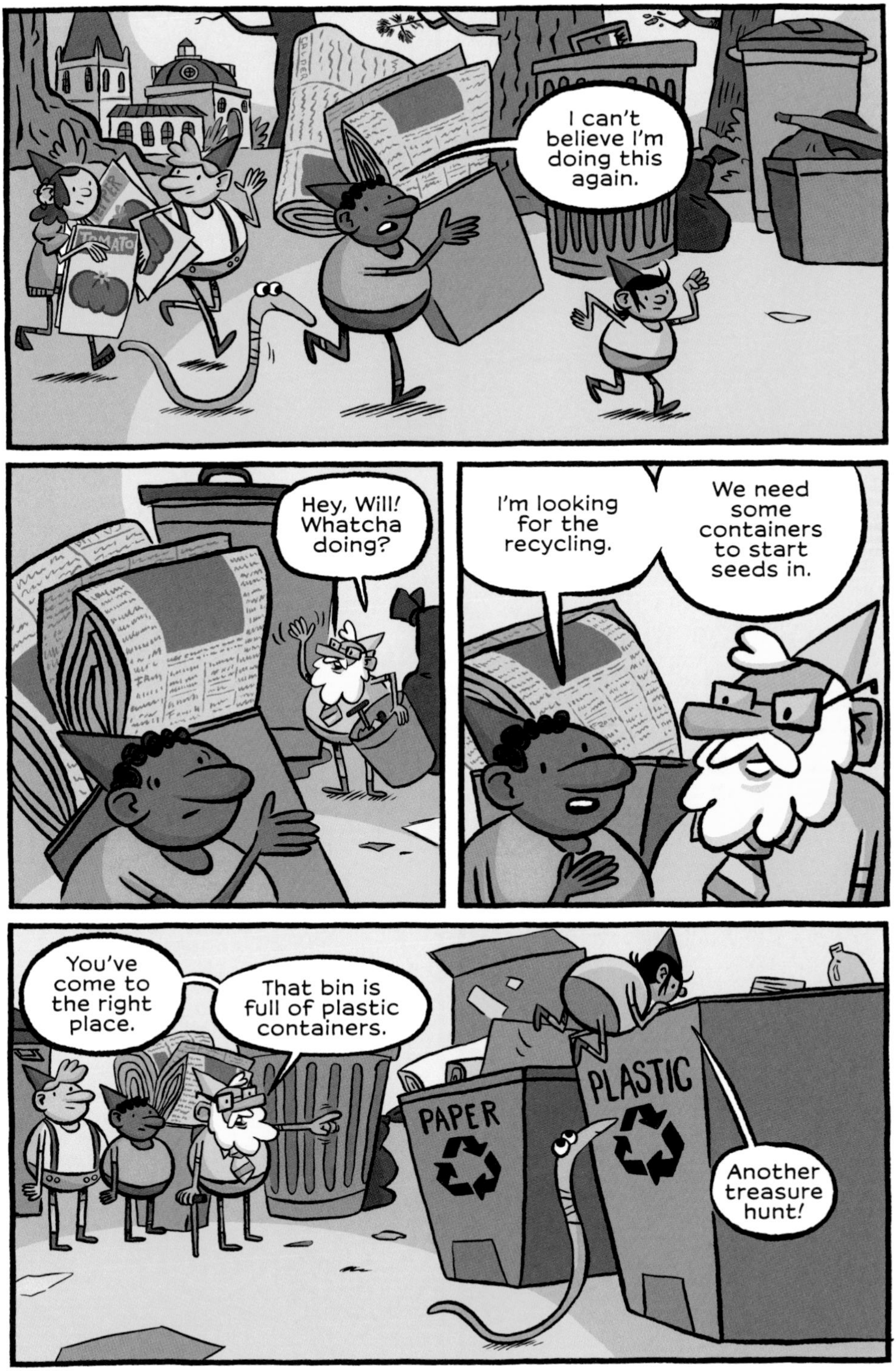
I can't believe I'm doing this again.
CALDER
TOMATO
Hey, Will! Whatcha doing?
I'm looking for the recycling.
We need some containers to start seeds in.
You've come to the right place.
That bin is full of plastic containers.
PAPER
PLASTIC
Another treasure hunt!

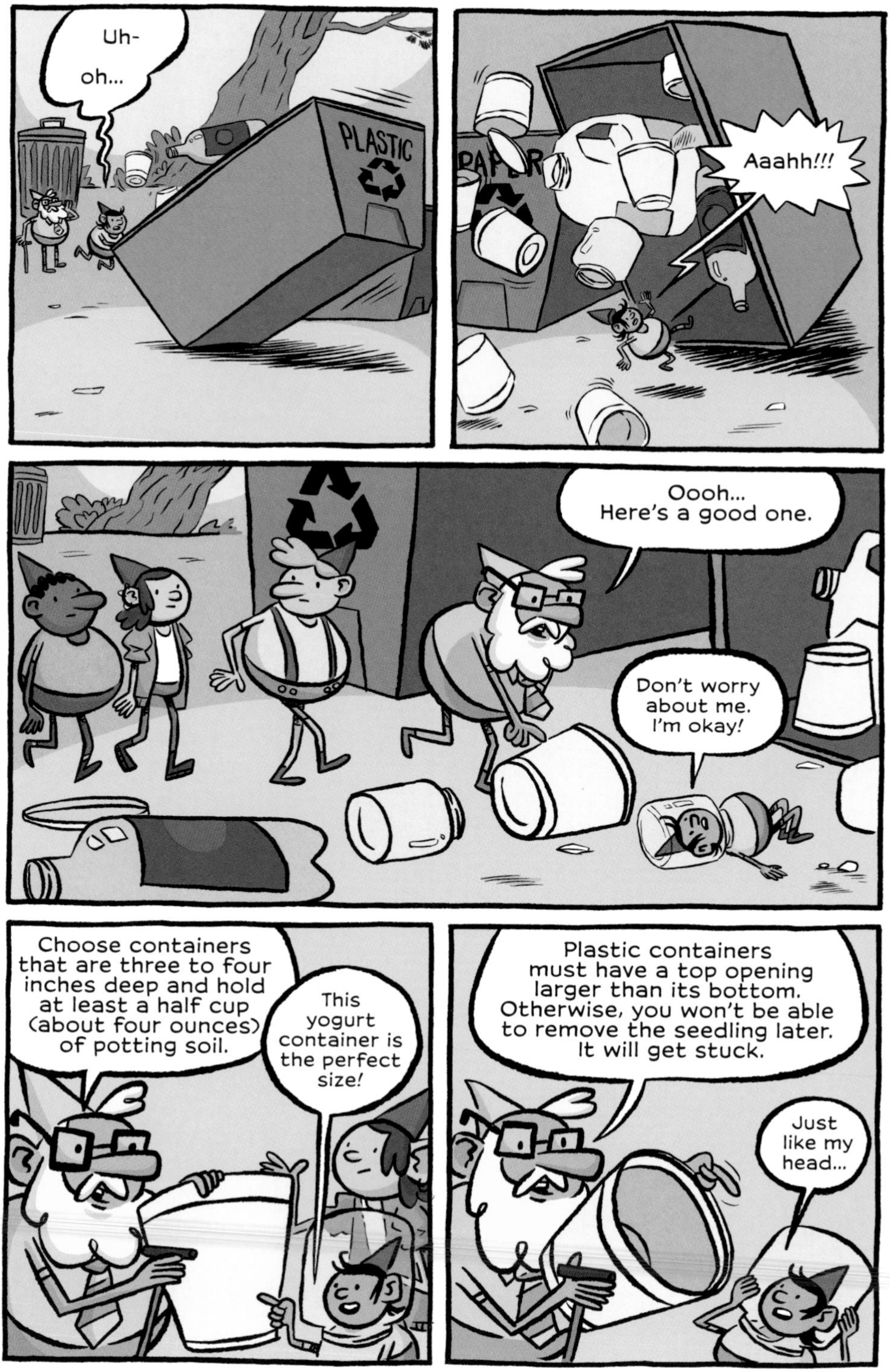
Uh-
oh...
Aaahh!!!
PLASTIC
PAPER
Oooh... Here's a good one.
Don't worry about me. I'm okay!
Choose containers that are three to four inches deep and hold at least a half cup (about four ounces) of potting soil.
This yogurt container is the perfect size!
Plastic containers must have a top opening larger than its bottom. Otherwise, you won't be able to remove the seedling later. It will get stuck.
Just like my head...

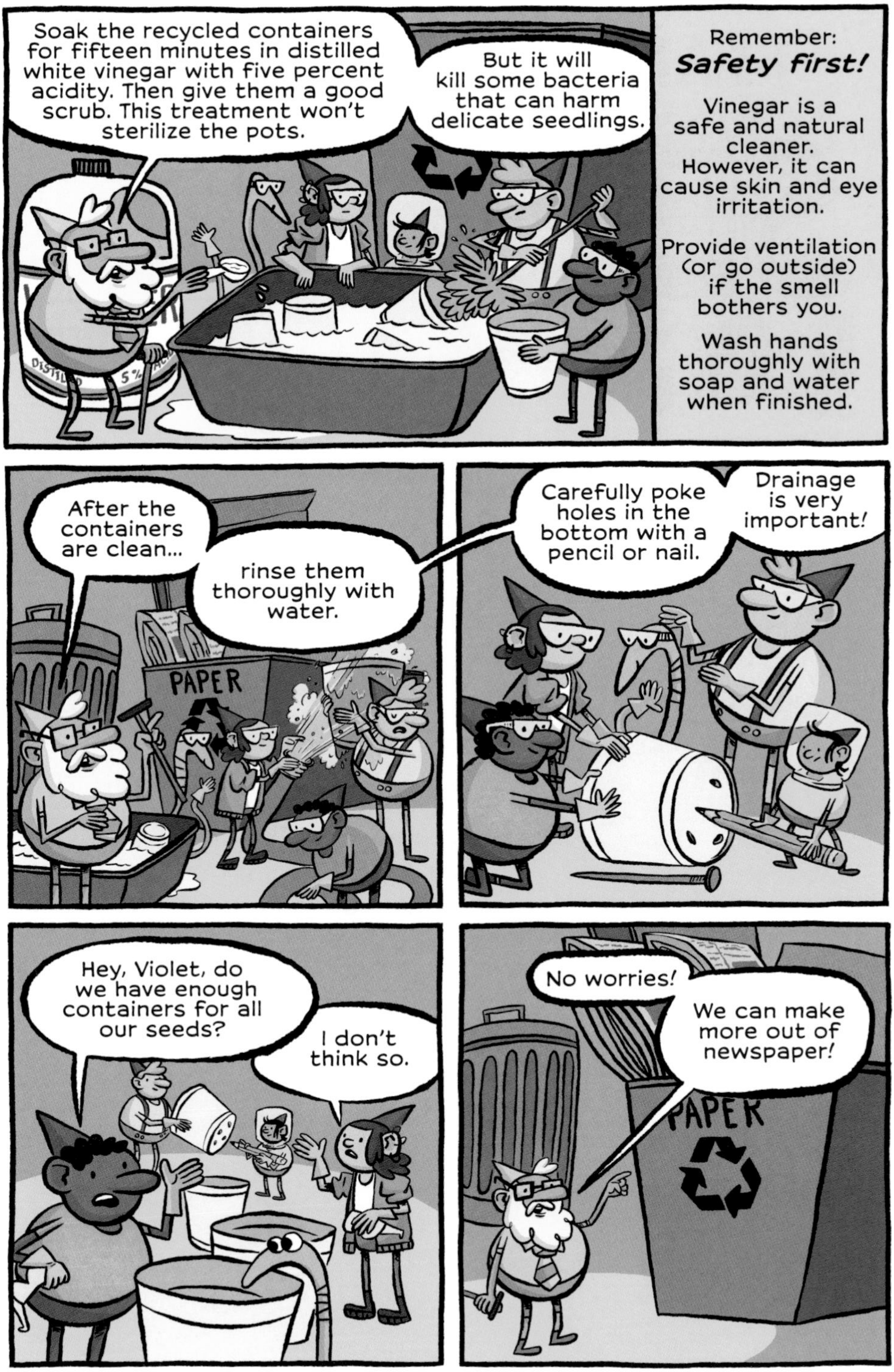
Soak the recycled containers for fifteen minutes in distilled white vinegar with five percent acidity. Then give them a good scrub. This treatment won't sterilize the pots.
But it will kill some bacteria that can harm delicate seedlings.
Remember: ***Safety first!***
Vinegar is a safe and natural cleaner. However, it can cause skin and eye irritation.
Provide ventilation (or go outside) if the smell bothers you.
Wash hands thoroughly with soap and water when finished.
After the containers are clean...
rinse them thoroughly with water.
PAPER
Carefully poke holes in the bottom with a pencil or nail.
Drainage is very important!
Hey, Violet, do we have enough containers for all our seeds?
I don't think so.
No worries!
We can make more out of newspaper!
PAPER

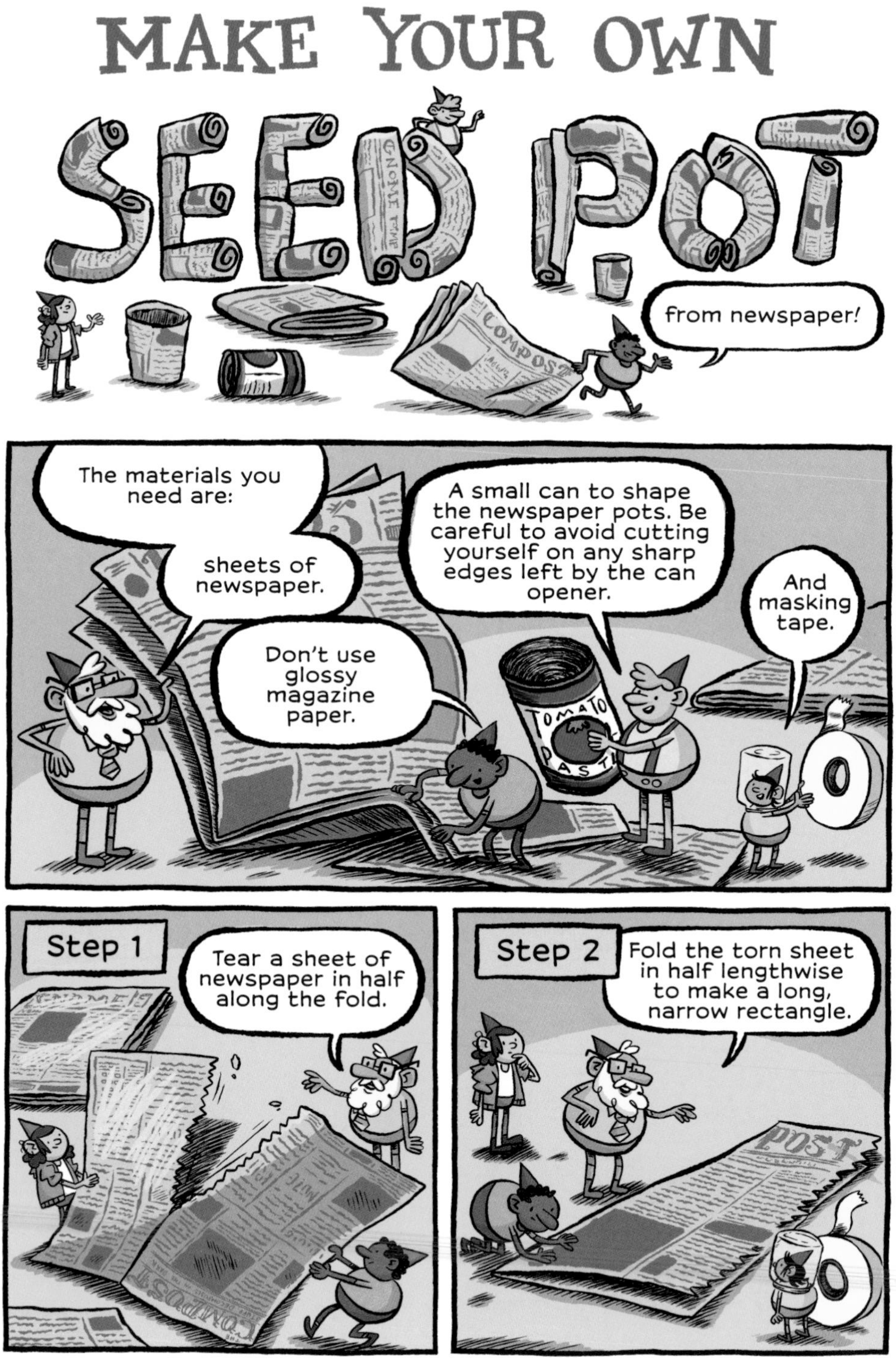
MAKE YOUR OWN
SEED POT
from newspaper!
The materials you need are:
sheets of newspaper.
Don't use glossy magazine paper.
A small can to shape the newspaper pots. Be careful to avoid cutting yourself on any sharp edges left by the can opener.
And masking tape.
Step 1
Tear a sheet of newspaper in half along the fold.
Step 2
Fold the torn sheet in half lengthwise to make a long, narrow rectangle.

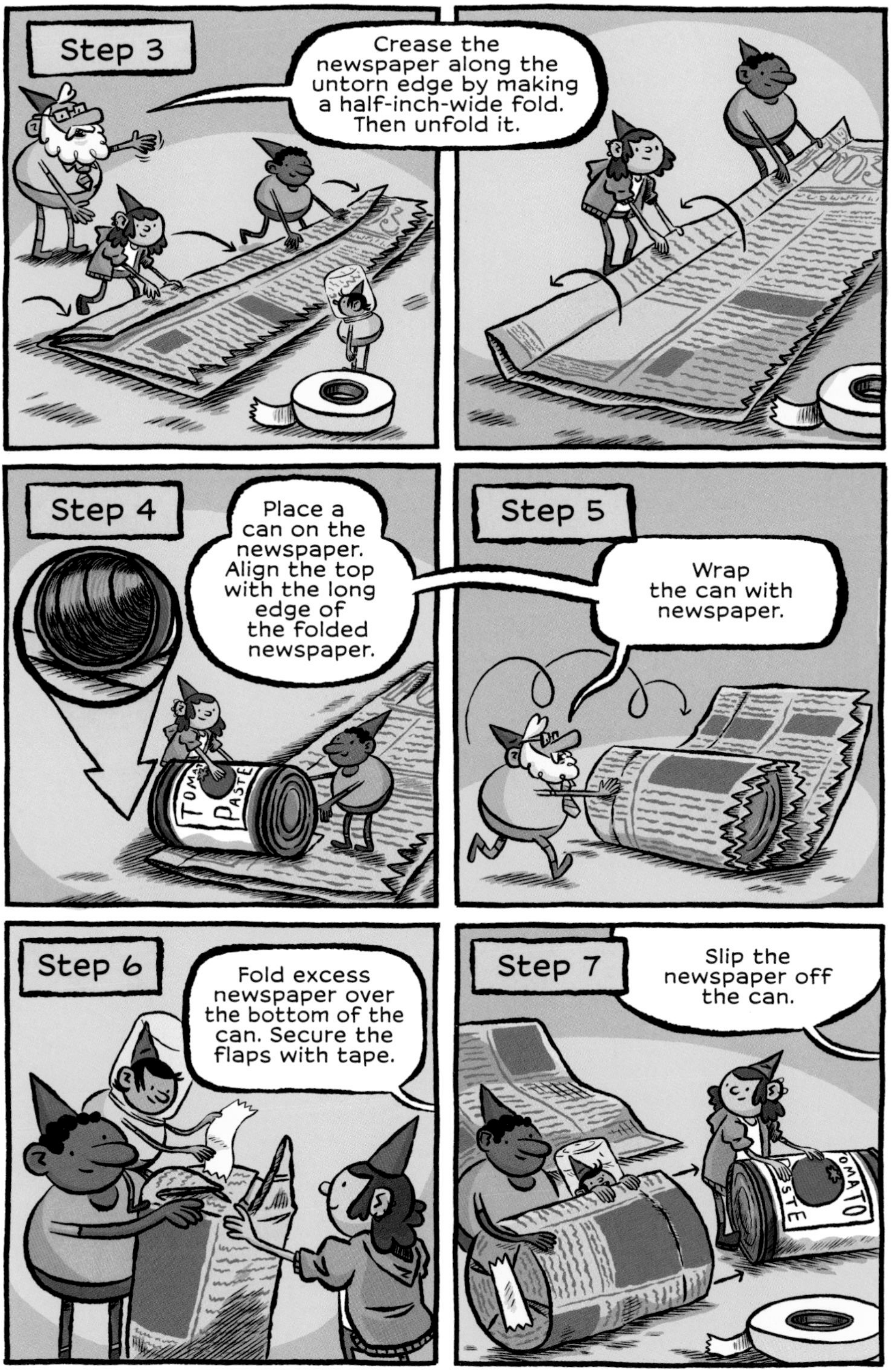
Step 3
Crease the newspaper along the untorn edge by making a half-inch-wide fold. Then unfold it.
Step 4
Place a can on the newspaper. Align the top with the long edge of the folded newspaper.
TOMATO PASTE
Step 5
Wrap the can with newspaper.
Step 6
Fold excess newspaper over the bottom of the can. Secure the flaps with tape.
Step 7
Slip the newspaper off the can.
TOMATO PASTE

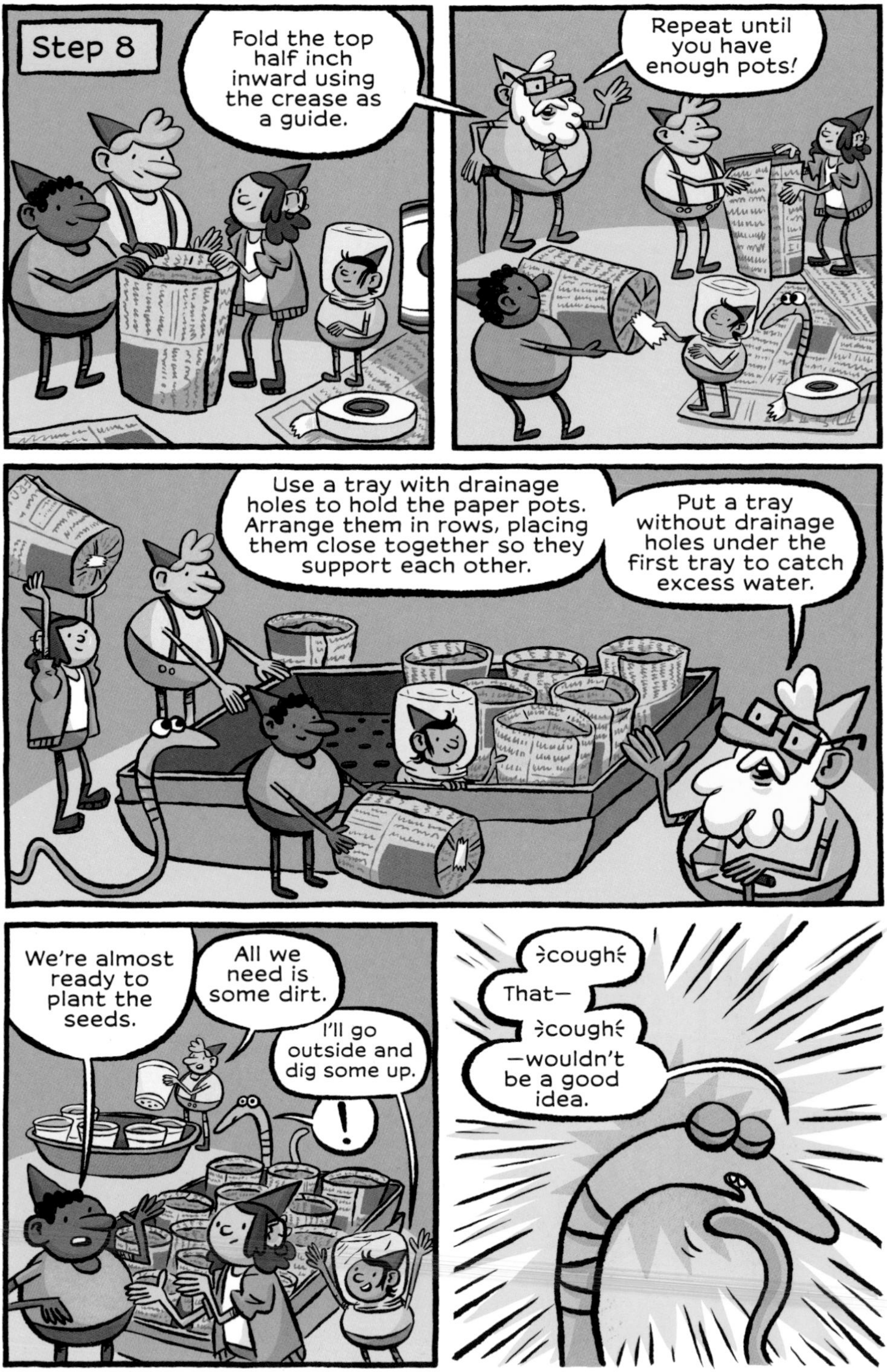

Step 8
Fold the top half inch inward using the crease as a guide.
Repeat until you have enough pots!
Use a tray with drainage holes to hold the paper pots. Arrange them in rows, placing them close together so they support each other.
Put a tray without drainage holes under the first tray to catch excess water.
We're almost ready to plant the seeds.
All we need is some dirt.
I'll go outside and dig some up.
!
cough
That—
cough
—wouldn't be a good idea.

Wrigley! I didn't know you could speak.

I'm just getting my voice back after having that thing stuck in my throat.

My name is Sir Wigglesworth Slimyington the Third...

but you can still call me Wrigley.

I am somewhat of a soil connoisseur.

Is a connoisseur like a dinosaur?!

No, it means he knows a lot about soil.

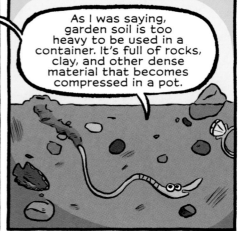

As I was saying, garden soil is too heavy to be used in a container. It's full of rocks, clay, and other dense material that becomes compressed in a pot.

A pot filled with dirt does not drain well and often will become waterlogged.

Saturated soil can kill seeds and the roots of plants.

dense dirt

waterlogged

Even worse, soil from outside might contain mold spores, fungus, or bugs that could harm tender seedlings.

Errk!

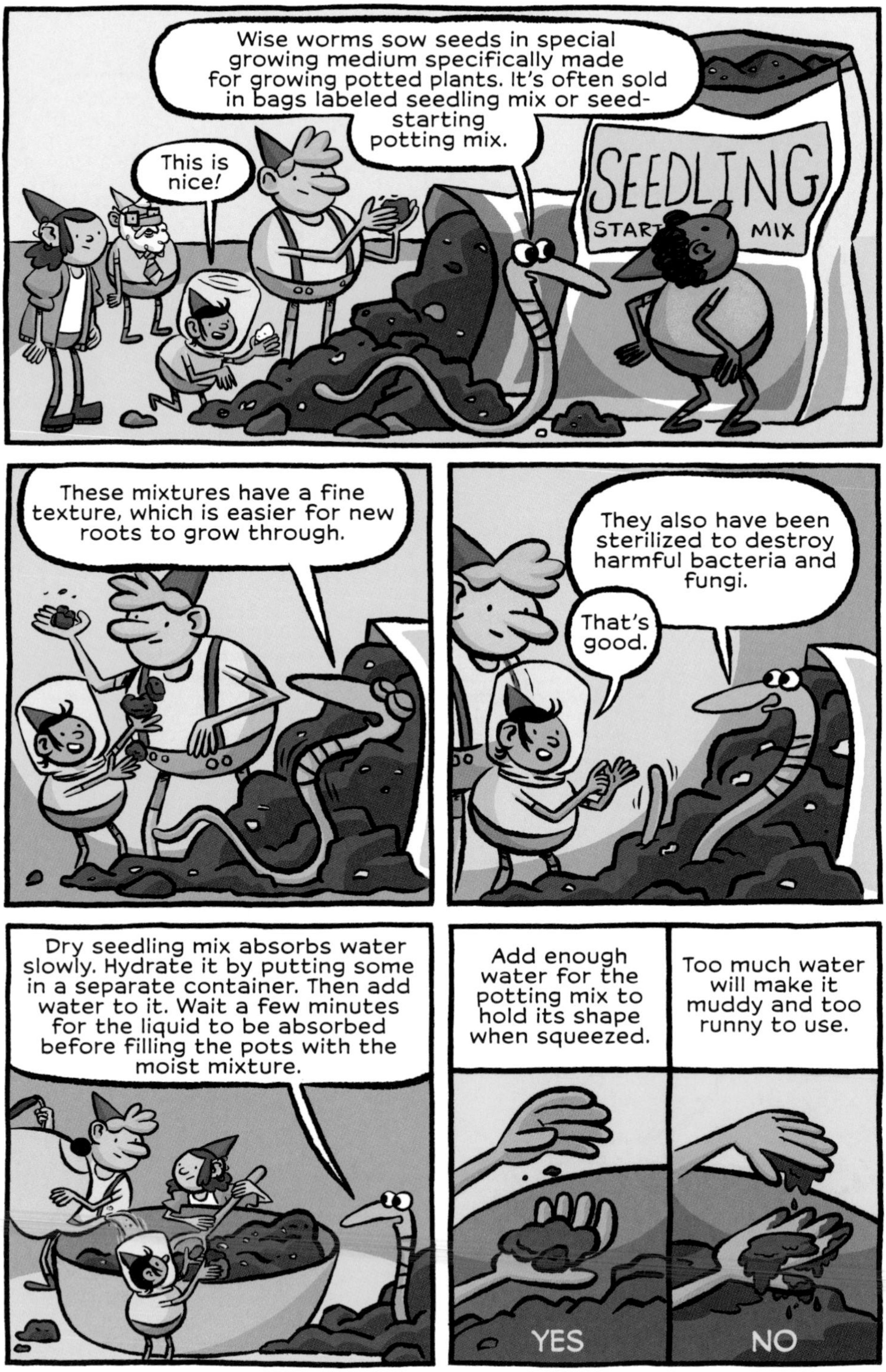
Wise worms sow seeds in special growing medium specifically made for growing potted plants. It's often sold in bags labeled seedling mix or seed-starting potting mix.
This is nice!
SEEDLING
START
MIX
These mixtures have a fine texture, which is easier for new roots to grow through.
They also have been sterilized to destroy harmful bacteria and fungi.
That's good.
Dry seedling mix absorbs water slowly. Hydrate it by putting some in a separate container. Then add water to it. Wait a few minutes for the liquid to be absorbed before filling the pots with the moist mixture.
Add enough water for the potting mix to hold its shape when squeezed.
Too much water will make it muddy and too runny to use.
YES
NO

MAKE YOUR OWN POTTING MIX

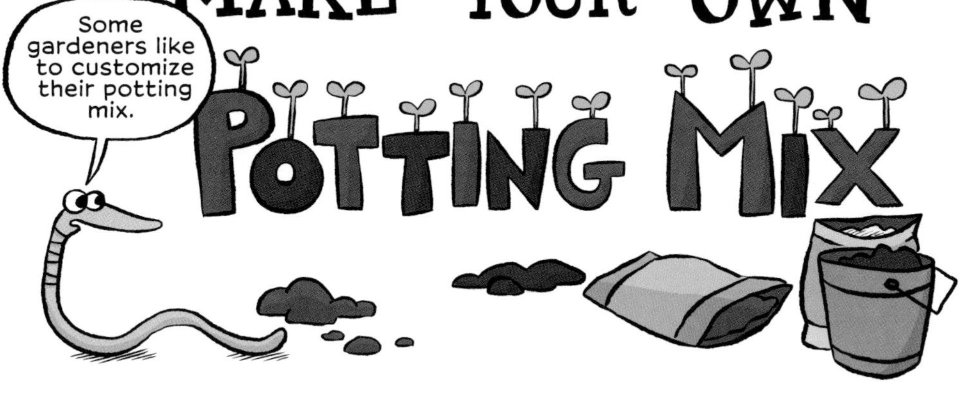
Some gardeners like to customize their potting mix.

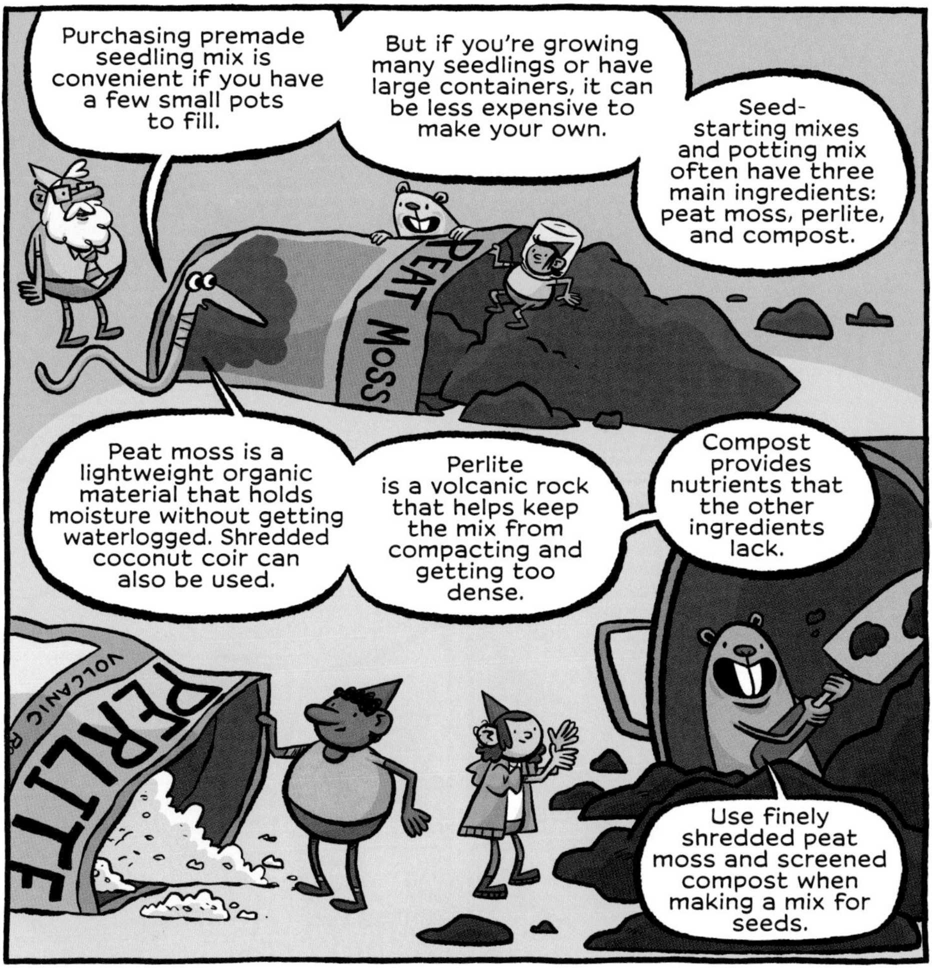
Purchasing premade seedling mix is convenient if you have a few small pots to fill.
But if you're growing many seedlings or have large containers, it can be less expensive to make your own.
Seed-starting mixes and potting mix often have three main ingredients: peat moss, perlite, and compost.
PEAT MOSS
Peat moss is a lightweight organic material that holds moisture without getting waterlogged. Shredded coconut coir can also be used.
Perlite is a volcanic rock that helps keep the mix from compacting and getting too dense.
Compost provides nutrients that the other ingredients lack.
PERLITE
Use finely shredded peat moss and screened compost when making a mix for seeds.

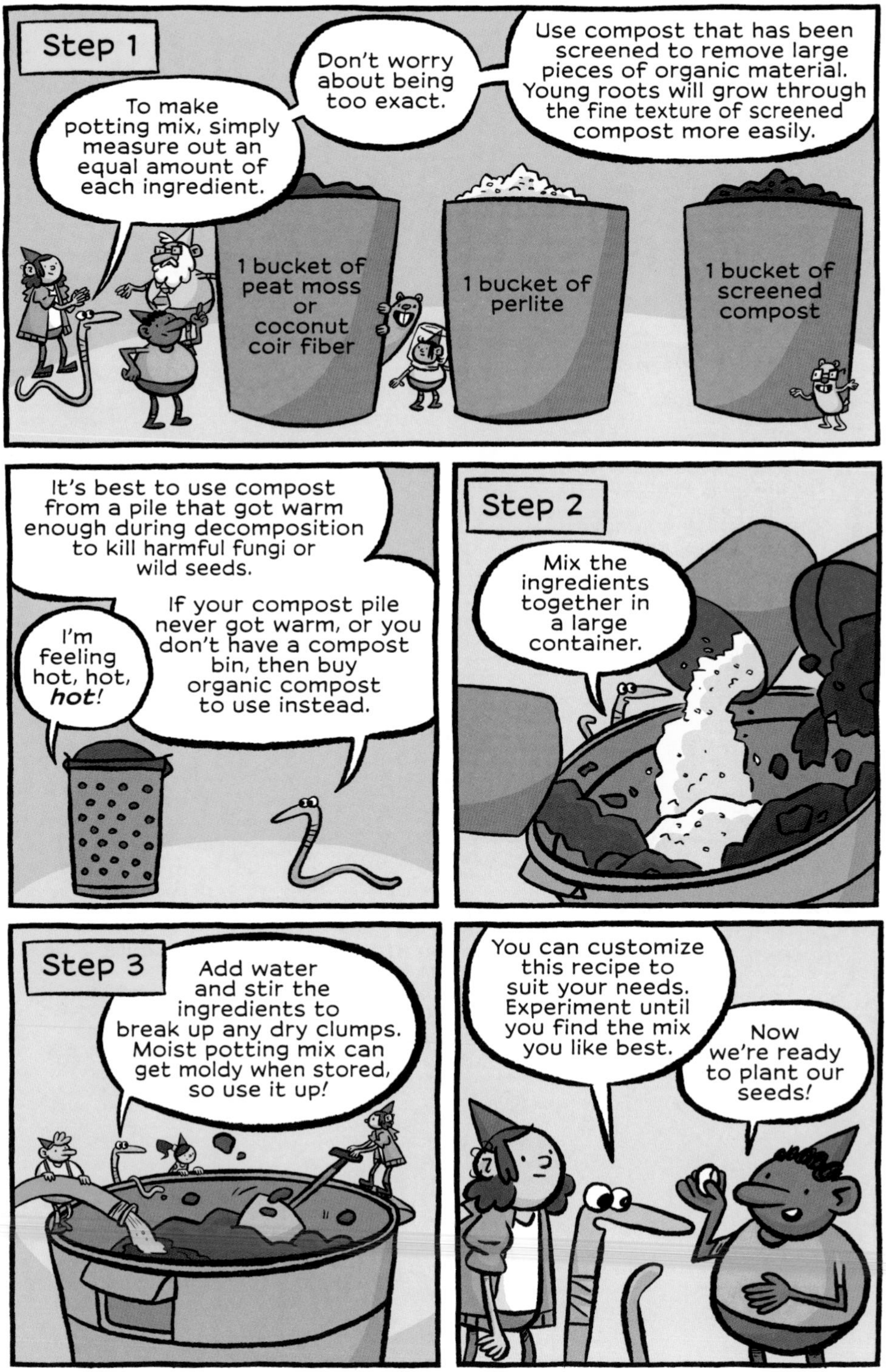
Step 1
To make potting mix, simply measure out an equal amount of each ingredient.
Don't worry about being too exact.
Use compost that has been screened to remove large pieces of organic material. Young roots will grow through the fine texture of screened compost more easily.
1 bucket of peat moss or coconut coir fiber
1 bucket of perlite
1 bucket of screened compost
It's best to use compost from a pile that got warm enough during decomposition to kill harmful fungi or wild seeds.
I'm feeling hot, hot, *hot*!
If your compost pile never got warm, or you don't have a compost bin, then buy organic compost to use instead.
Step 2
Mix the ingredients together in a large container.
Step 3
Add water and stir the ingredients to break up any dry clumps. Moist potting mix can get moldy when stored, so use it up!
You can customize this recipe to suit your needs. Experiment until you find the mix you like best.
Now we're ready to plant our seeds!

Fill the pots completely with potting mix. Then press the mix down about a half inch. The mix should be firm enough to support a plant...

...but loose enough for roots to grow through easily.

Make two shallow holes a quarter inch deep and a quarter inch apart near the center of the pot.

1/4 inch

Place a seed in each hole and cover with soil. Label each pot before you forget which type of seeds you sowed.

PEPPER

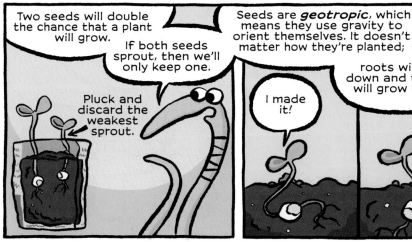

Two seeds will double the chance that a plant will grow.

If both seeds sprout, then we'll only keep one.

Pluck and discard the weakest sprout.

Seeds are *geotropic*, which means they use gravity to orient themselves. It doesn't matter how they're planted;

roots will grow down and the stem will grow upward.

I made it!

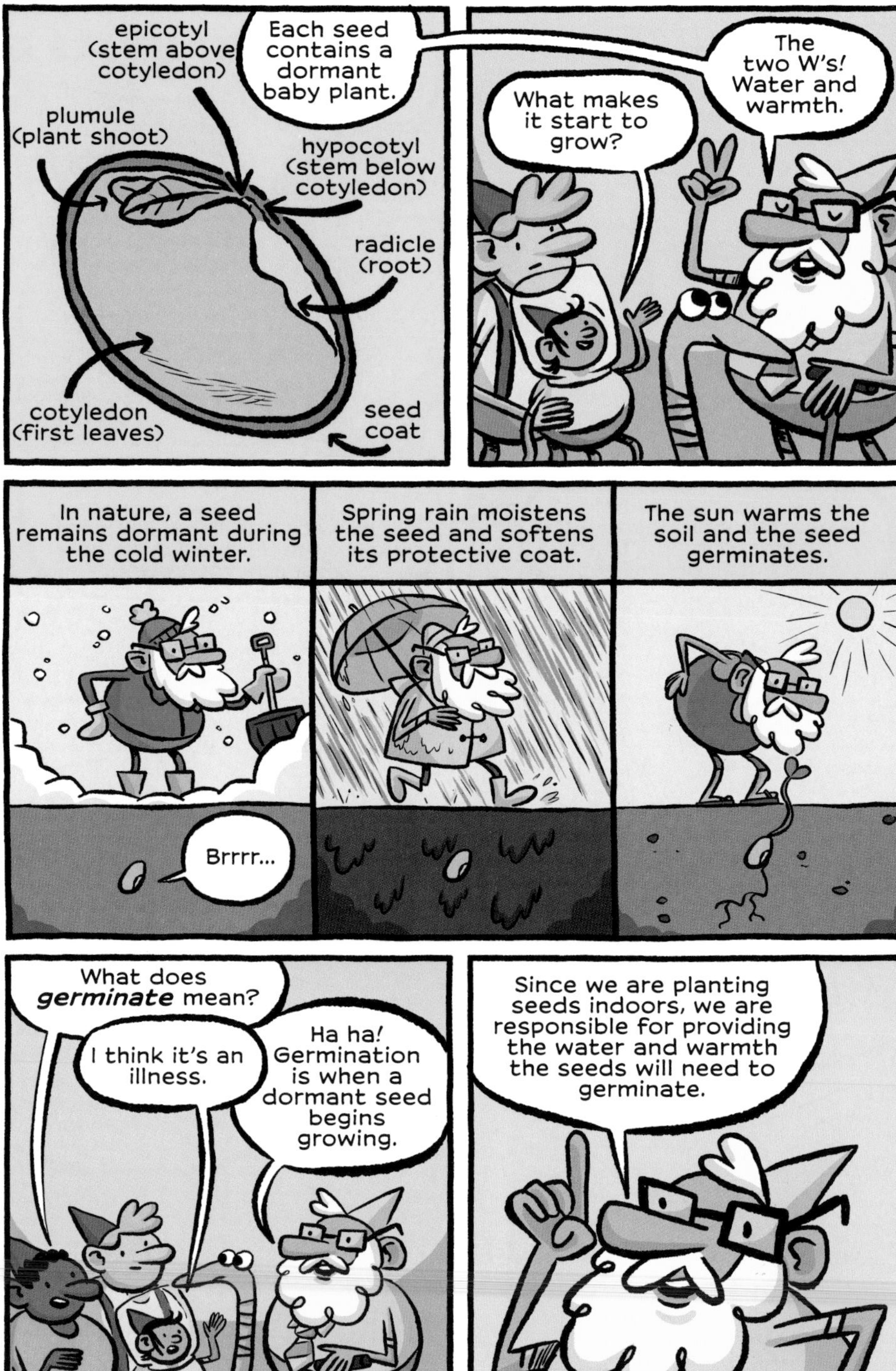

Each seed contains a dormant baby plant.
epicotyl (stem above cotyledon)
plumule (plant shoot)
hypocotyl (stem below cotyledon)
radicle (root)
cotyledon (first leaves)
seed coat
What makes it start to grow?
The two W's! Water and warmth.
In nature, a seed remains dormant during the cold winter.
Brrrr...
Spring rain moistens the seed and softens its protective coat.
The sun warms the soil and the seed germinates.
What does ***germinate*** mean?
I think it's an illness.
Ha ha! Germination is when a dormant seed begins growing.
Since we are planting seeds indoors, we are responsible for providing the water and warmth the seeds will need to germinate.

In general, seeds need temperatures above seventy-five degrees Fahrenheit during the day and sixty-five degrees at night to germinate.

← 75 degrees

← 65 degrees

That's warm, which is why the perfect place to start seeds is in a greenhouse!

Luckily, the school has one!

Let's take the tray of paper pots first. We will come back for the others.

The four of you can carry it together.

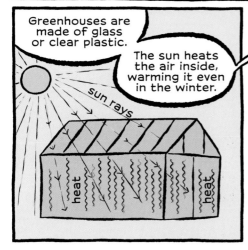

Greenhouses are made of glass or clear plastic.

The sun heats the air inside, warming it even in the winter.

sun rays

heat

heat

Hmm... For some reason, the door is locked.

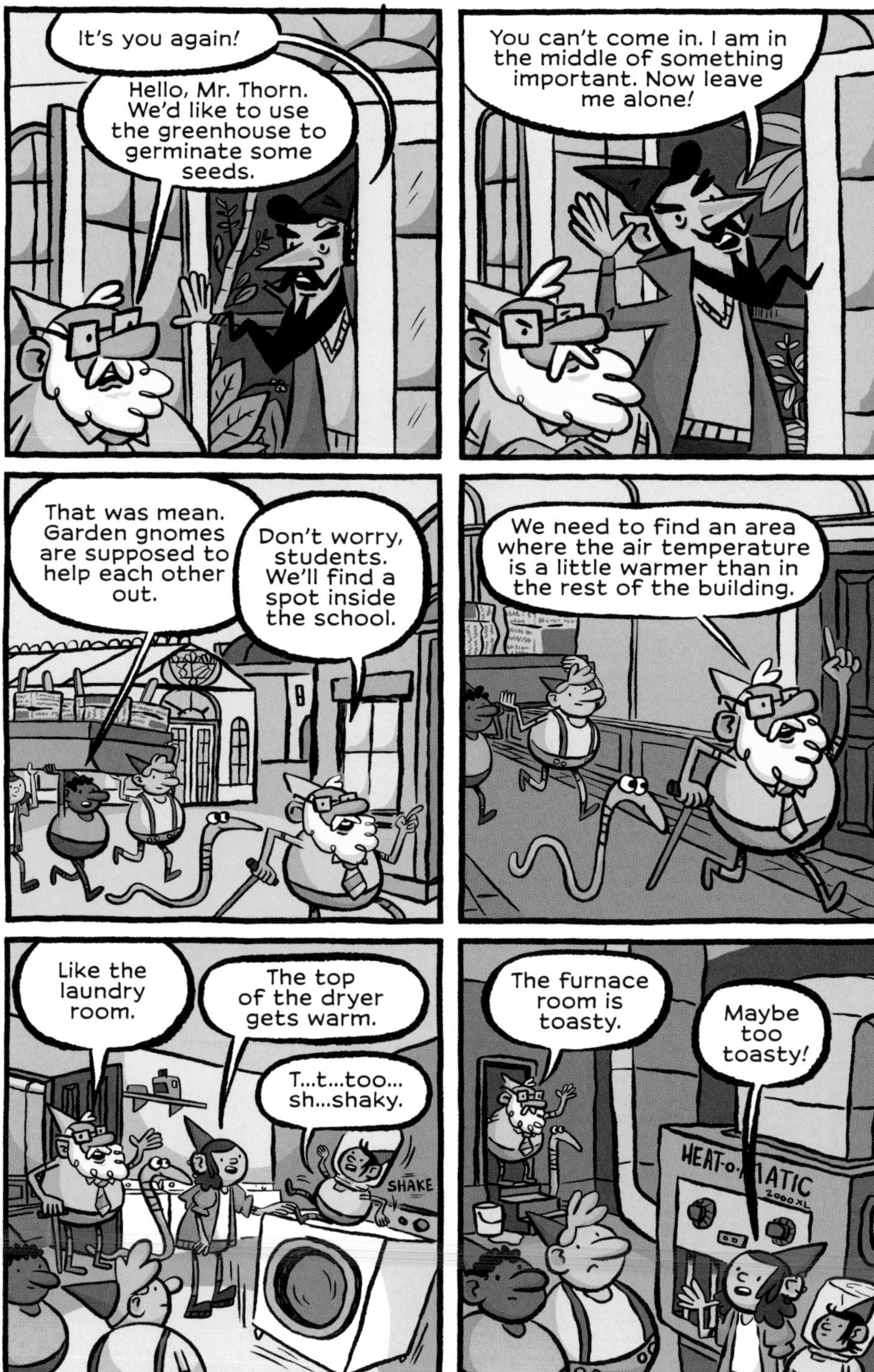
It's you again!
Hello, Mr. Thorn. We'd like to use the greenhouse to germinate some seeds.
You can't come in. I am in the middle of something important. Now leave me alone!
That was mean. Garden gnomes are supposed to help each other out.
Don't worry, students. We'll find a spot inside the school.
We need to find an area where the air temperature is a little warmer than in the rest of the building.
Like the laundry room.
The top of the dryer gets warm.
T...t...too... sh...shaky.
SHAKE
The furnace room is toasty.
Maybe too toasty!
HEAT-o-MATIC
2000XL

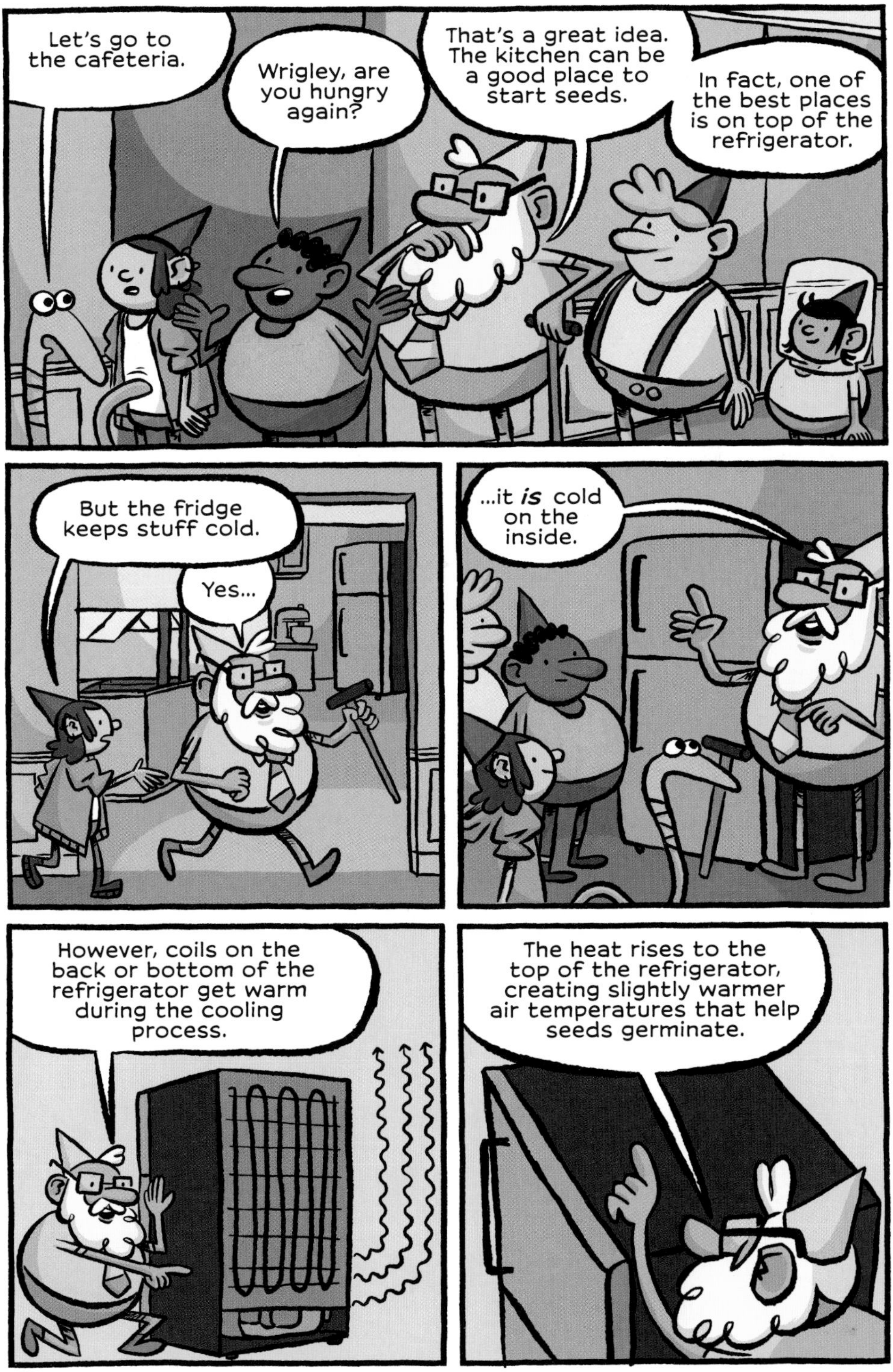
Let's go to the cafeteria.
Wrigley, are you hungry again?
That's a great idea. The kitchen can be a good place to start seeds.
In fact, one of the best places is on top of the refrigerator.
But the fridge keeps stuff cold.
Yes...
...it *is* cold on the inside.
However, coils on the back or bottom of the refrigerator get warm during the cooling process.
The heat rises to the top of the refrigerator, creating slightly warmer air temperatures that help seeds germinate.

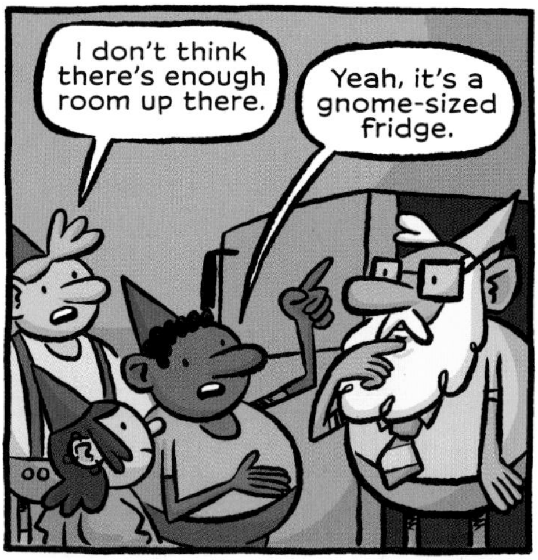
I don't think there's enough room up there.
Yeah, it's a gnome-sized fridge.

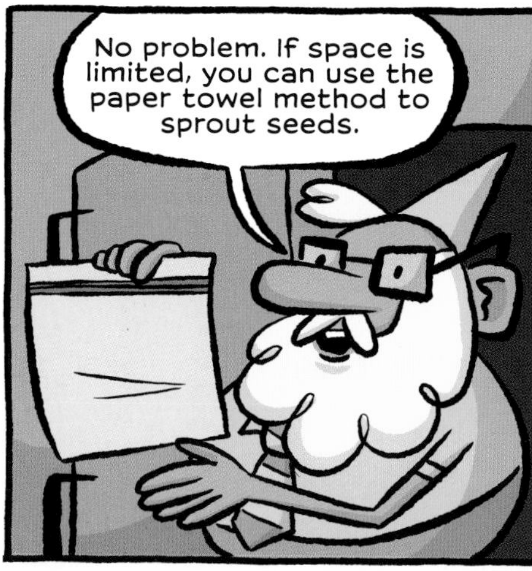
No problem. If space is limited, you can use the paper towel method to sprout seeds.

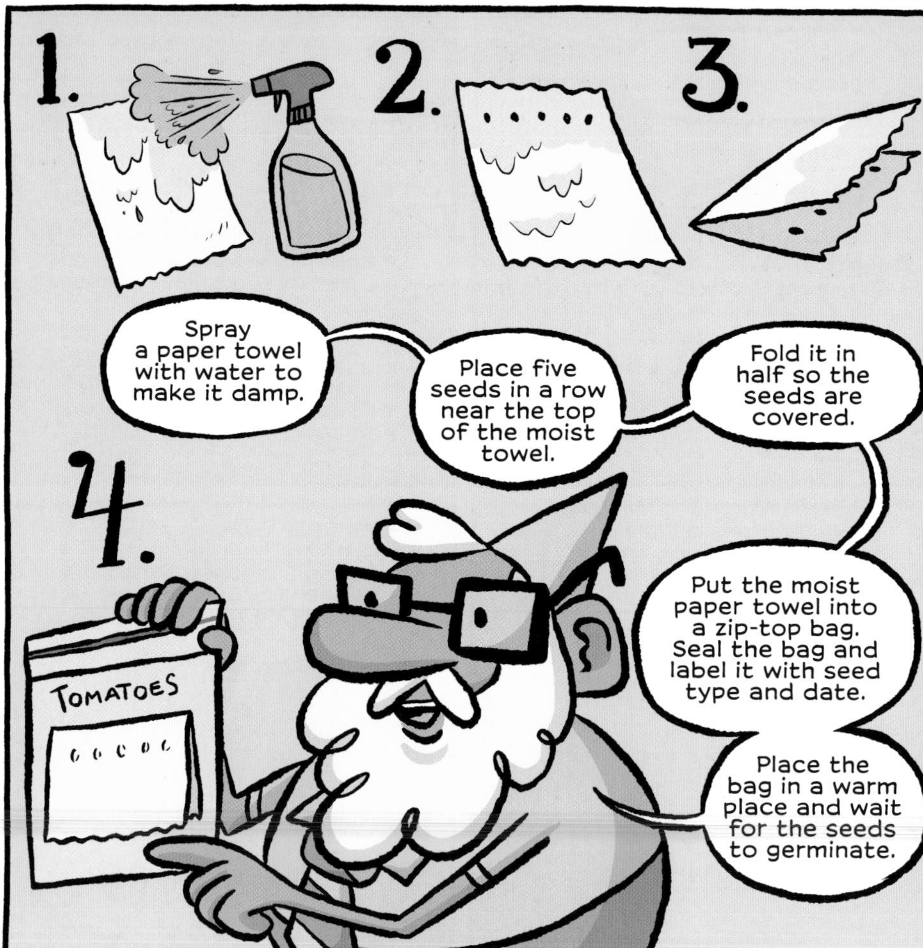
1.
2.
3.
Spray a paper towel with water to make it damp.
Place five seeds in a row near the top of the moist towel.
Fold it in half so the seeds are covered.
4.
TOMATOES
Put the moist paper towel into a zip-top bag. Seal the bag and label it with seed type and date.
Place the bag in a warm place and wait for the seeds to germinate.

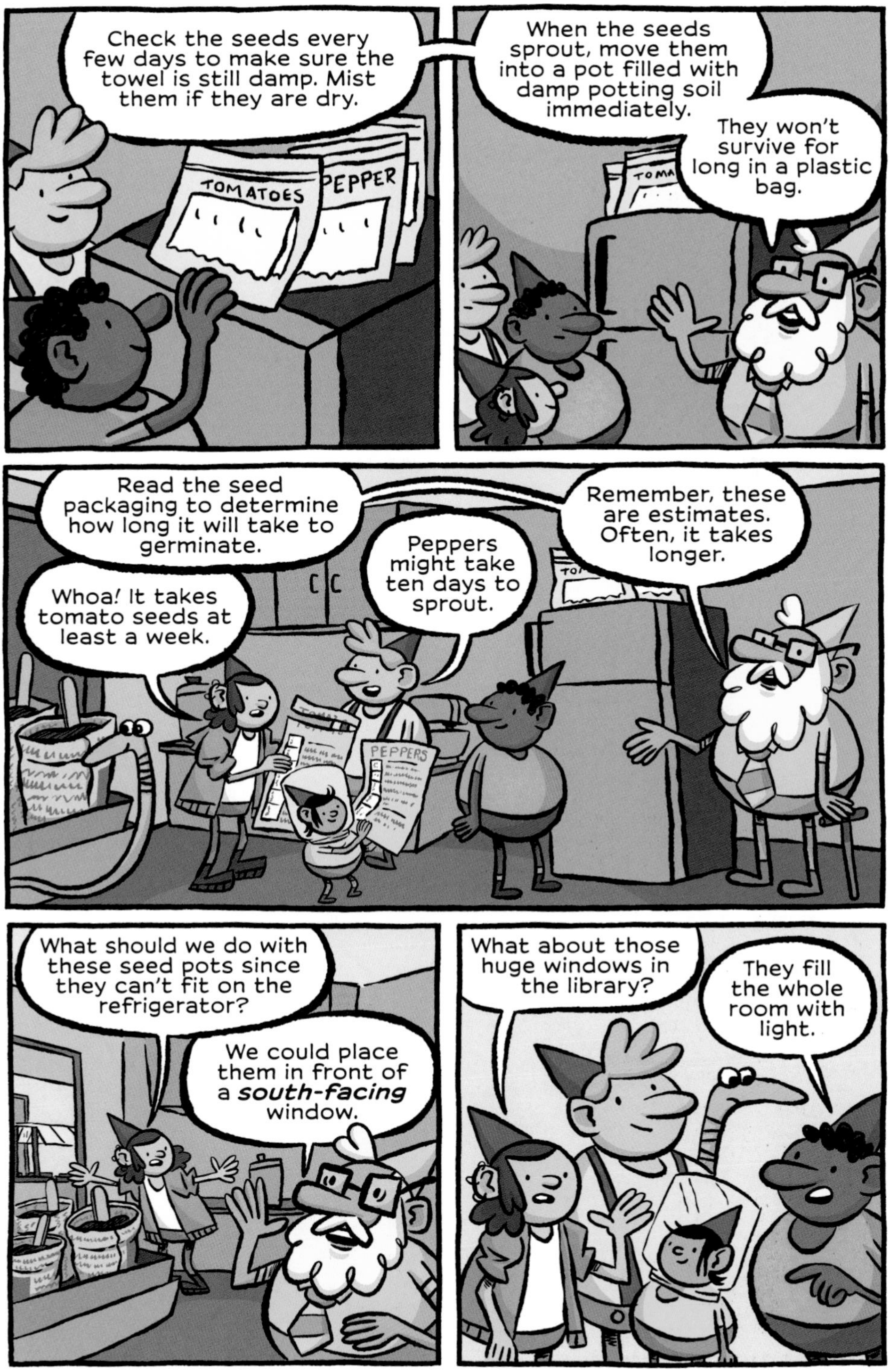
Check the seeds every few days to make sure the towel is still damp. Mist them if they are dry.
TOMATOES
PEPPER
When the seeds sprout, move them into a pot filled with damp potting soil immediately.
They won't survive for long in a plastic bag.
Read the seed packaging to determine how long it will take to germinate.
Remember, these are estimates. Often, it takes longer.
Peppers might take ten days to sprout.
Whoa! It takes tomato seeds at least a week.
PEPPERS
What should we do with these seed pots since they can't fit on the refrigerator?
We could place them in front of a *south-facing* window.
What about those huge windows in the library?
They fill the whole room with light.

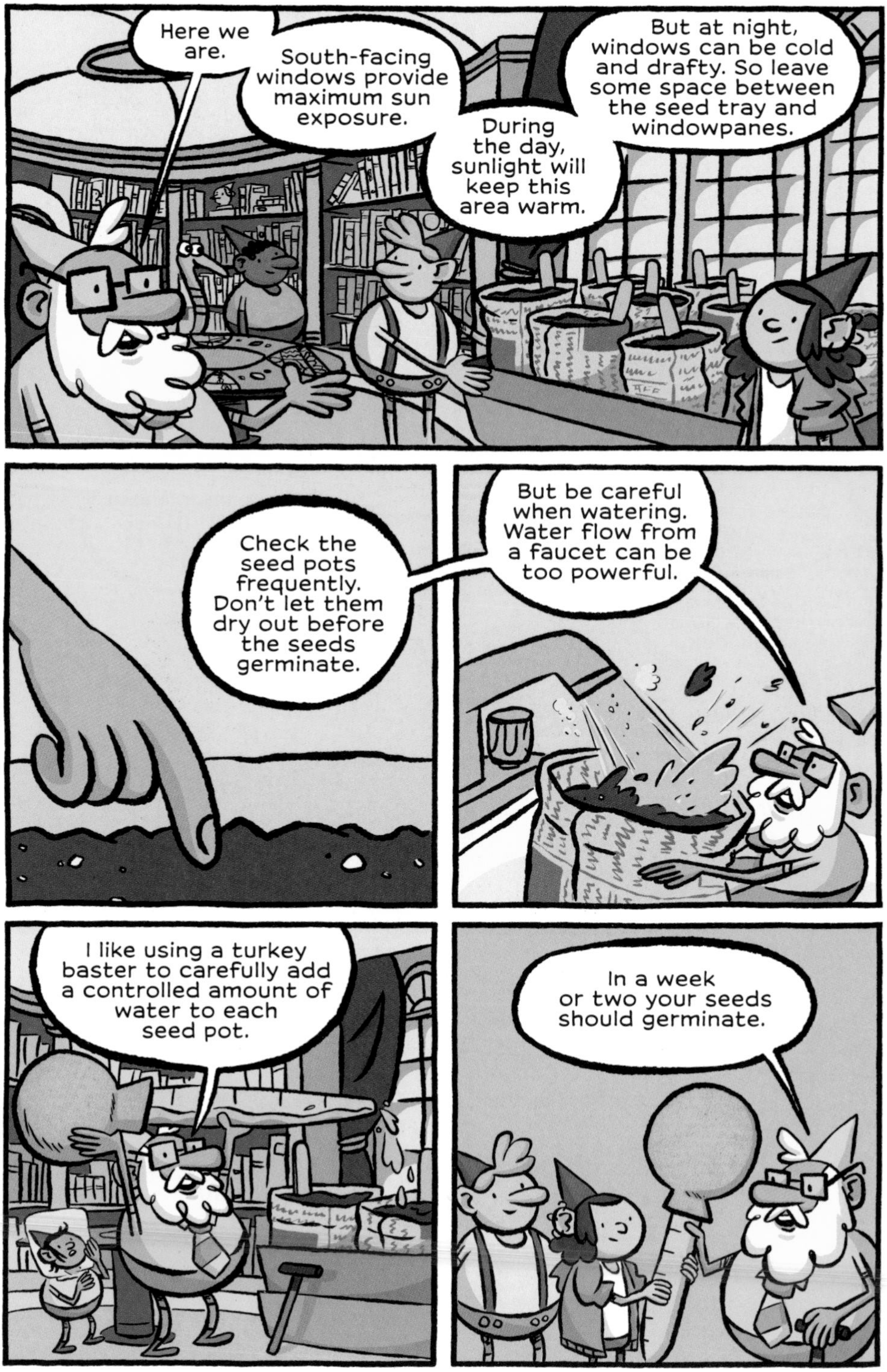
Here we are.
South-facing windows provide maximum sun exposure.
During the day, sunlight will keep this area warm.
But at night, windows can be cold and drafty. So leave some space between the seed tray and windowpanes.
Check the seed pots frequently. Don't let them dry out before the seeds germinate.
But be careful when watering. Water flow from a faucet can be too powerful.
I like using a turkey baster to carefully add a controlled amount of water to each seed pot.
In a week or two your seeds should germinate.

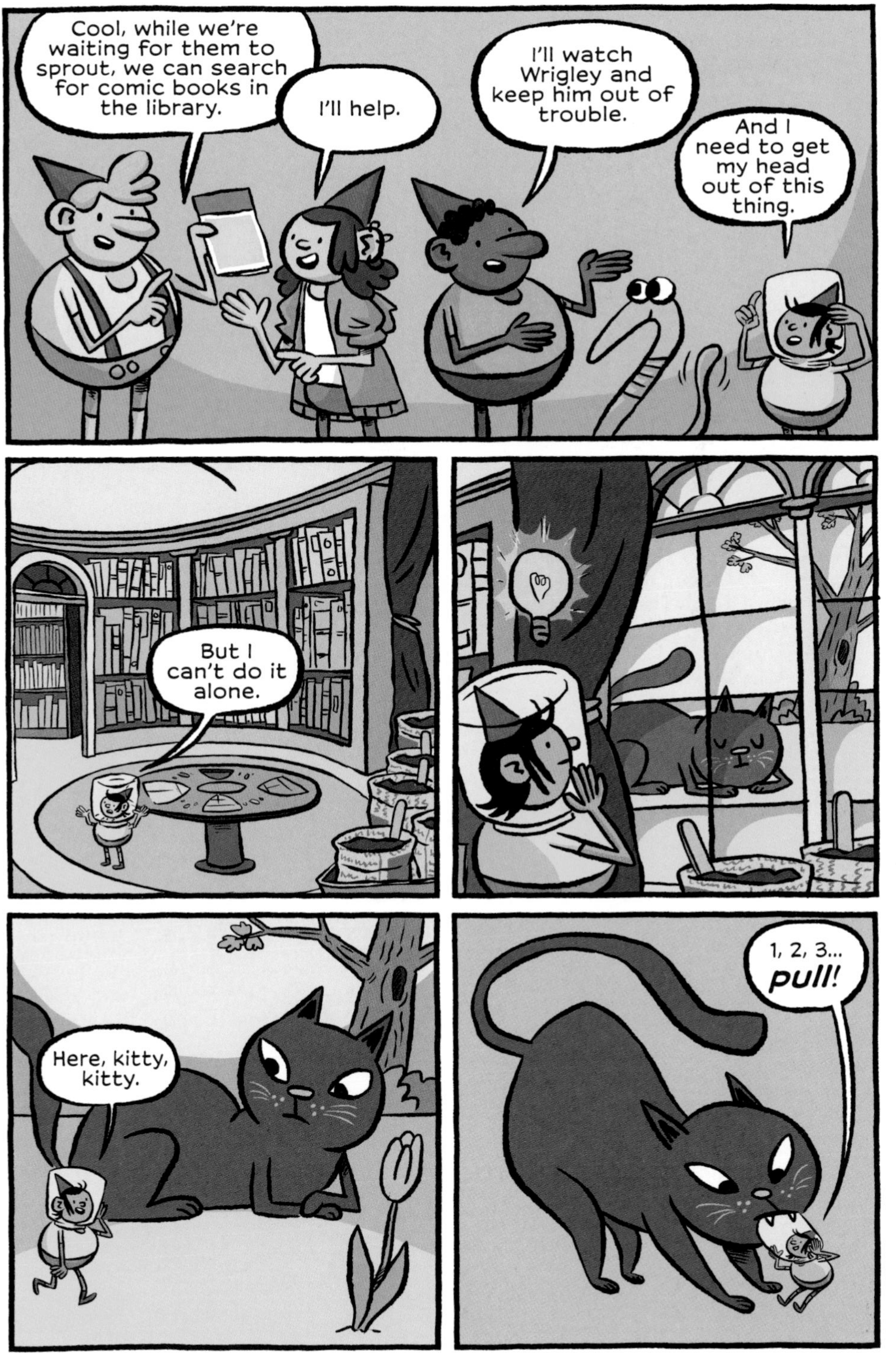
Cool, while we're waiting for them to sprout, we can search for comic books in the library.
I'll help.
I'll watch Wrigley and keep him out of trouble.
And I need to get my head out of this thing.
But I can't do it alone.
Here, kitty, kitty.
1, 2, 3... ***pull!***

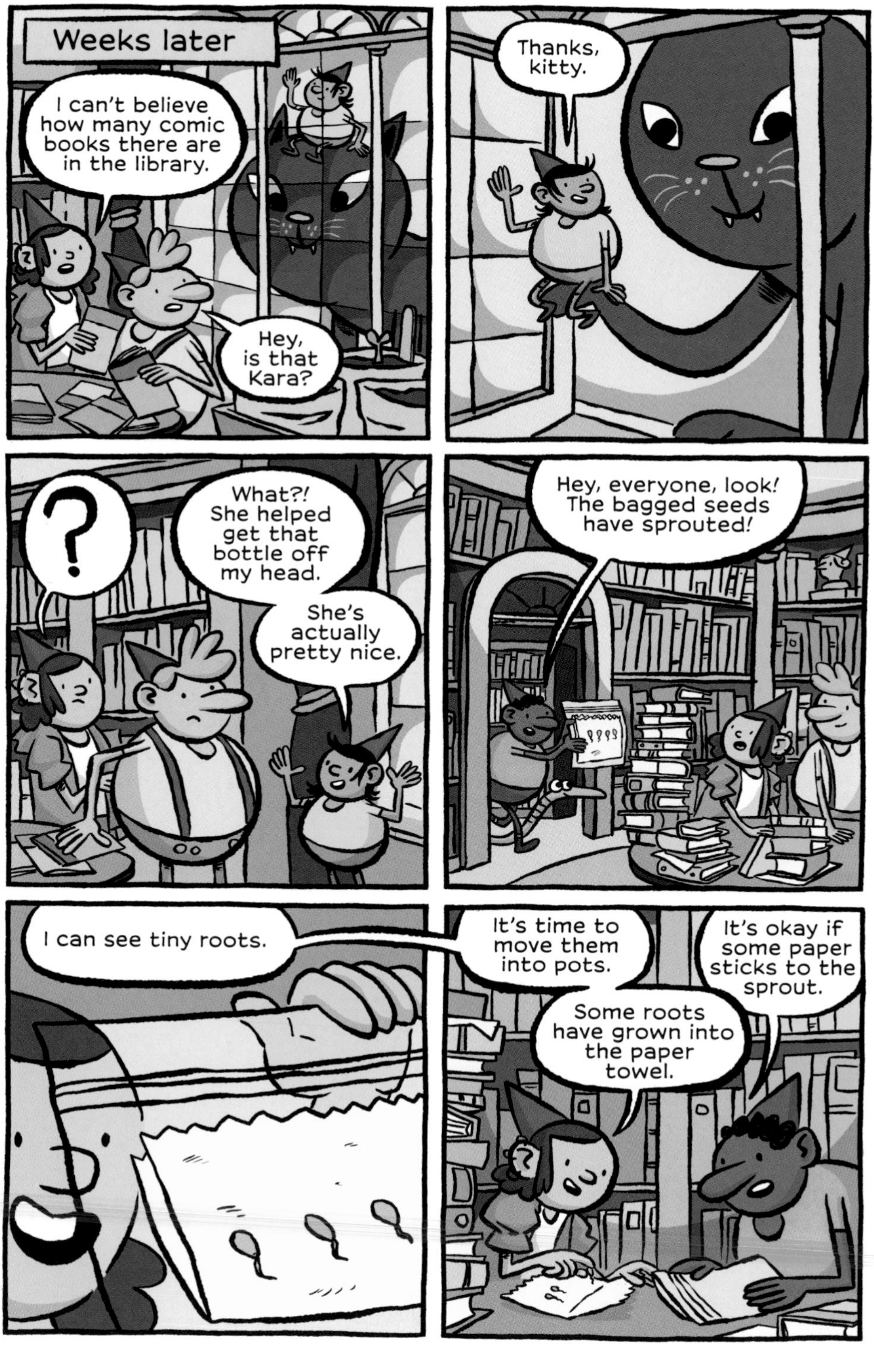
Weeks later
I can't believe how many comic books there are in the library.
Hey, is that Kara?
Thanks, kitty.
?
What?! She helped get that bottle off my head.
She's actually pretty nice.
Hey, everyone, look! The bagged seeds have sprouted!
I can see tiny roots.
It's time to move them into pots.
Some roots have grown into the paper towel.
It's okay if some paper sticks to the sprout.

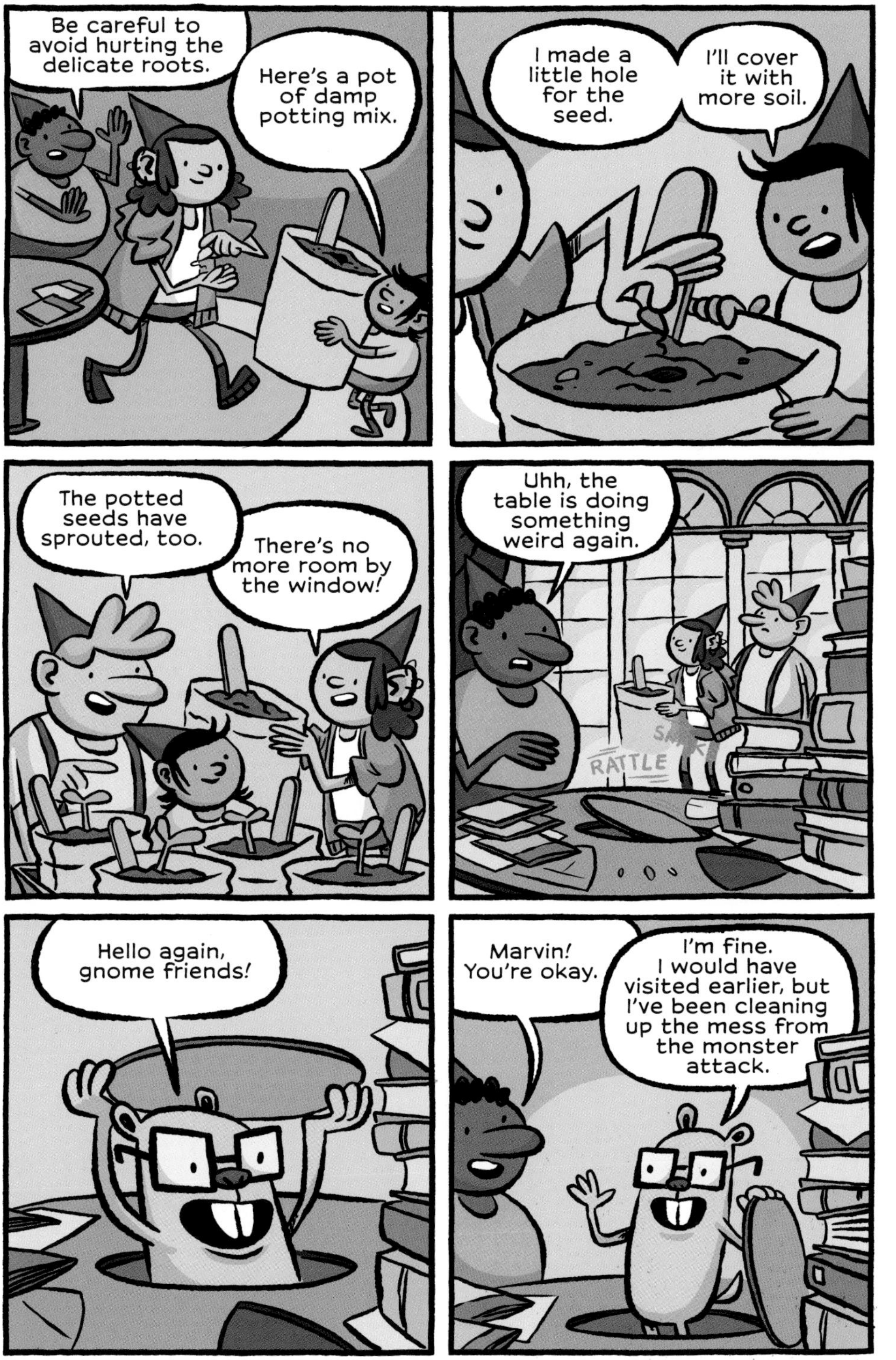
Be careful to avoid hurting the delicate roots.
Here's a pot of damp potting mix.
I made a little hole for the seed.
I'll cover it with more soil.
The potted seeds have sprouted, too.
There's no more room by the window!
Uhh, the table is doing something weird again.
RATTLE
Hello again, gnome friends!
Marvin! You're okay.
I'm fine. I would have visited earlier, but I've been cleaning up the mess from the monster attack.

So how are your seeds? Have they sprouted?

Yes, but we're running out of space for them.

Hmmm... I see.

This *is* a problem.

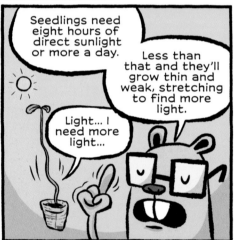

Seedlings need eight hours of direct sunlight or more a day.

Less than that and they'll grow thin and weak, stretching to find more light.

Light... I need more light...

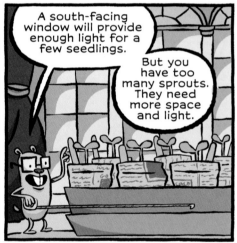

A south-facing window will provide enough light for a few seedlings.

But you have too many sprouts. They need more space and light.

A grow shelf could provide the additional light they crave.

Does the school have one?

No, but we can make one ourselves!

Naked mole rats, assemble!

MAKE YOUR OWN Grow Light SHELF

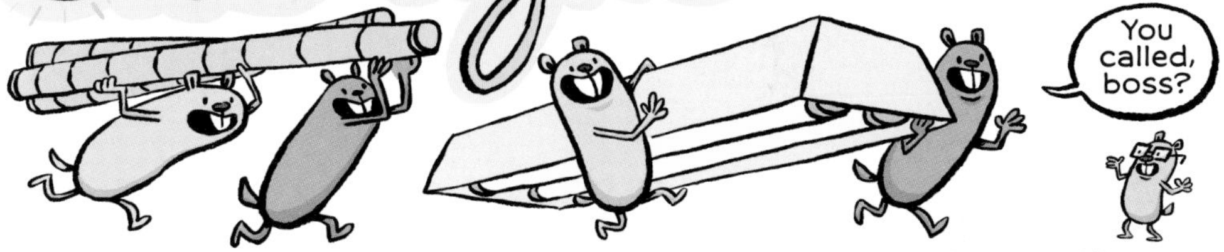
You called, boss?

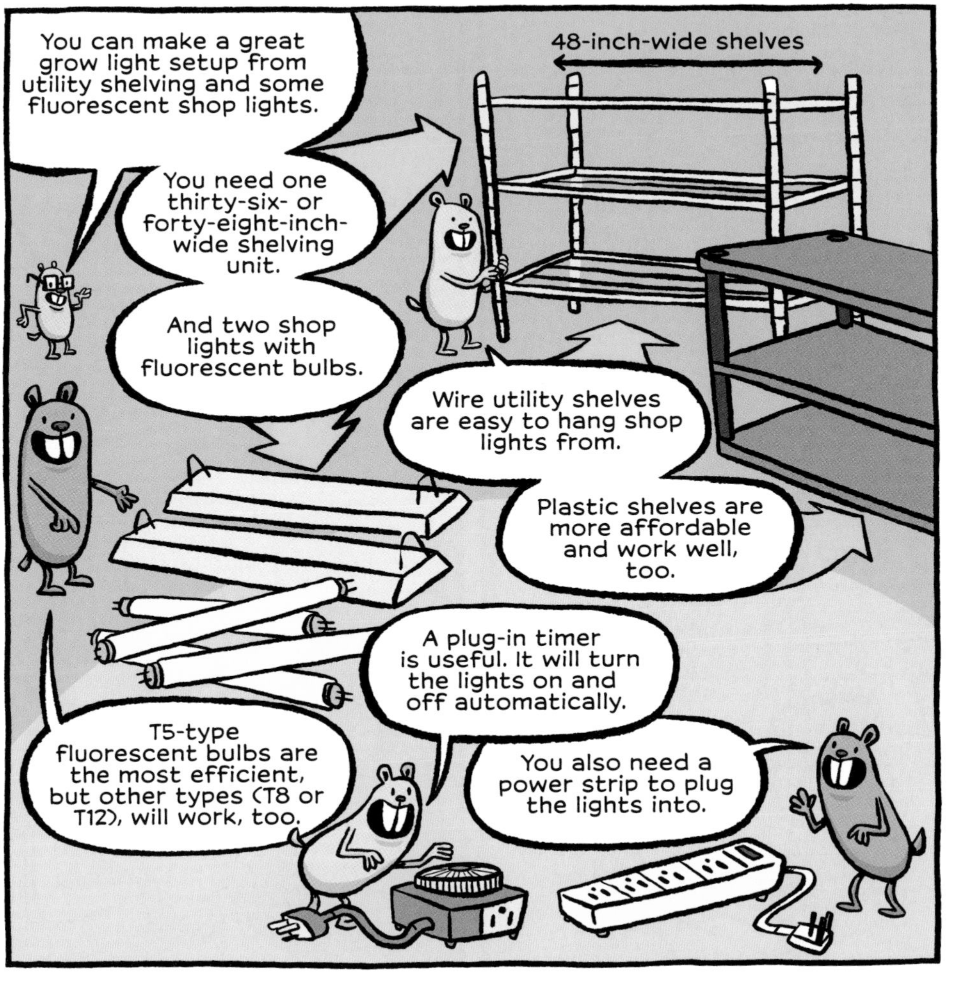
You can make a great grow light setup from utility shelving and some fluorescent shop lights.
48-inch-wide shelves
You need one thirty-six- or forty-eight-inch-wide shelving unit.
And two shop lights with fluorescent bulbs.
Wire utility shelves are easy to hang shop lights from.
Plastic shelves are more affordable and work well, too.
A plug-in timer is useful. It will turn the lights on and off automatically.
T5-type fluorescent bulbs are the most efficient, but other types (T8 or T12), will work, too.
You also need a power strip to plug the lights into.

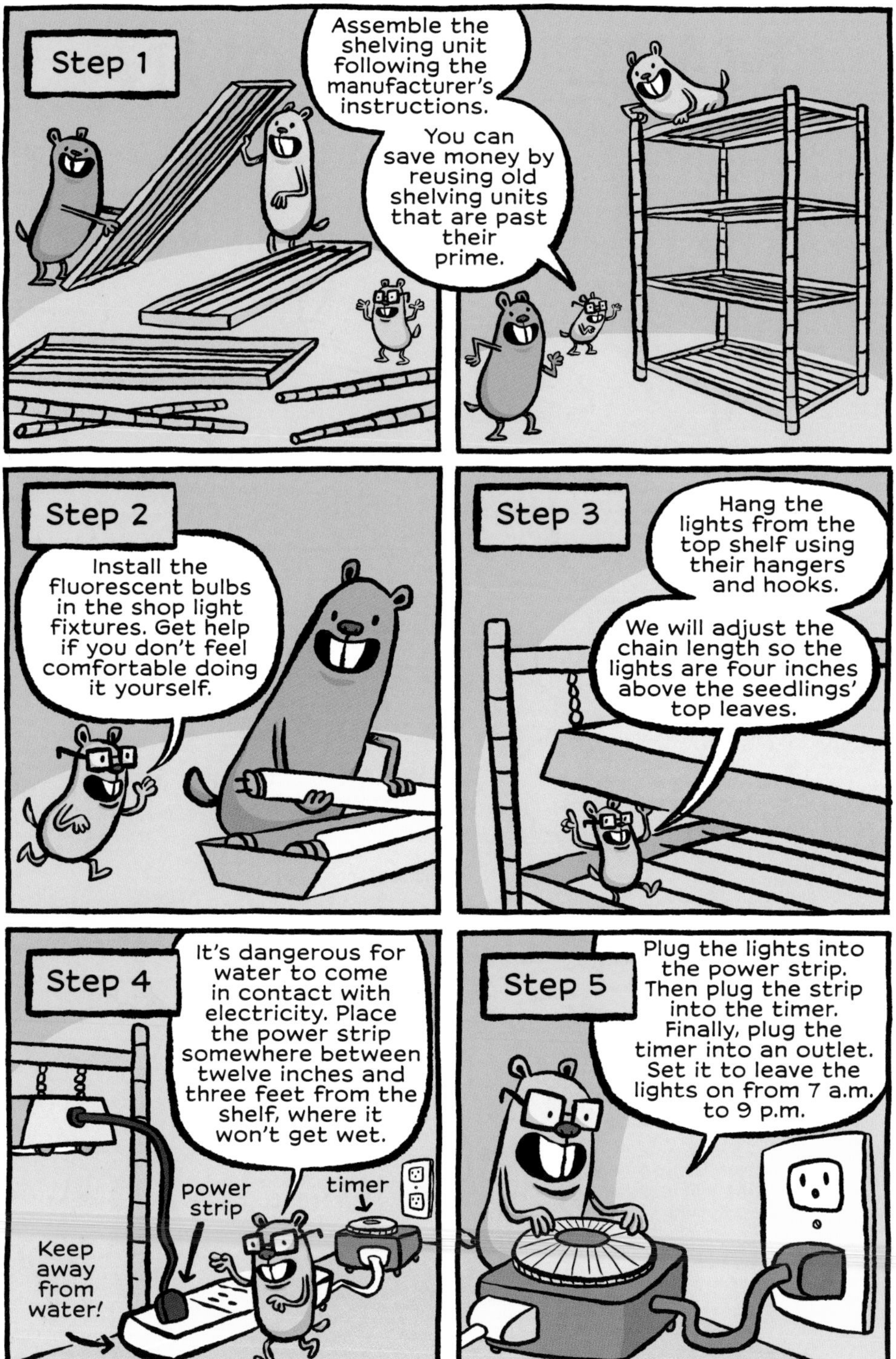

Step 1
Assemble the shelving unit following the manufacturer's instructions.
You can save money by reusing old shelving units that are past their prime.
Step 2
Install the fluorescent bulbs in the shop light fixtures. Get help if you don't feel comfortable doing it yourself.
Step 3
Hang the lights from the top shelf using their hangers and hooks.
We will adjust the chain length so the lights are four inches above the seedlings' top leaves.
Step 4
It's dangerous for water to come in contact with electricity. Place the power strip somewhere between twelve inches and three feet from the shelf, where it won't get wet.
power strip
timer
Keep away from water!
Step 5
Plug the lights into the power strip. Then plug the strip into the timer. Finally, plug the timer into an outlet. Set it to leave the lights on from 7 a.m. to 9 p.m.

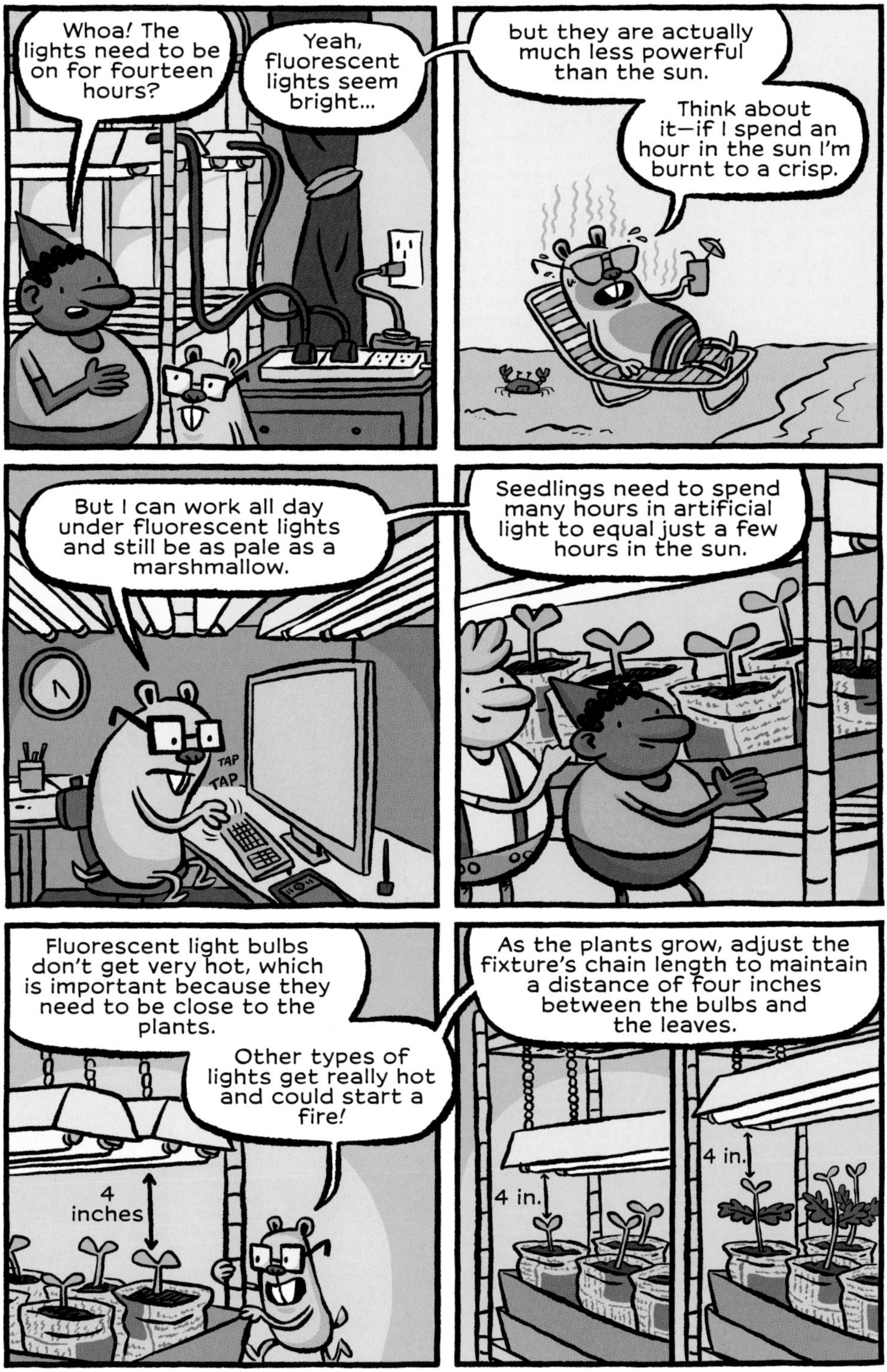
Whoa! The lights need to be on for fourteen hours?
Yeah, fluorescent lights seem bright...
but they are actually much less powerful than the sun.
Think about it—if I spend an hour in the sun I'm burnt to a crisp.
But I can work all day under fluorescent lights and still be as pale as a marshmallow.
TAP
TAP
Seedlings need to spend many hours in artificial light to equal just a few hours in the sun.
Fluorescent light bulbs don't get very hot, which is important because they need to be close to the plants.
Other types of lights get really hot and could start a fire!
4 inches
As the plants grow, adjust the fixture's chain length to maintain a distance of four inches between the bulbs and the leaves.
4 in.
4 in.

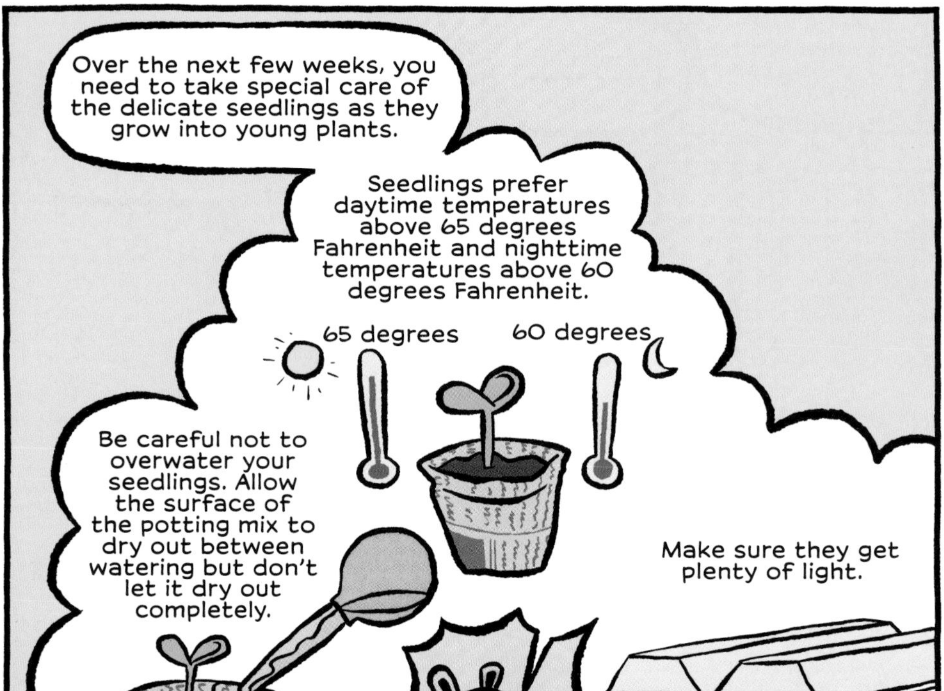
Over the next few weeks, you need to take special care of the delicate seedlings as they grow into young plants.
Seedlings prefer daytime temperatures above 65 degrees Fahrenheit and nighttime temperatures above 60 degrees Fahrenheit.
65 degrees
60 degrees
Be careful not to overwater your seedlings. Allow the surface of the potting mix to dry out between watering but don't let it dry out completely.
Make sure they get plenty of light.

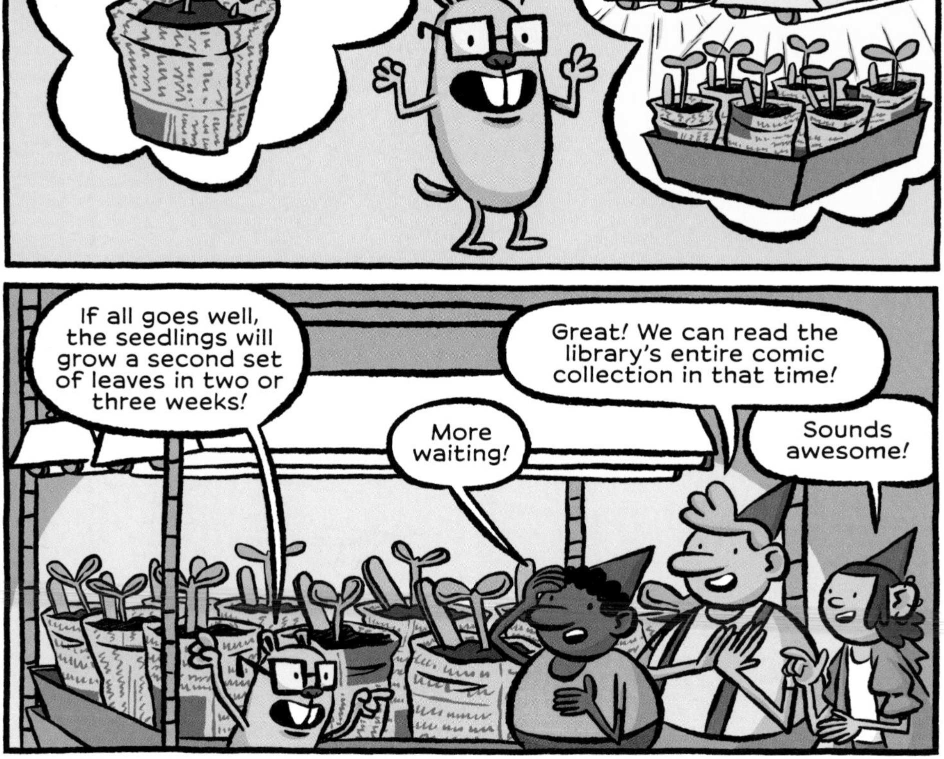
If all goes well, the seedlings will grow a second set of leaves in two or three weeks!
More waiting!
Great! We can read the library's entire comic collection in that time!
Sounds awesome!

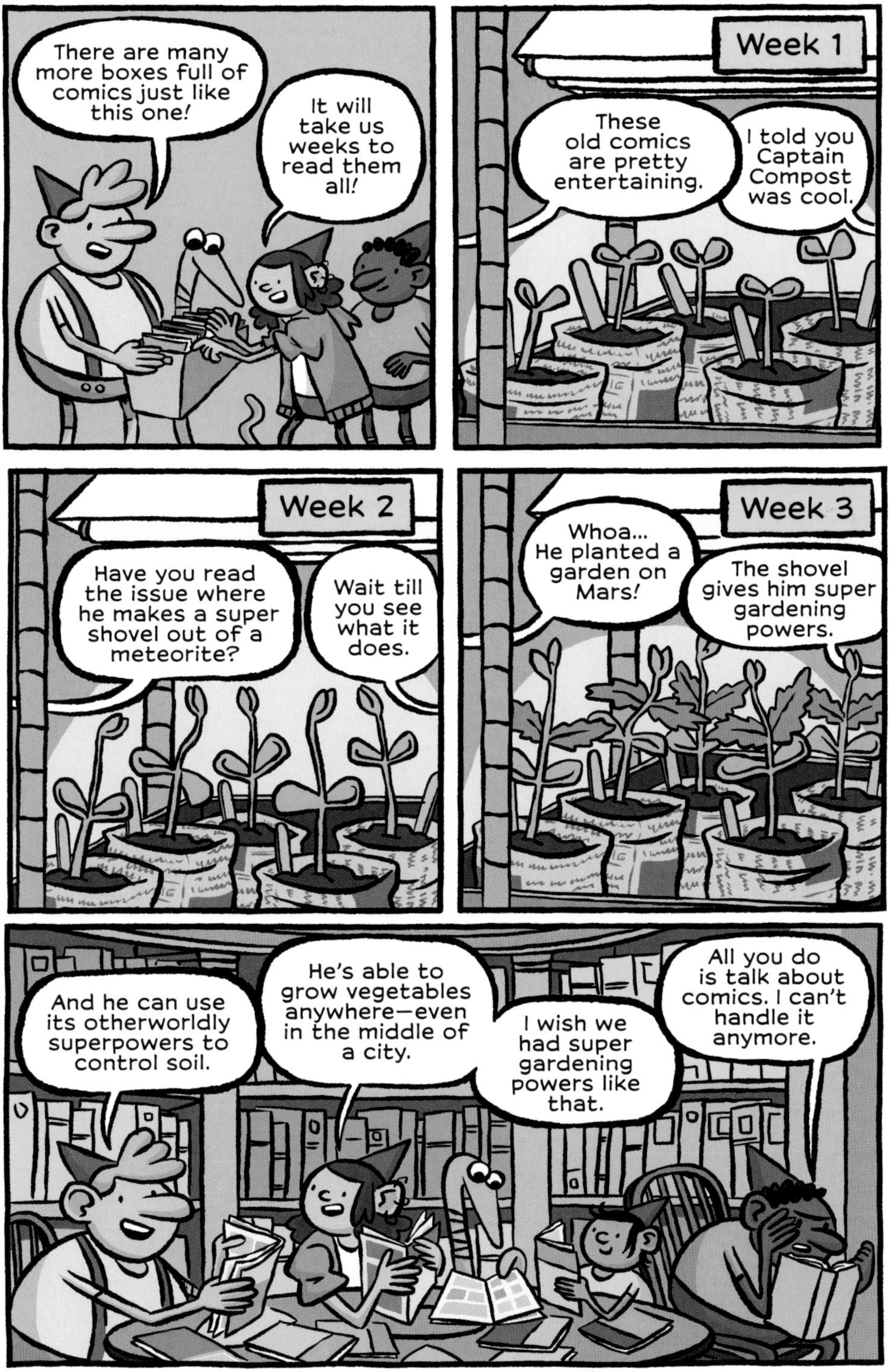
There are many more boxes full of comics just like this one!
It will take us weeks to read them all!
Week 1
These old comics are pretty entertaining.
I told you Captain Compost was cool.
Week 2
Have you read the issue where he makes a super shovel out of a meteorite?
Wait till you see what it does.
Week 3
Whoa... He planted a garden on Mars!
The shovel gives him super gardening powers.
And he can use its otherworldly superpowers to control soil.
He's able to grow vegetables anywhere—even in the middle of a city.
I wish we had super gardening powers like that.
All you do is talk about comics. I can't handle it anymore.

Let's take a break and get some food.

You're always hungry, Wrigley.

I'm not hungry but the seedlings probably are. They've been growing for a while and need more food to continue.

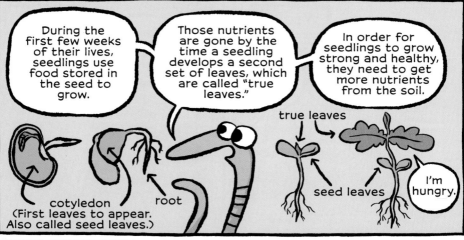

During the first few weeks of their lives, seedlings use food stored in the seed to grow.

Those nutrients are gone by the time a seedling develops a second set of leaves, which are called "true leaves."

In order for seedlings to grow strong and healthy, they need to get more nutrients from the soil.

true leaves

cotyledon
(First leaves to appear. Also called seed leaves.)

root

seed leaves

I'm hungry.

Some seed mixes contain fertilizer, but many don't. You have to provide additional nutrients by using liquid fertilizer.

SEEDLING STARTING MIX

Fertilizers can either be synthetic, which have been manufactured from minerals and inorganic material, or organic, which come from plant or animal sources.

TOMATO GROW

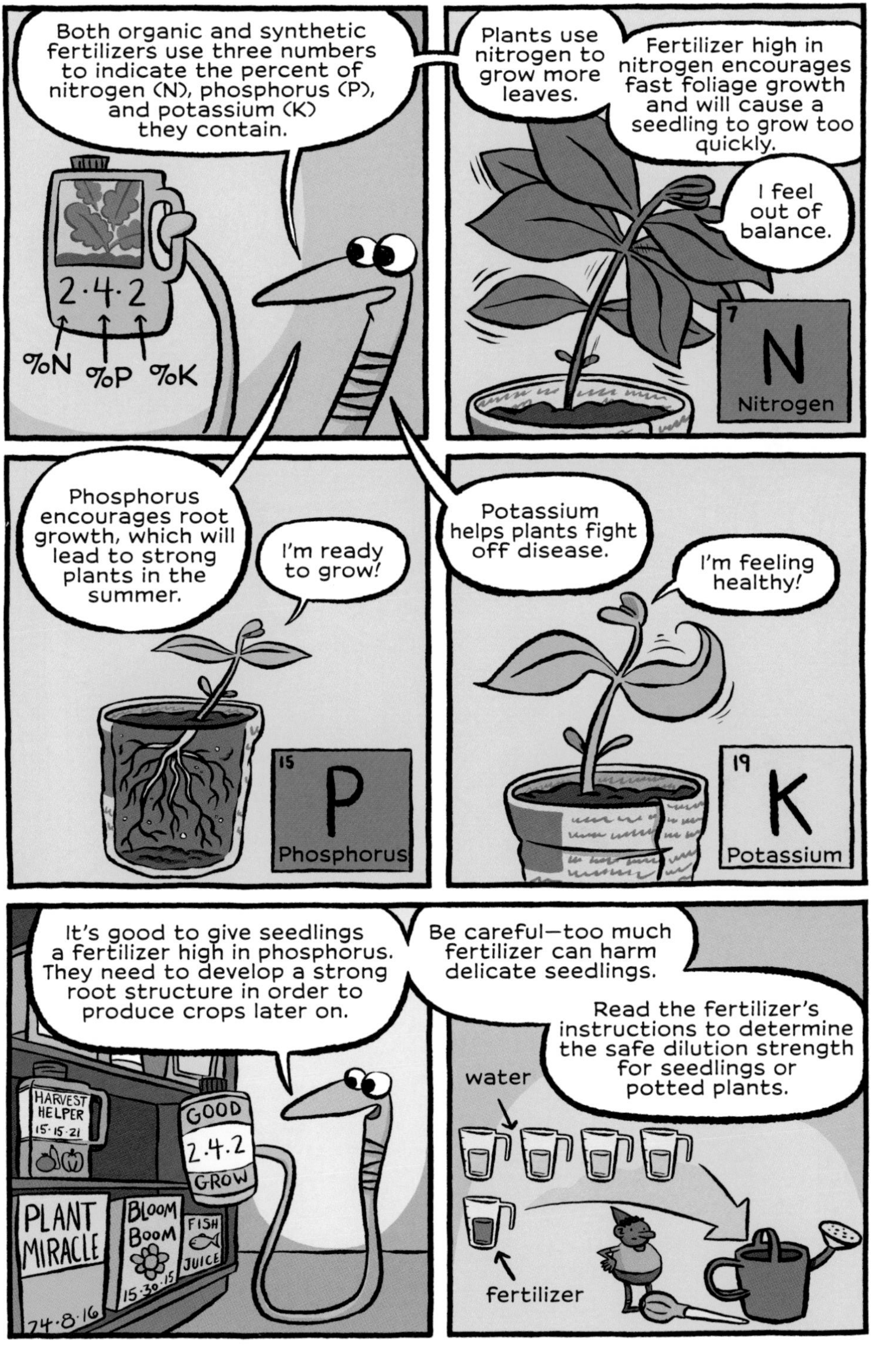

Both organic and synthetic fertilizers use three numbers to indicate the percent of nitrogen (N), phosphorus (P), and potassium (K) they contain.
2·4·2
%N %P %K
Plants use nitrogen to grow more leaves.
Fertilizer high in nitrogen encourages fast foliage growth and will cause a seedling to grow too quickly.
I feel out of balance.
7 N Nitrogen
Phosphorus encourages root growth, which will lead to strong plants in the summer.
I'm ready to grow!
15 P Phosphorus
Potassium helps plants fight off disease.
I'm feeling healthy!
19 K Potassium
It's good to give seedlings a fertilizer high in phosphorus. They need to develop a strong root structure in order to produce crops later on.
HARVEST HELPER 15·15·21
GOOD 2·4·2 GROW
PLANT MIRACLE 24·8·16
BLOOM BOOM 15·30·15
FISH JUICE
Be careful—too much fertilizer can harm delicate seedlings.
Read the fertilizer's instructions to determine the safe dilution strength for seedlings or potted plants.
water
fertilizer

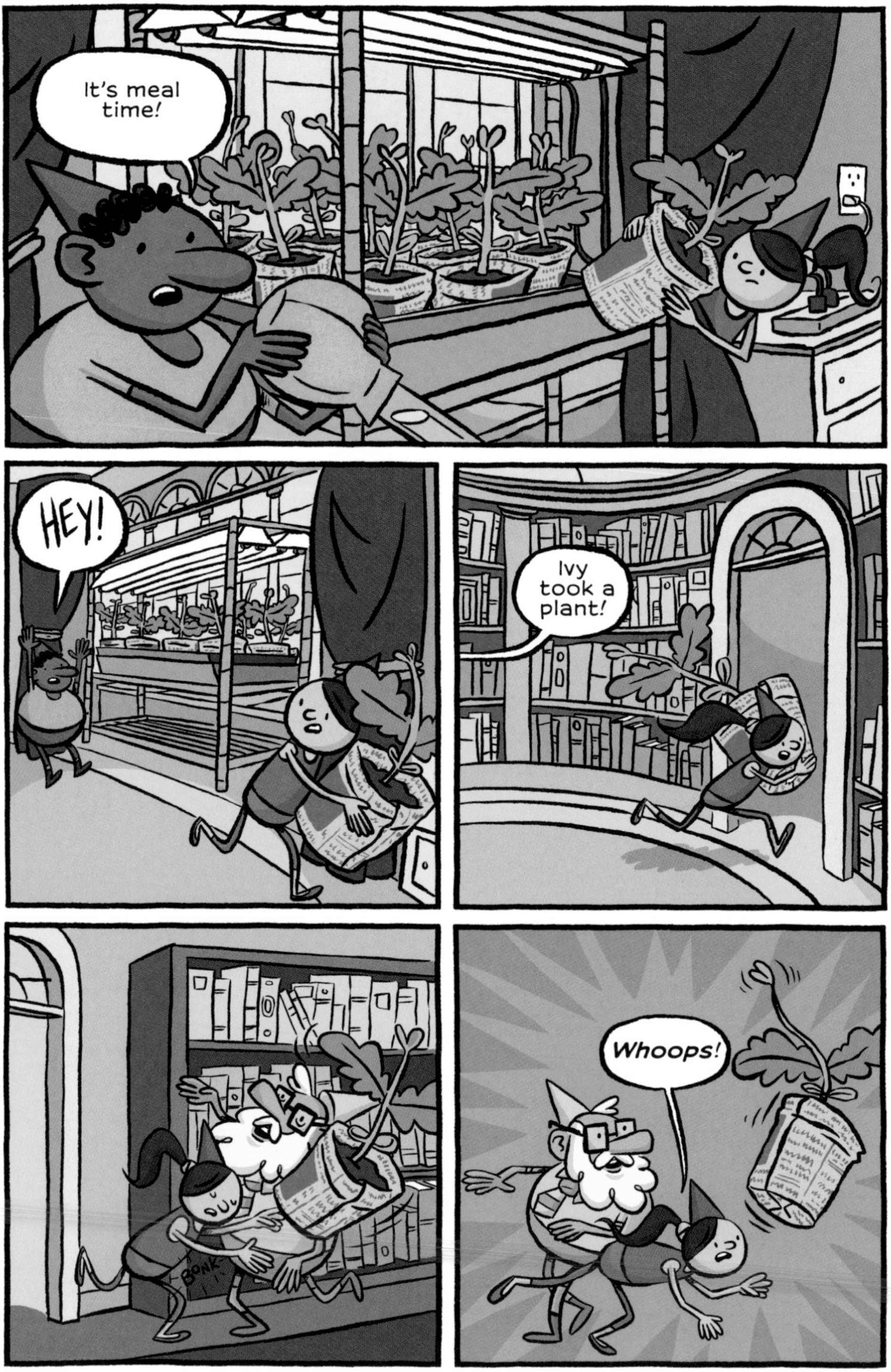
It's meal time!
HEY!
Ivy took a plant!
BONK
Whoops!

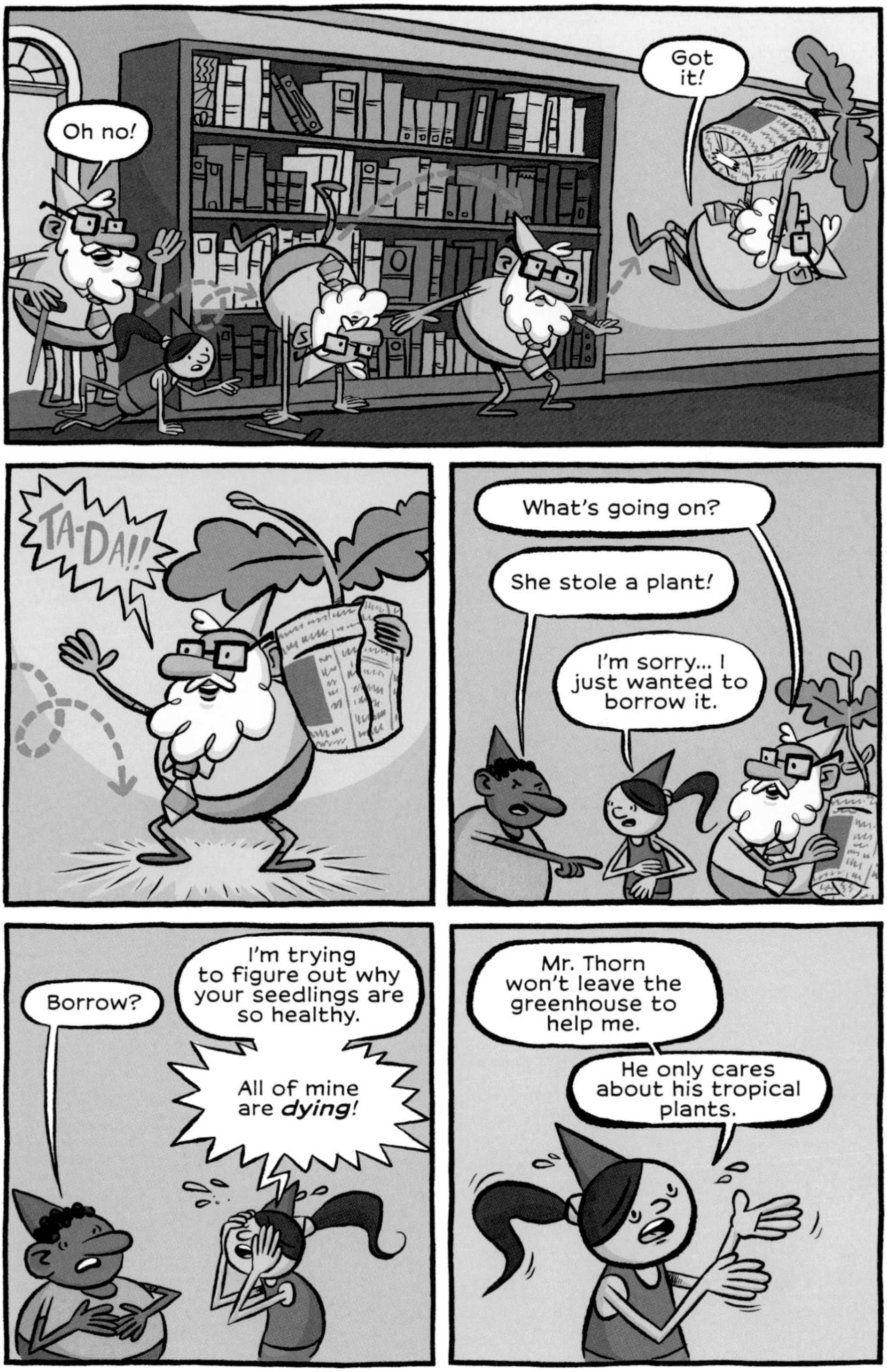
Oh no!
Got it!
TA-DA!!
What's going on?
She stole a plant!
I'm sorry... I just wanted to borrow it.
Borrow?
I'm trying to figure out why your seedlings are so healthy.
All of mine are *dying*!
Mr. Thorn won't leave the greenhouse to help me.
He only cares about his tropical plants.

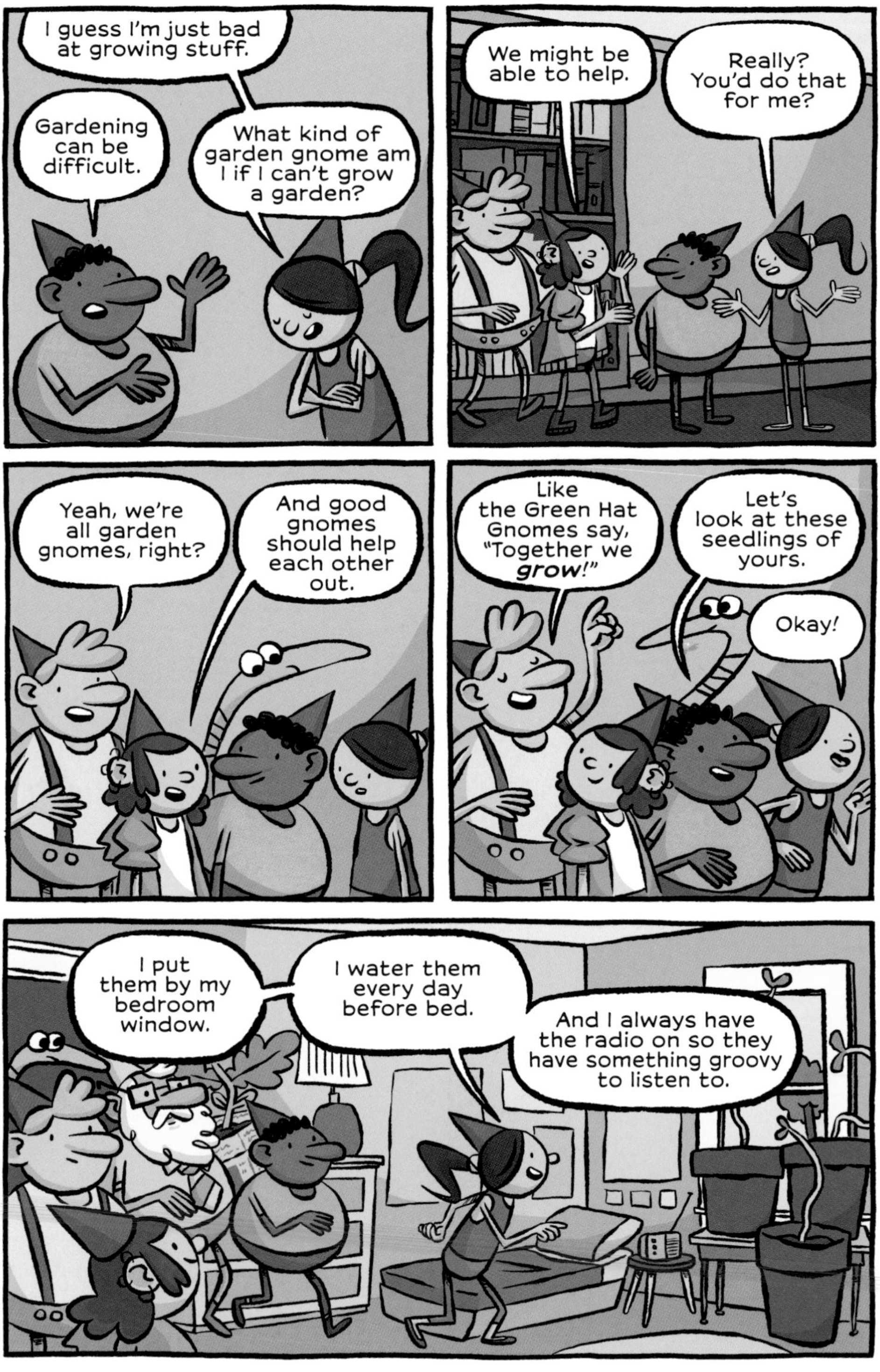

I guess I'm just bad at growing stuff.
Gardening can be difficult.
What kind of garden gnome am I if I can't grow a garden?
We might be able to help.
Really? You'd do that for me?
Yeah, we're all garden gnomes, right?
And good gnomes should help each other out.
Like the Green Hat Gnomes say, "Together we *grow*!"
Let's look at these seedlings of yours.
Okay!
I put them by my bedroom window.
I water them every day before bed.
And I always have the radio on so they have something groovy to listen to.

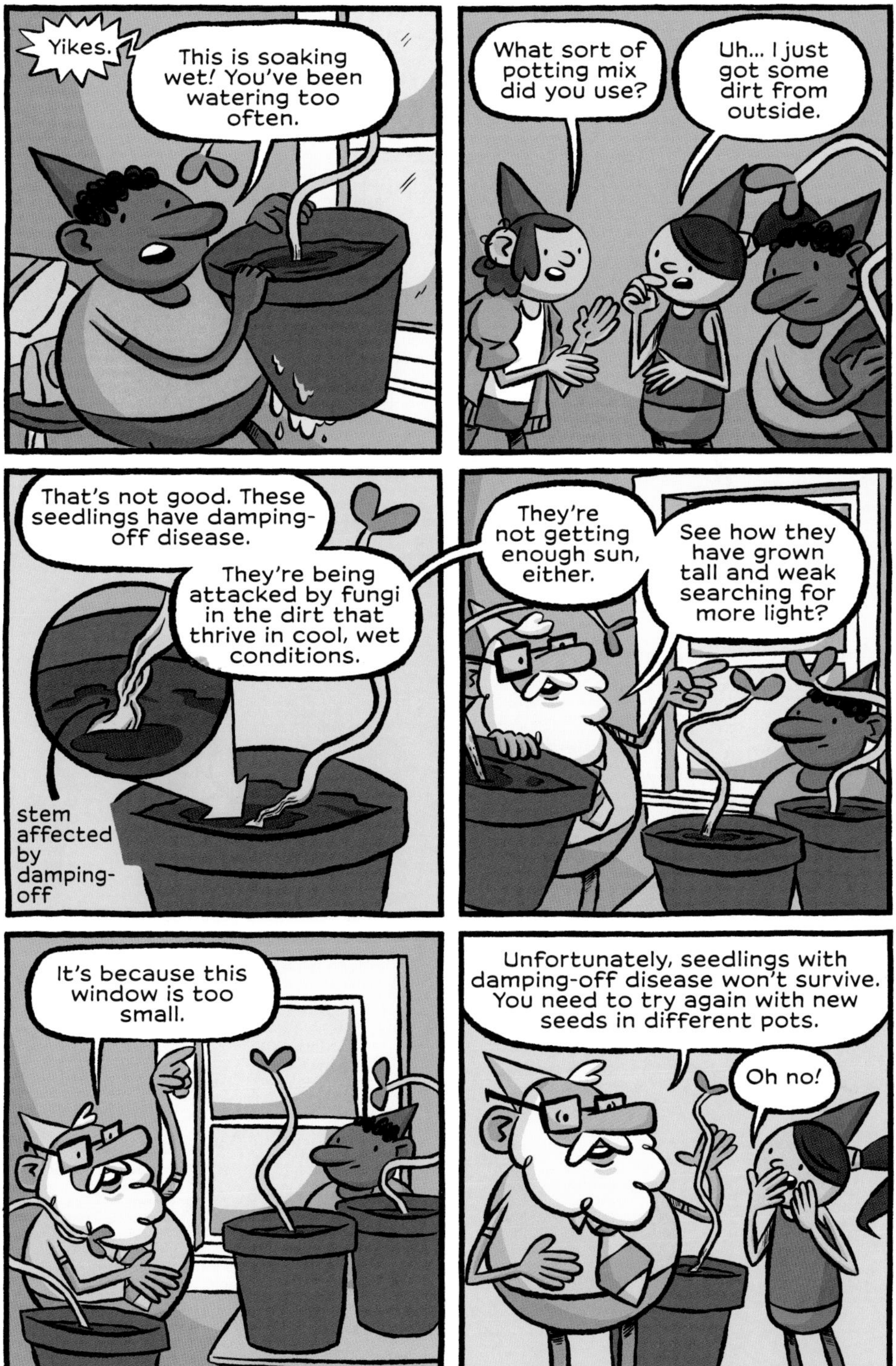
Yikes.
This is soaking wet! You've been watering too often.
What sort of potting mix did you use?
Uh... I just got some dirt from outside.
That's not good. These seedlings have damping-off disease.
They're being attacked by fungi in the dirt that thrive in cool, wet conditions.
stem affected by damping-off
They're not getting enough sun, either.
See how they have grown tall and weak searching for more light?
It's because this window is too small.
Unfortunately, seedlings with damping-off disease won't survive. You need to try again with new seeds in different pots.
Oh no!

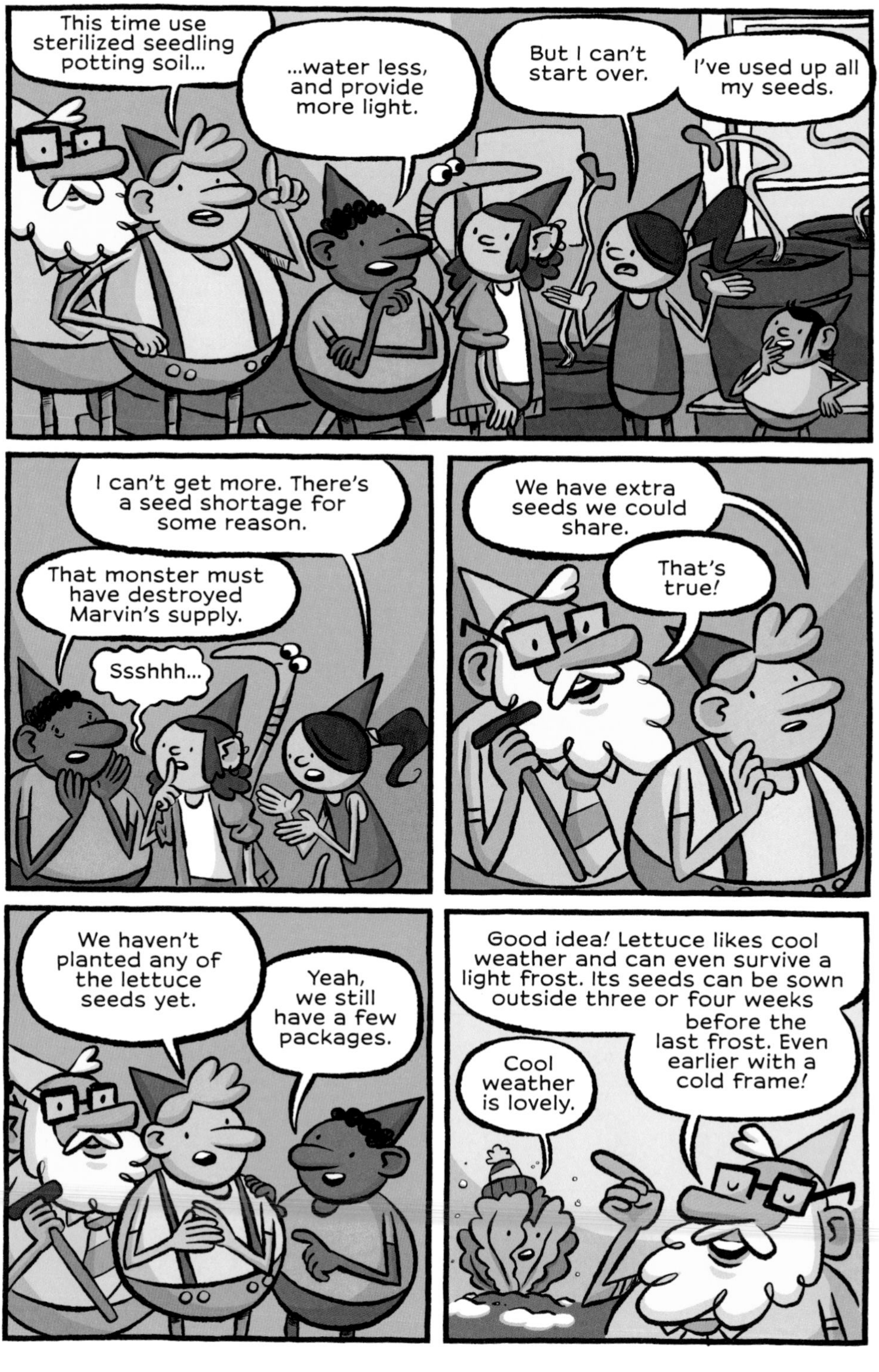
This time use sterilized seedling potting soil...
...water less, and provide more light.
But I can't start over.
I've used up all my seeds.
I can't get more. There's a seed shortage for some reason.
That monster must have destroyed Marvin's supply.
Ssshhh...
We have extra seeds we could share.
That's true!
We haven't planted any of the lettuce seeds yet.
Yeah, we still have a few packages.
Good idea! Lettuce likes cool weather and can even survive a light frost. Its seeds can be sown outside three or four weeks before the last frost. Even earlier with a cold frame!
Cool weather is lovely.

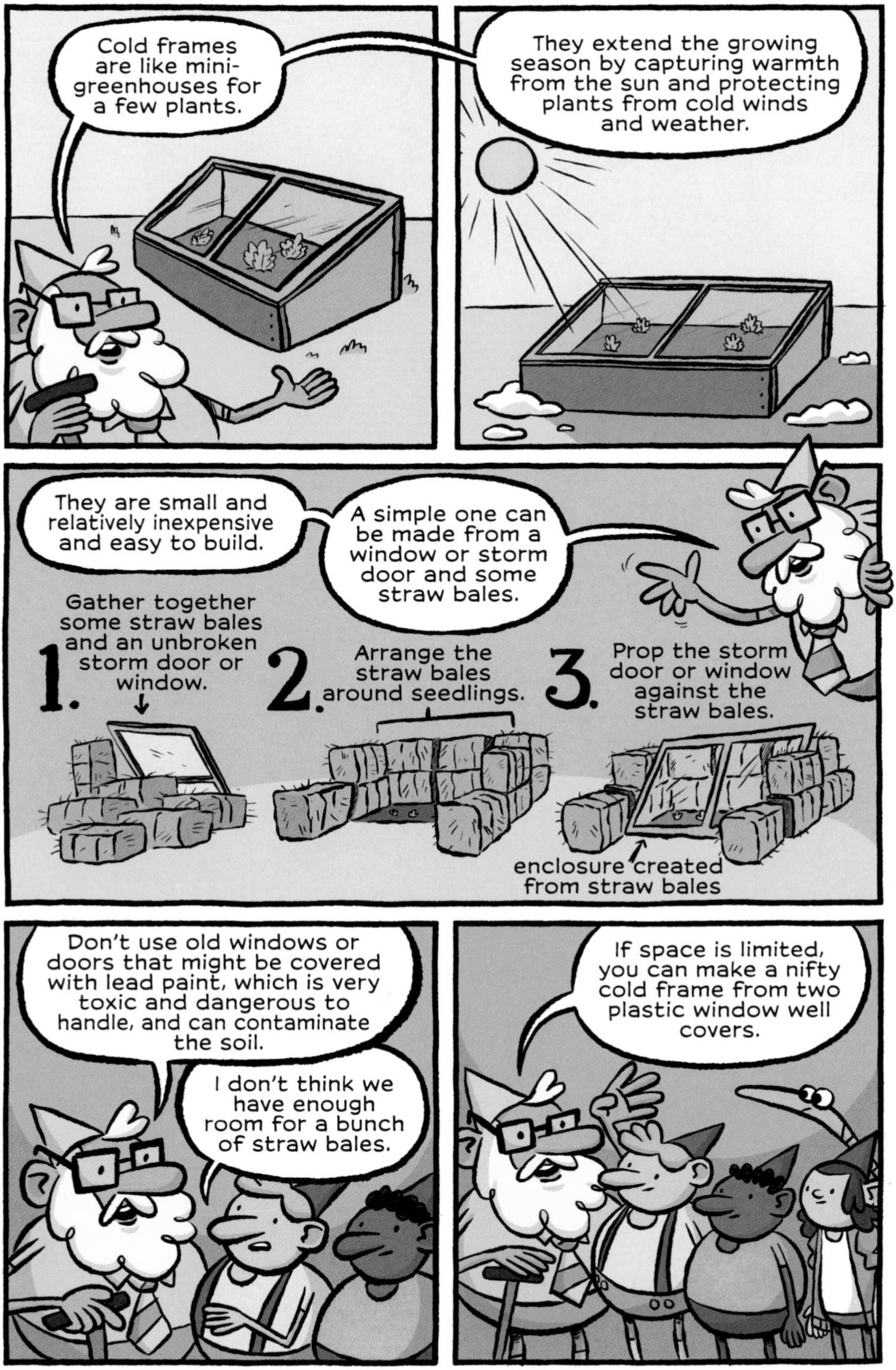
Cold frames are like mini-greenhouses for a few plants.
They extend the growing season by capturing warmth from the sun and protecting plants from cold winds and weather.
They are small and relatively inexpensive and easy to build.
A simple one can be made from a window or storm door and some straw bales.
1. Gather together some straw bales and an unbroken storm door or window.
2. Arrange the straw bales around seedlings.
3. Prop the storm door or window against the straw bales.
enclosure created from straw bales
Don't use old windows or doors that might be covered with lead paint, which is very toxic and dangerous to handle, and can contaminate the soil.
I don't think we have enough room for a bunch of straw bales.
If space is limited, you can make a nifty cold frame from two plastic window well covers.

MAKE YOUR OWN Cold Frame

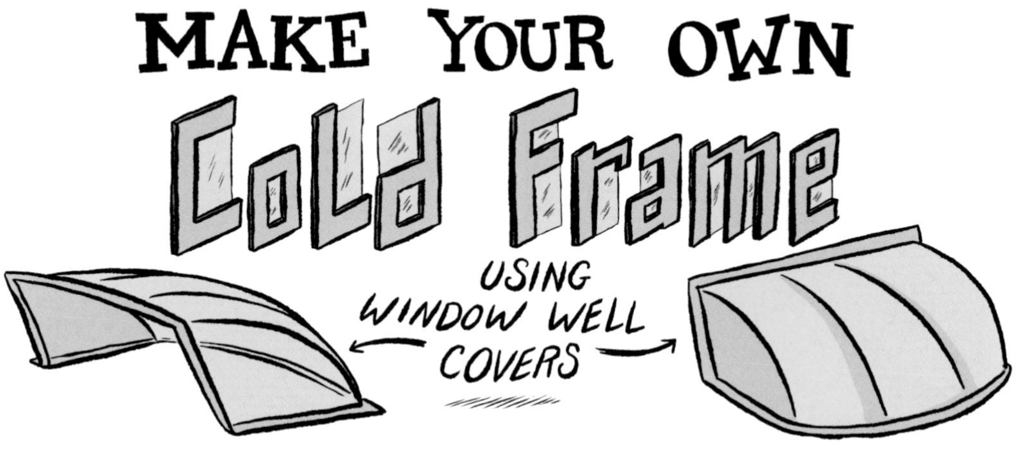
USING WINDOW WELL COVERS

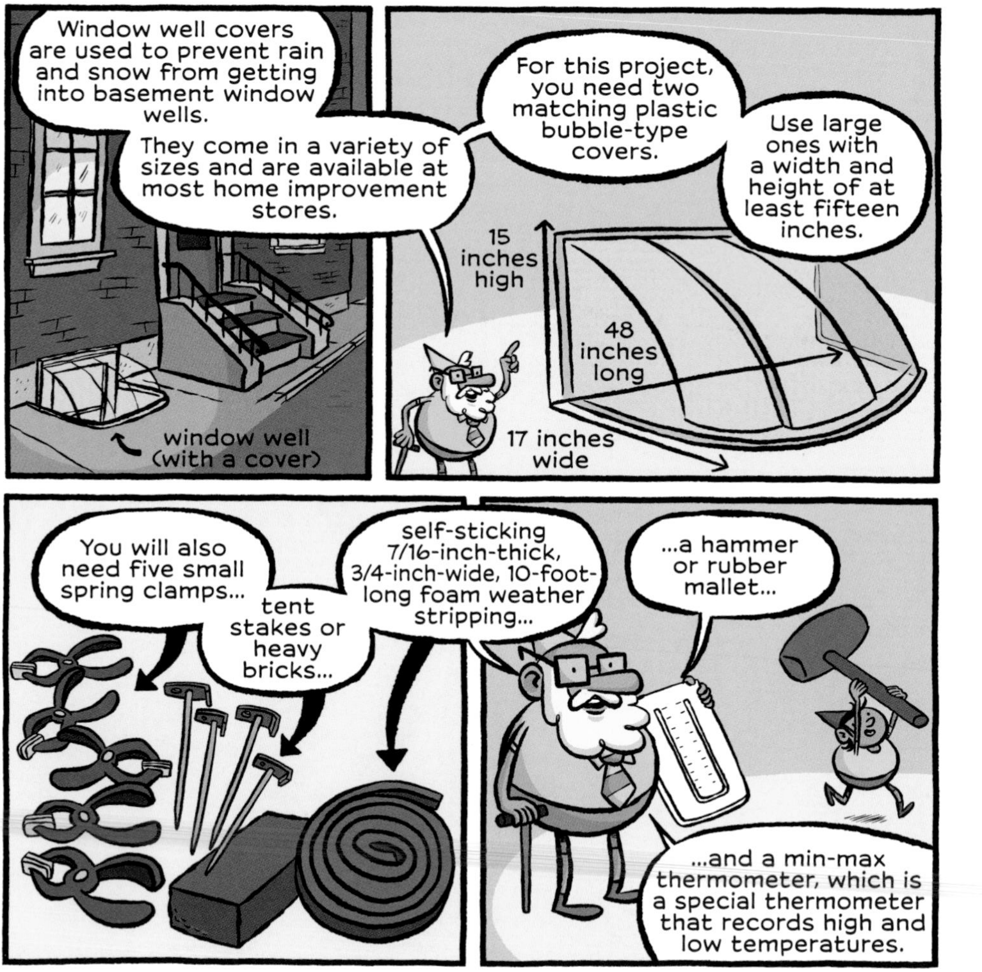
Window well covers are used to prevent rain and snow from getting into basement window wells.
They come in a variety of sizes and are available at most home improvement stores.
window well (with a cover)
For this project, you need two matching plastic bubble-type covers.
Use large ones with a width and height of at least fifteen inches.
15 inches high
48 inches long
17 inches wide
You will also need five small spring clamps...
tent stakes or heavy bricks...
self-sticking 7/16-inch-thick, 3/4-inch-wide, 10-foot-long foam weather stripping...
...a hammer or rubber mallet...
...and a min-max thermometer, which is a special thermometer that records high and low temperatures.

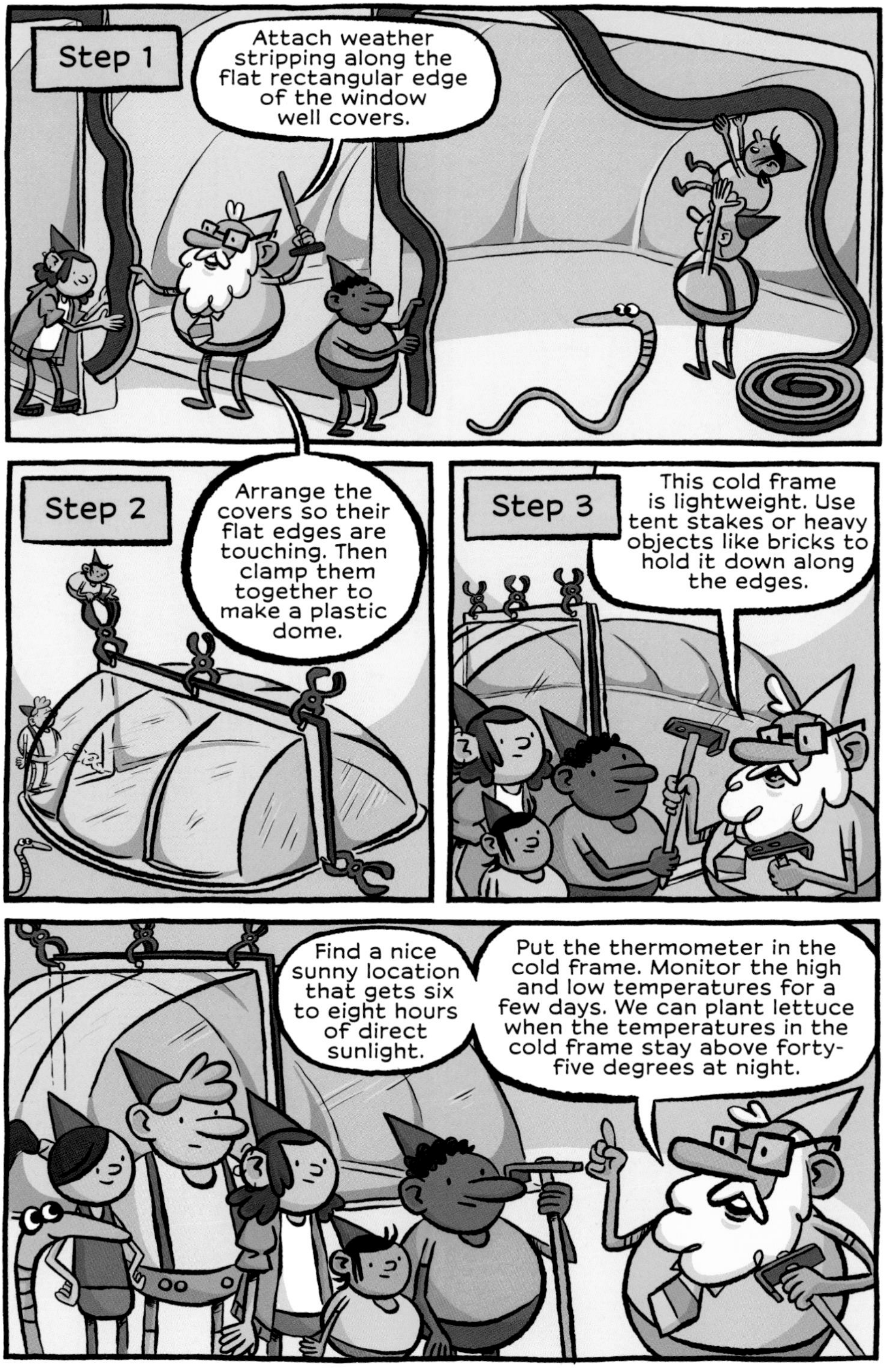
Step 1
Attach weather stripping along the flat rectangular edge of the window well covers.
Step 2
Arrange the covers so their flat edges are touching. Then clamp them together to make a plastic dome.
Step 3
This cold frame is lightweight. Use tent stakes or heavy objects like bricks to hold it down along the edges.
Find a nice sunny location that gets six to eight hours of direct sunlight.
Put the thermometer in the cold frame. Monitor the high and low temperatures for a few days. We can plant lettuce when the temperatures in the cold frame stay above forty-five degrees at night.

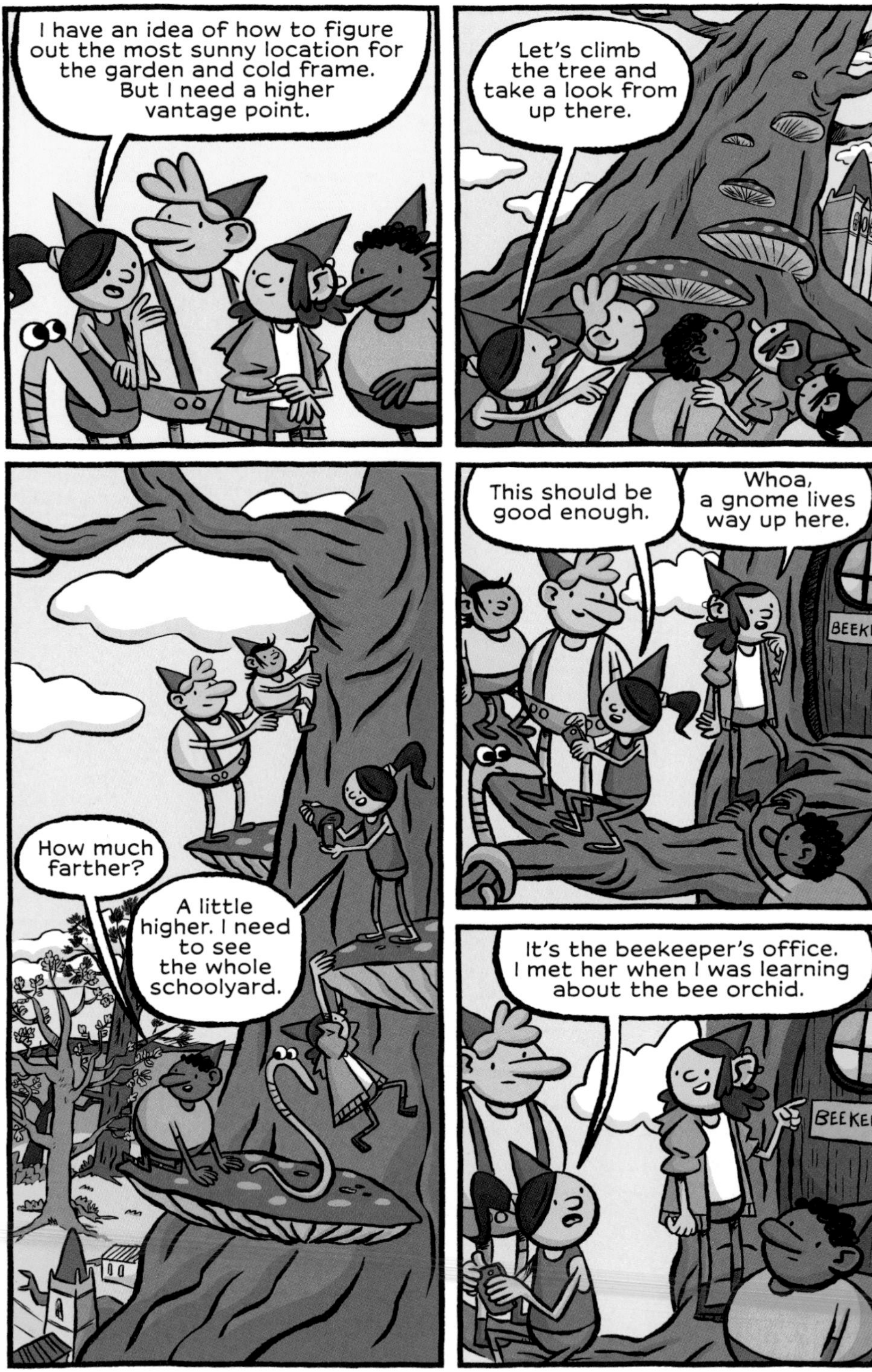
I have an idea of how to figure out the most sunny location for the garden and cold frame. But I need a higher vantage point.
Let's climb the tree and take a look from up there.
How much farther?
A little higher. I need to see the whole schoolyard.
This should be good enough.
Whoa, a gnome lives way up here.
BEEKEE
It's the beekeeper's office. I met her when I was learning about the bee orchid.
BEEKEEP

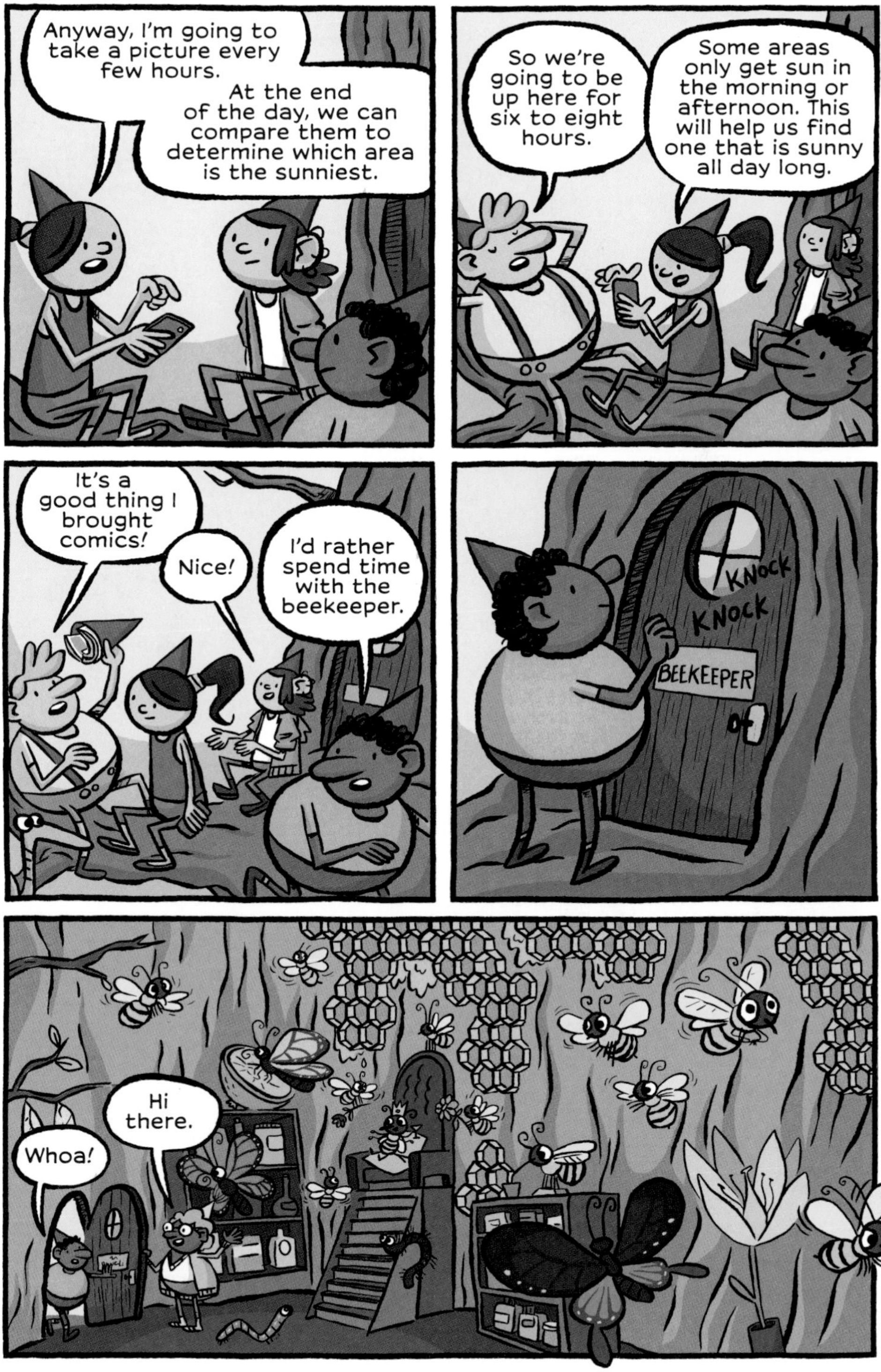
Anyway, I'm going to take a picture every few hours.
At the end of the day, we can compare them to determine which area is the sunniest.
So we're going to be up here for six to eight hours.
Some areas only get sun in the morning or afternoon. This will help us find one that is sunny all day long.
It's a good thing I brought comics!
Nice!
I'd rather spend time with the beekeeper.
KNOCK
KNOCK
BEEKEEPER
Whoa!
Hi there.

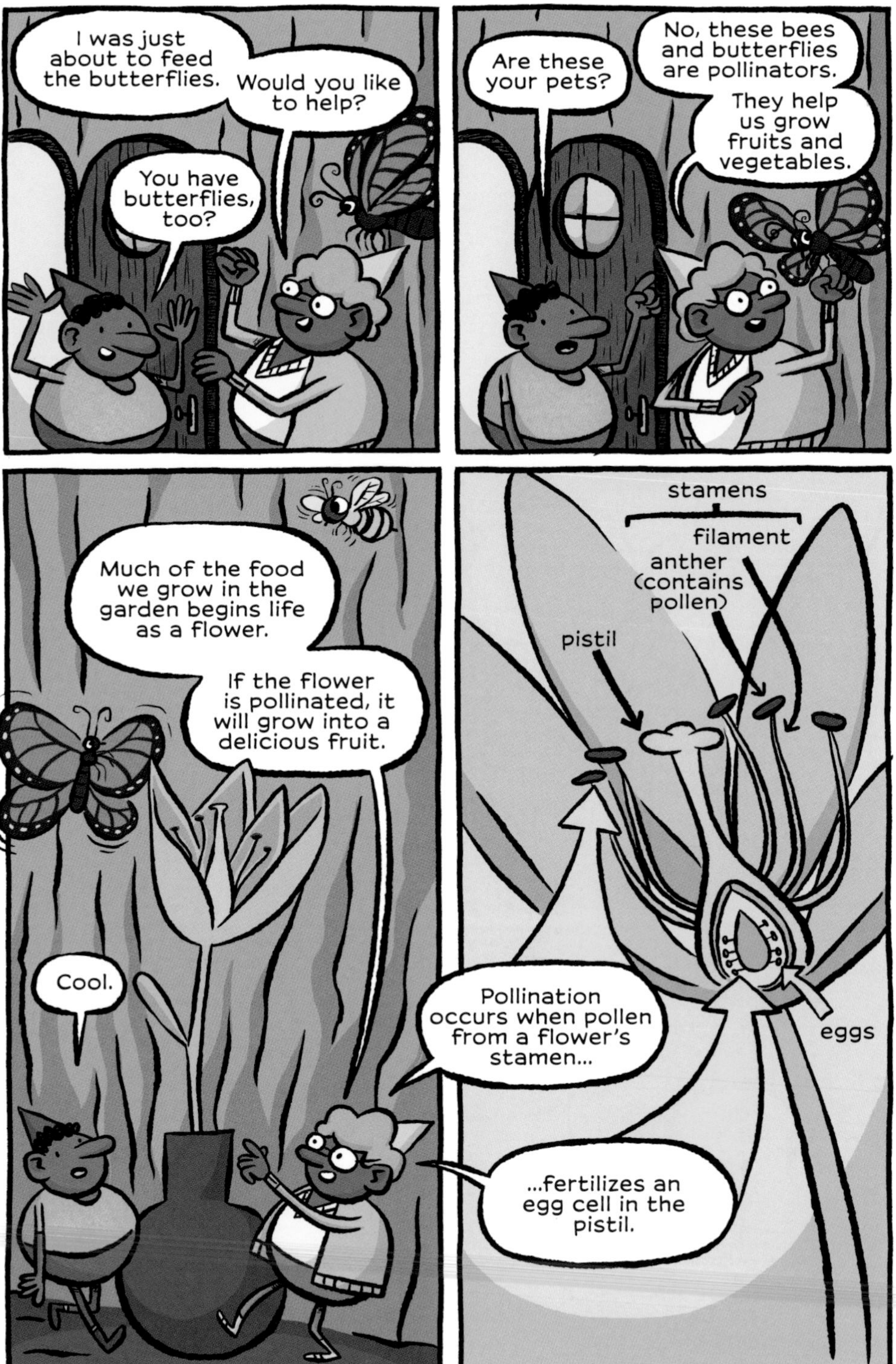
I was just about to feed the butterflies.
Would you like to help?
You have butterflies, too?
Are these your pets?
No, these bees and butterflies are pollinators.
They help us grow fruits and vegetables.
Much of the food we grow in the garden begins life as a flower.
If the flower is pollinated, it will grow into a delicious fruit.
Cool.
Pollination occurs when pollen from a flower's stamen...
stamens
filament
anther (contains pollen)
pistil
eggs
...fertilizes an egg cell in the pistil.

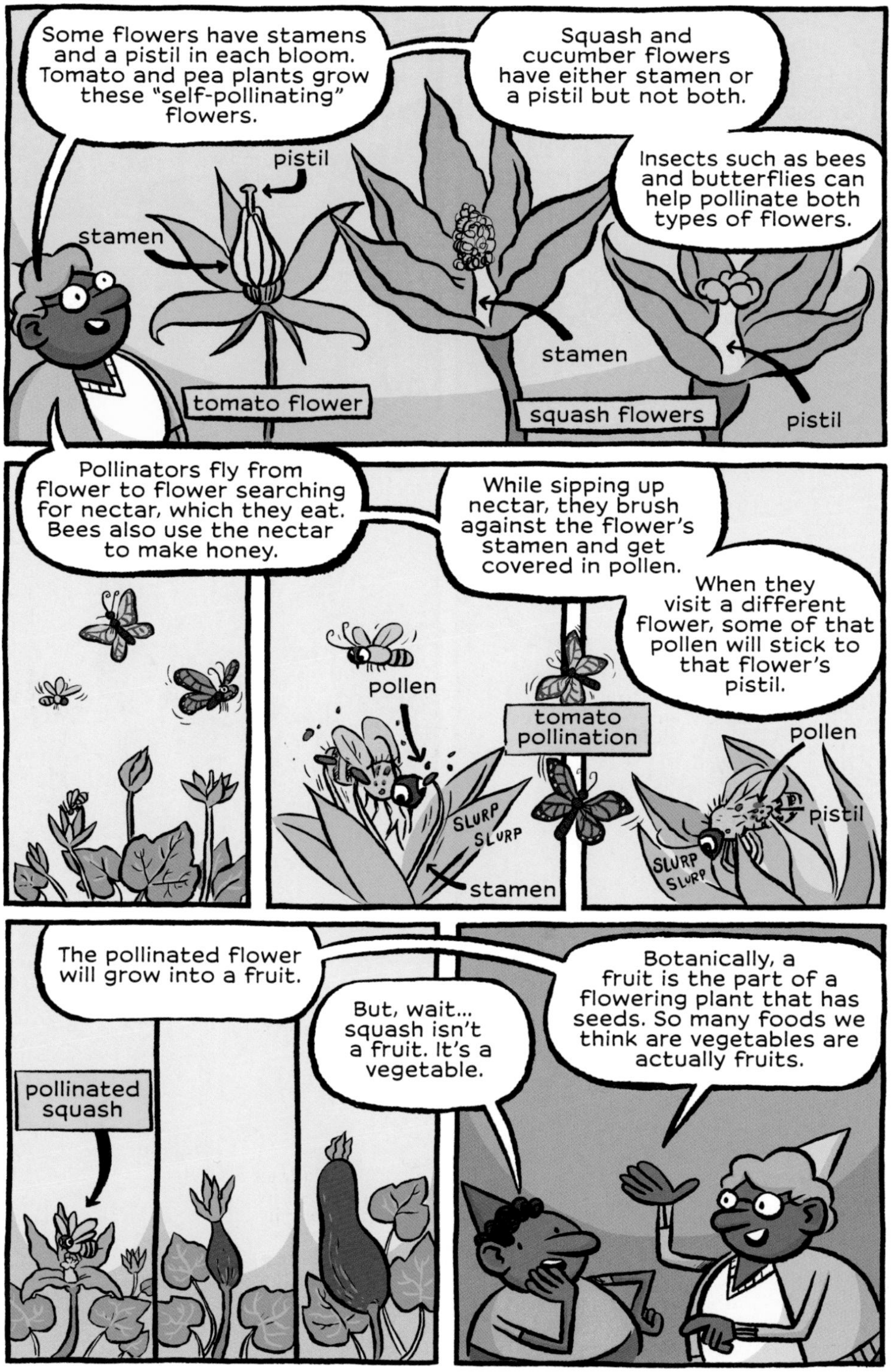
Some flowers have stamens and a pistil in each bloom. Tomato and pea plants grow these "self-pollinating" flowers.
Squash and cucumber flowers have either stamen or a pistil but not both.
Insects such as bees and butterflies can help pollinate both types of flowers.
pistil
stamen
tomato flower
stamen
squash flowers
pistil
Pollinators fly from flower to flower searching for nectar, which they eat. Bees also use the nectar to make honey.
While sipping up nectar, they brush against the flower's stamen and get covered in pollen.
When they visit a different flower, some of that pollen will stick to that flower's pistil.
pollen
tomato pollination
pollen
SLURP SLURP
stamen
pistil
SLURP SLURP
The pollinated flower will grow into a fruit.
pollinated squash
But, wait... squash isn't a fruit. It's a vegetable.
Botanically, a fruit is the part of a flowering plant that has seeds. So many foods we think are vegetables are actually fruits.

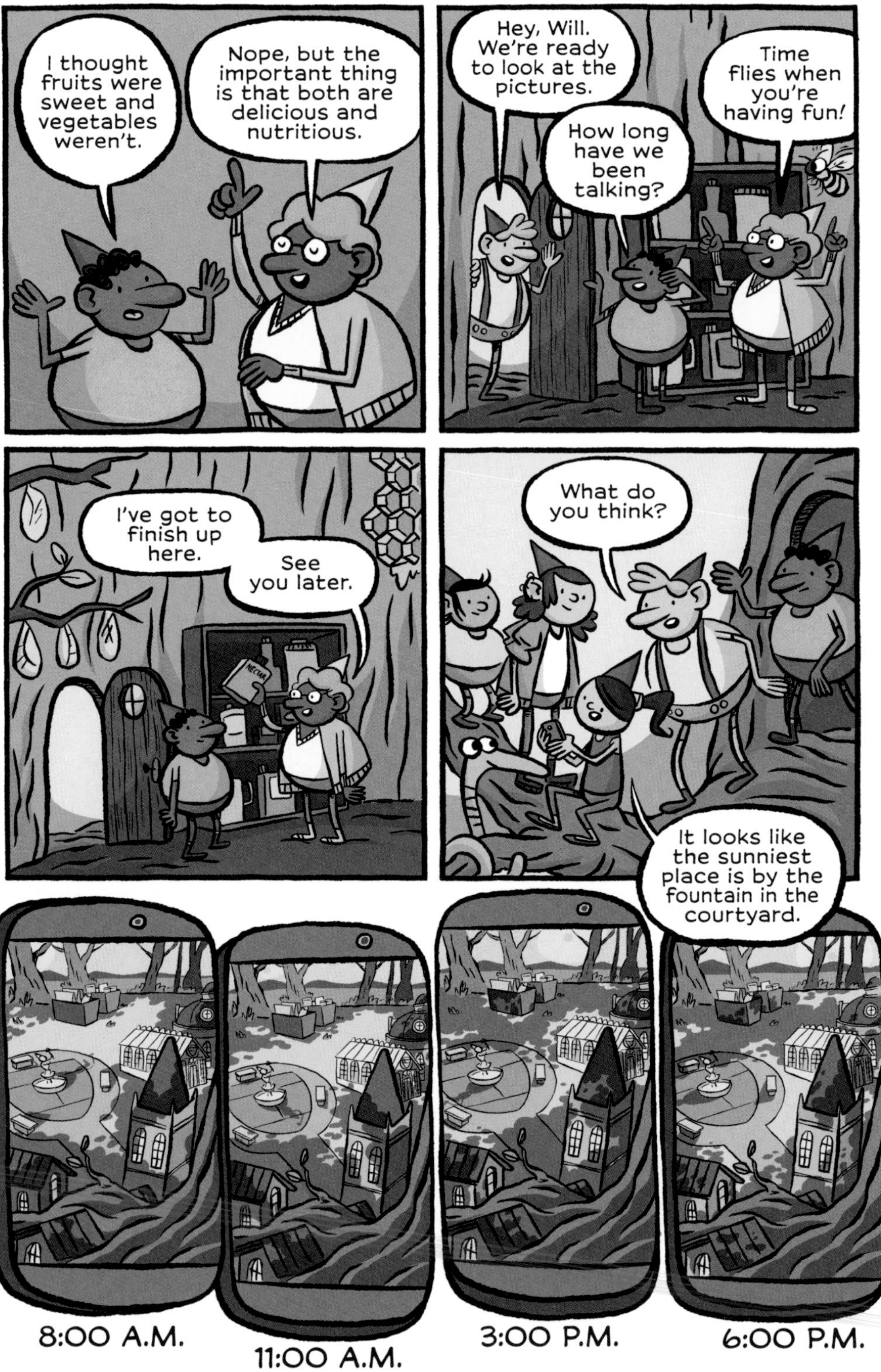
I thought fruits were sweet and vegetables weren't.
Nope, but the important thing is that both are delicious and nutritious.
Hey, Will. We're ready to look at the pictures.
How long have we been talking?
Time flies when you're having fun!
I've got to finish up here.
See you later.
NECTAR
What do you think?
It looks like the sunniest place is by the fountain in the courtyard.
8:00 A.M.
11:00 A.M.
3:00 P.M.
6:00 P.M.

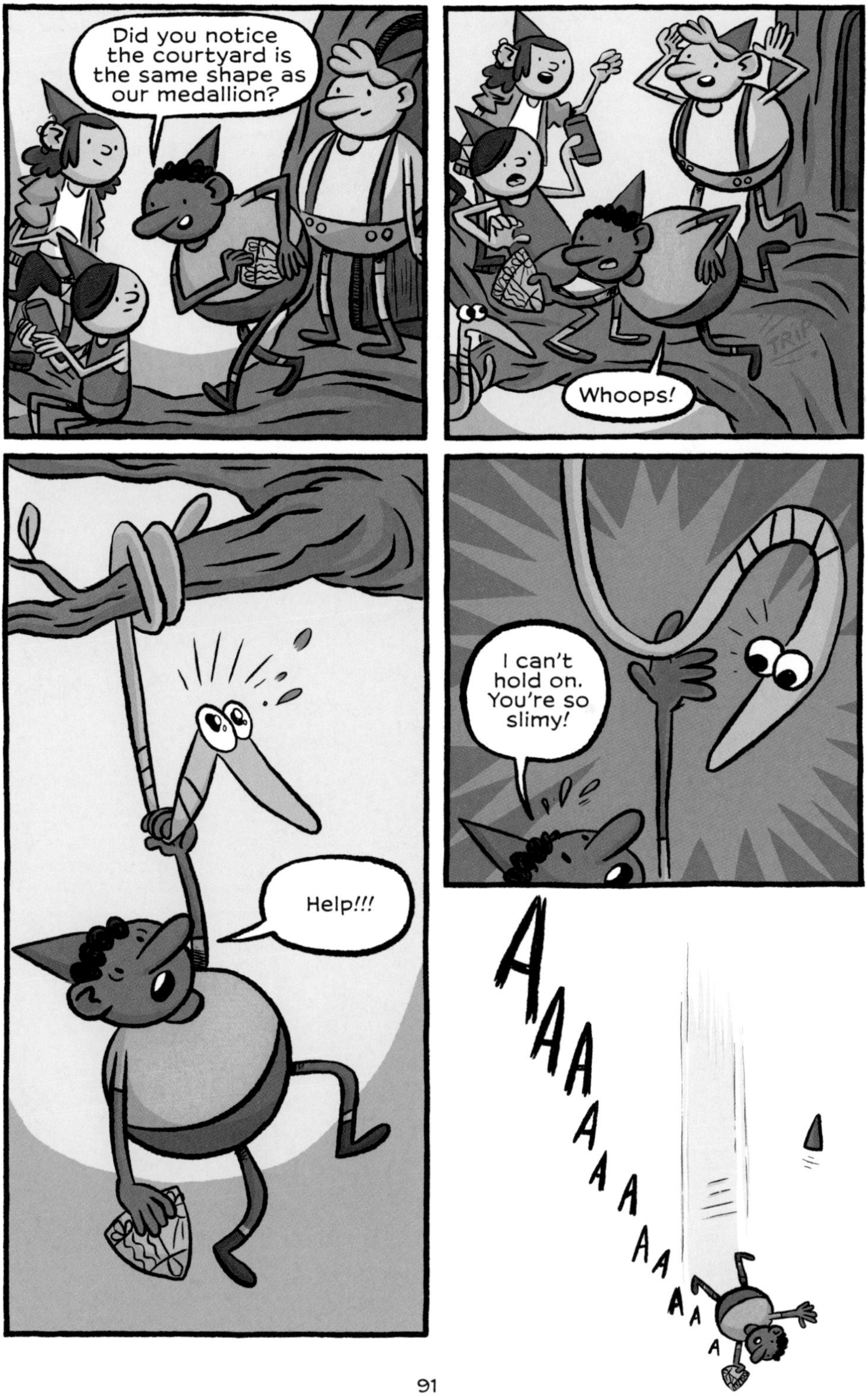

Did you notice the courtyard is the same shape as our medallion?
TRIP
Whoops!
Help!!!
I can't hold on. You're so slimy!
AAAAAAAAAAAAAA

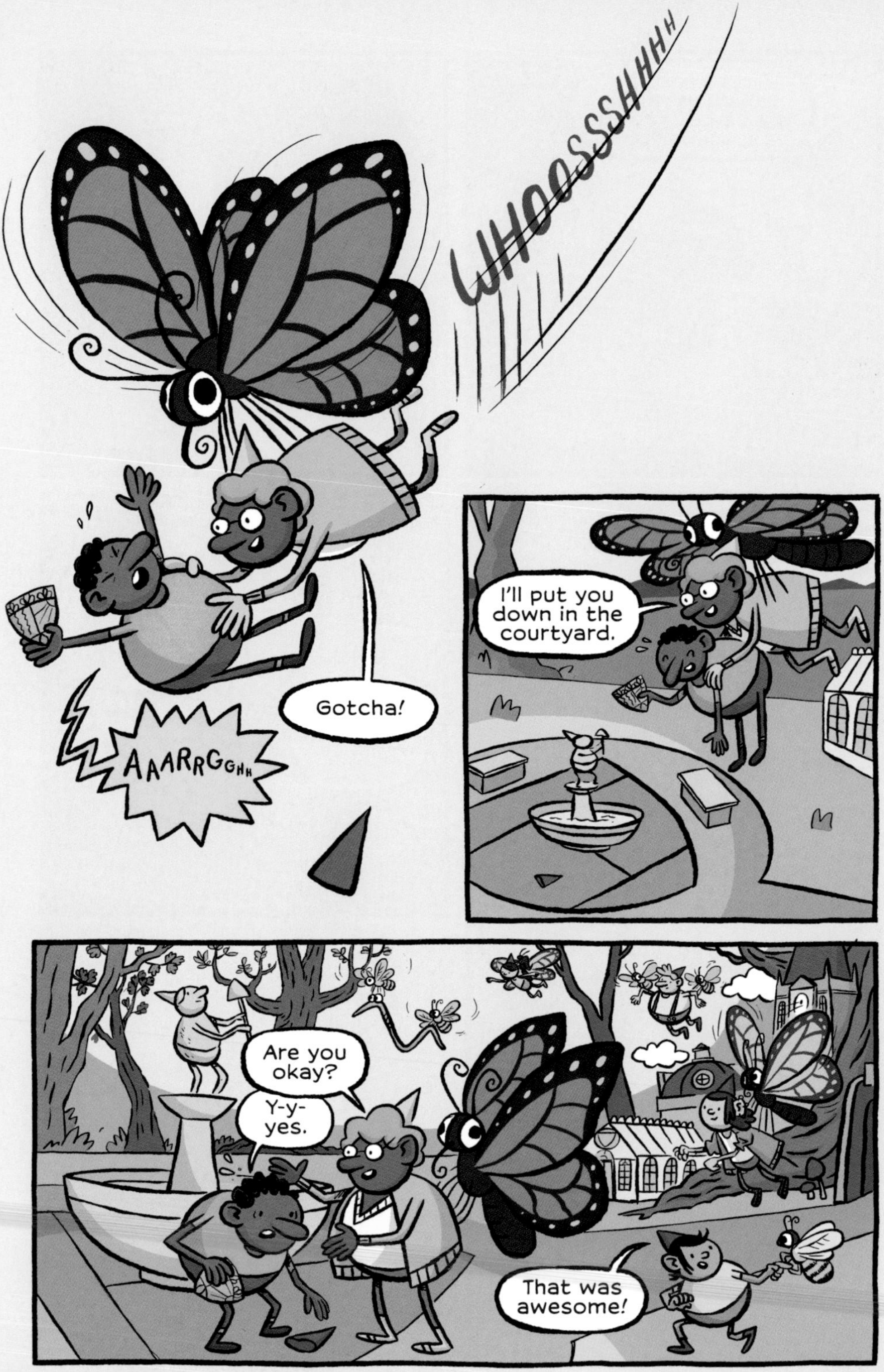
WHOOSSHHHH
Gotcha!
AAARRGGHH
I'll put you down in the courtyard.
Are you okay?
Y-y-yes.
That was awesome!

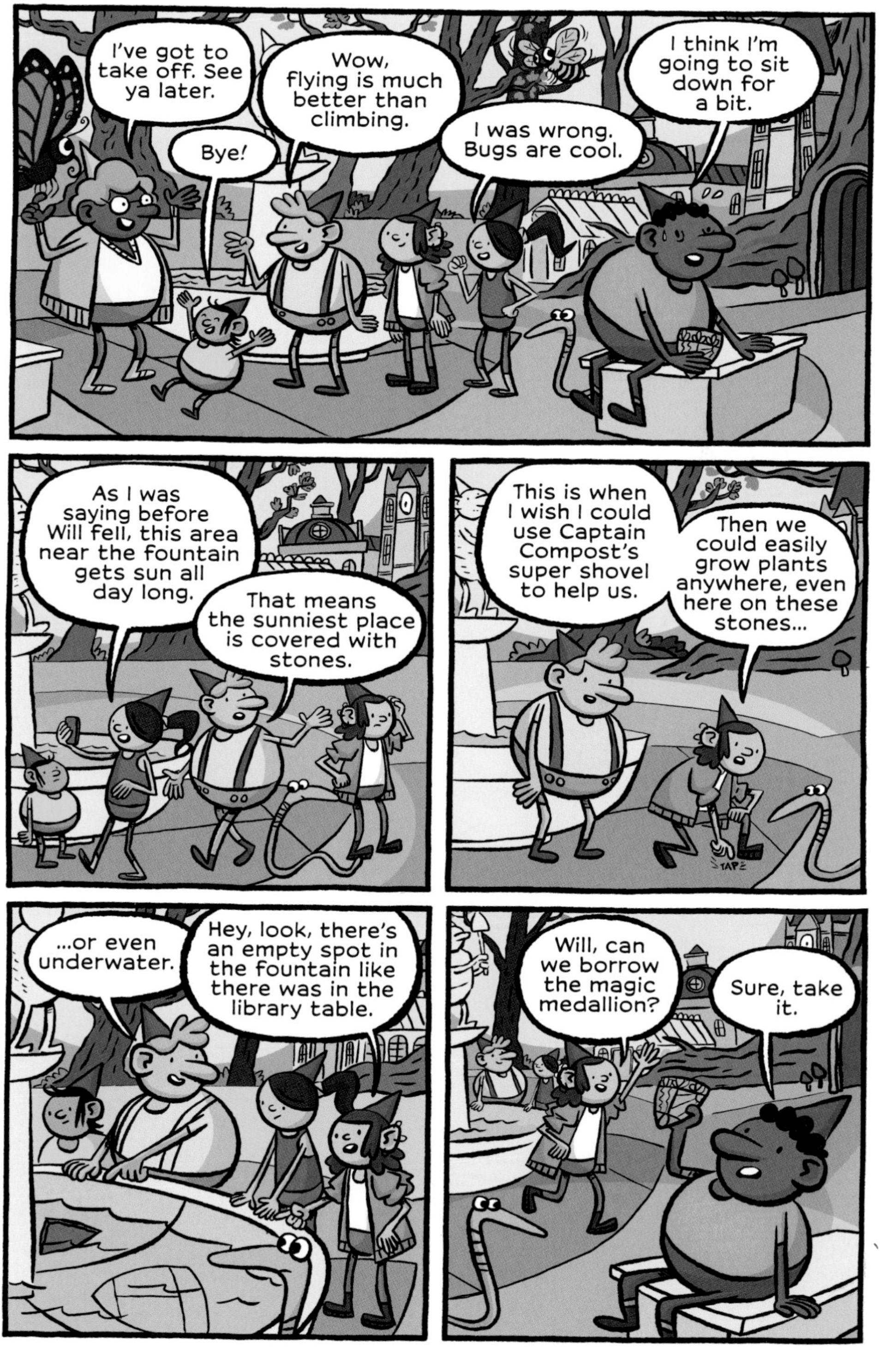
I've got to take off. See ya later.
Bye!
Wow, flying is much better than climbing.
I was wrong. Bugs are cool.
I think I'm going to sit down for a bit.
As I was saying before Will fell, this area near the fountain gets sun all day long.
That means the sunniest place is covered with stones.
This is when I wish I could use Captain Compost's super shovel to help us.
Then we could easily grow plants anywhere, even here on these stones...
TAP
...or even underwater.
Hey, look, there's an empty spot in the fountain like there was in the library table.
Will, can we borrow the magic medallion?
Sure, take it.

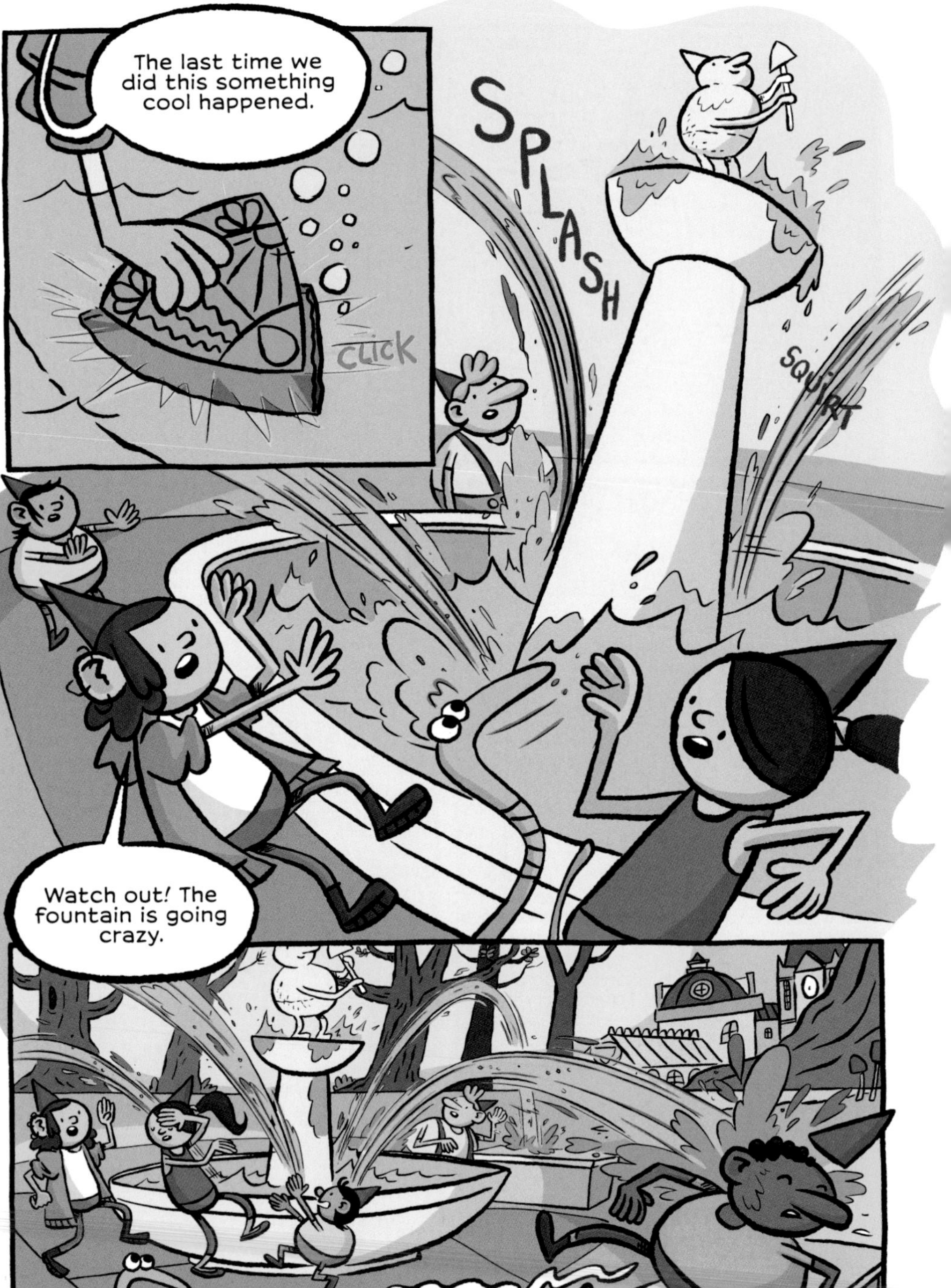

The last time we did this something cool happened.
CLICK
SPLASH
SQUIRT
Watch out! The fountain is going crazy.
Oooofff...

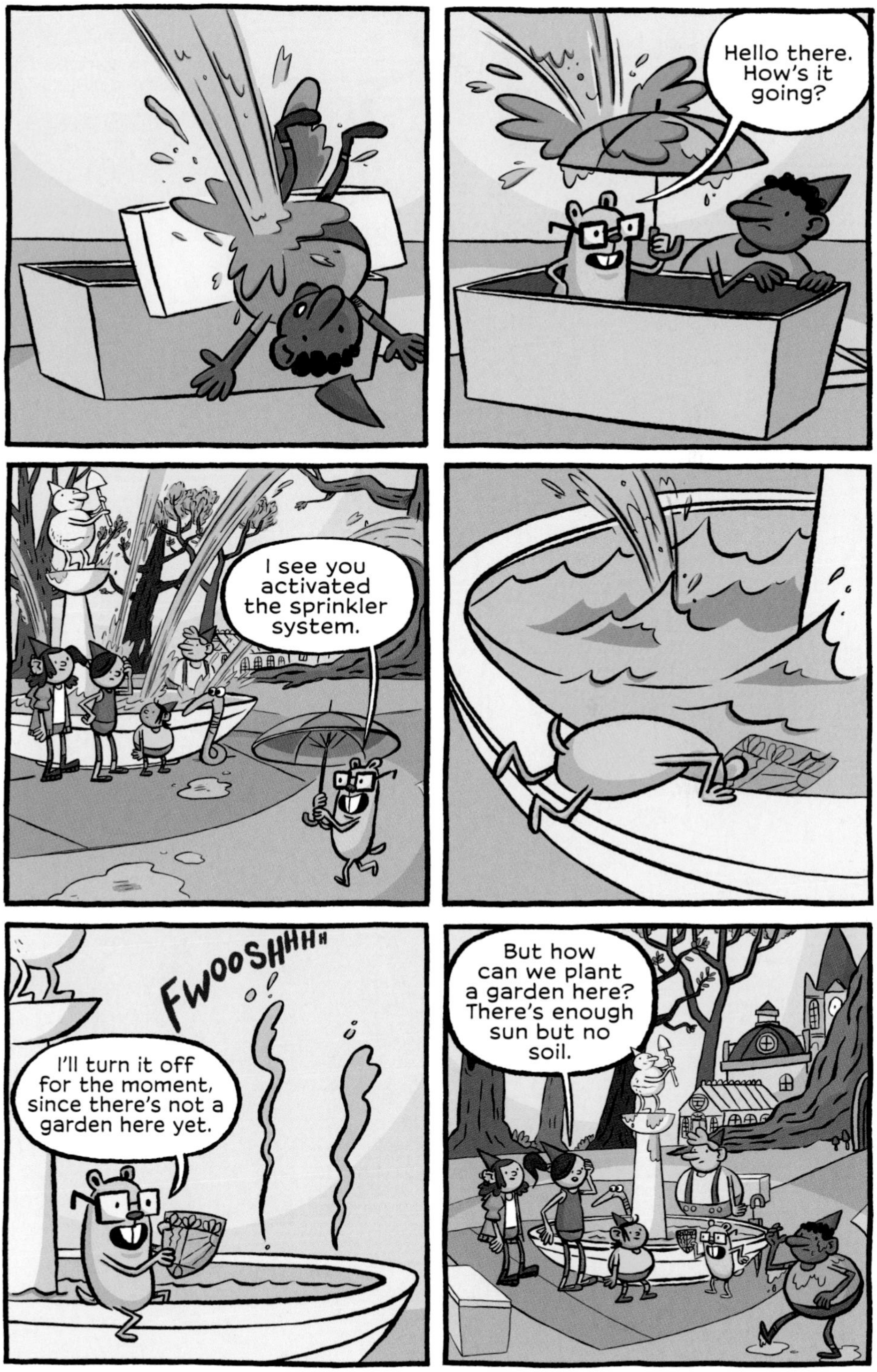
Hello there. How's it going?
I see you activated the sprinkler system.
FWOOSHHHH
I'll turn it off for the moment, since there's not a garden here yet.
But how can we plant a garden here? There's enough sun but no soil.

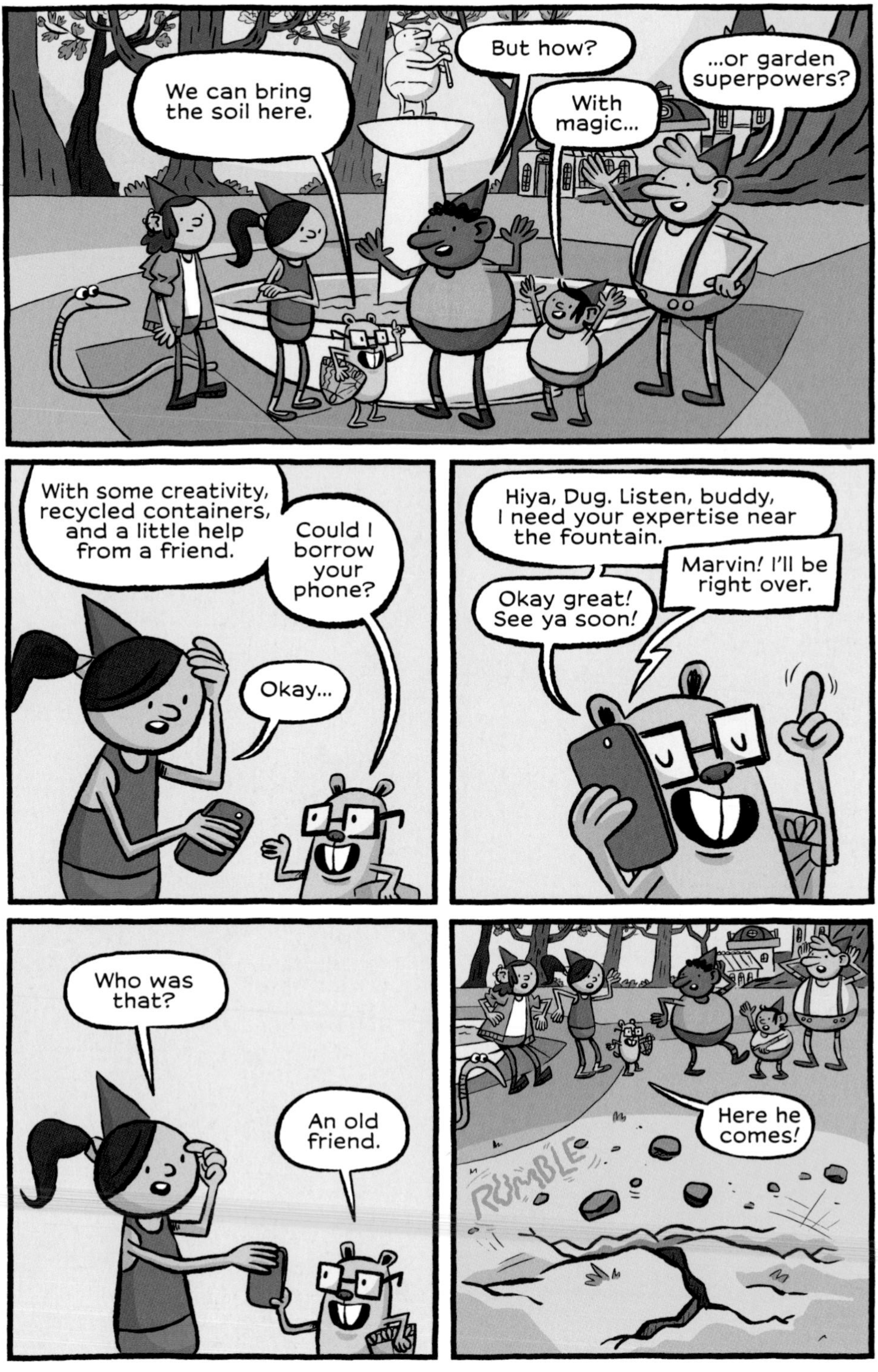
We can bring the soil here.
But how?
With magic...
...or garden superpowers?
With some creativity, recycled containers, and a little help from a friend.
Could I borrow your phone?
Okay...
Hiya, Dug. Listen, buddy, I need your expertise near the fountain.
Marvin! I'll be right over.
Okay great! See ya soon!
Who was that?
An old friend.
Here he comes!
RUMBLE

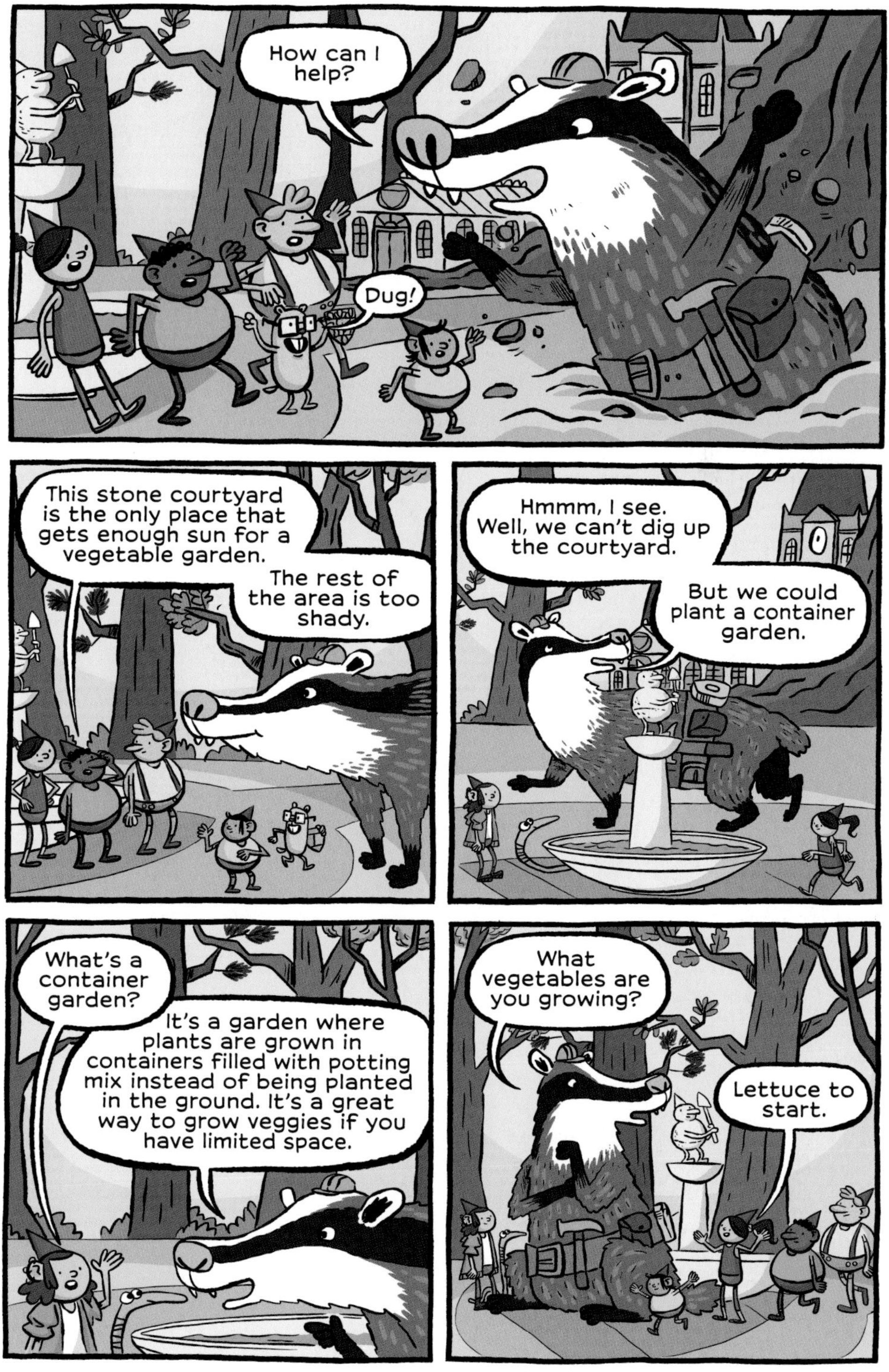

How can I help?
Dug!
This stone courtyard is the only place that gets enough sun for a vegetable garden.
The rest of the area is too shady.
Hmmm, I see. Well, we can't dig up the courtyard.
But we could plant a container garden.
What's a container garden?
It's a garden where plants are grown in containers filled with potting mix instead of being planted in the ground. It's a great way to grow veggies if you have limited space.
What vegetables are you growing?
Lettuce to start.

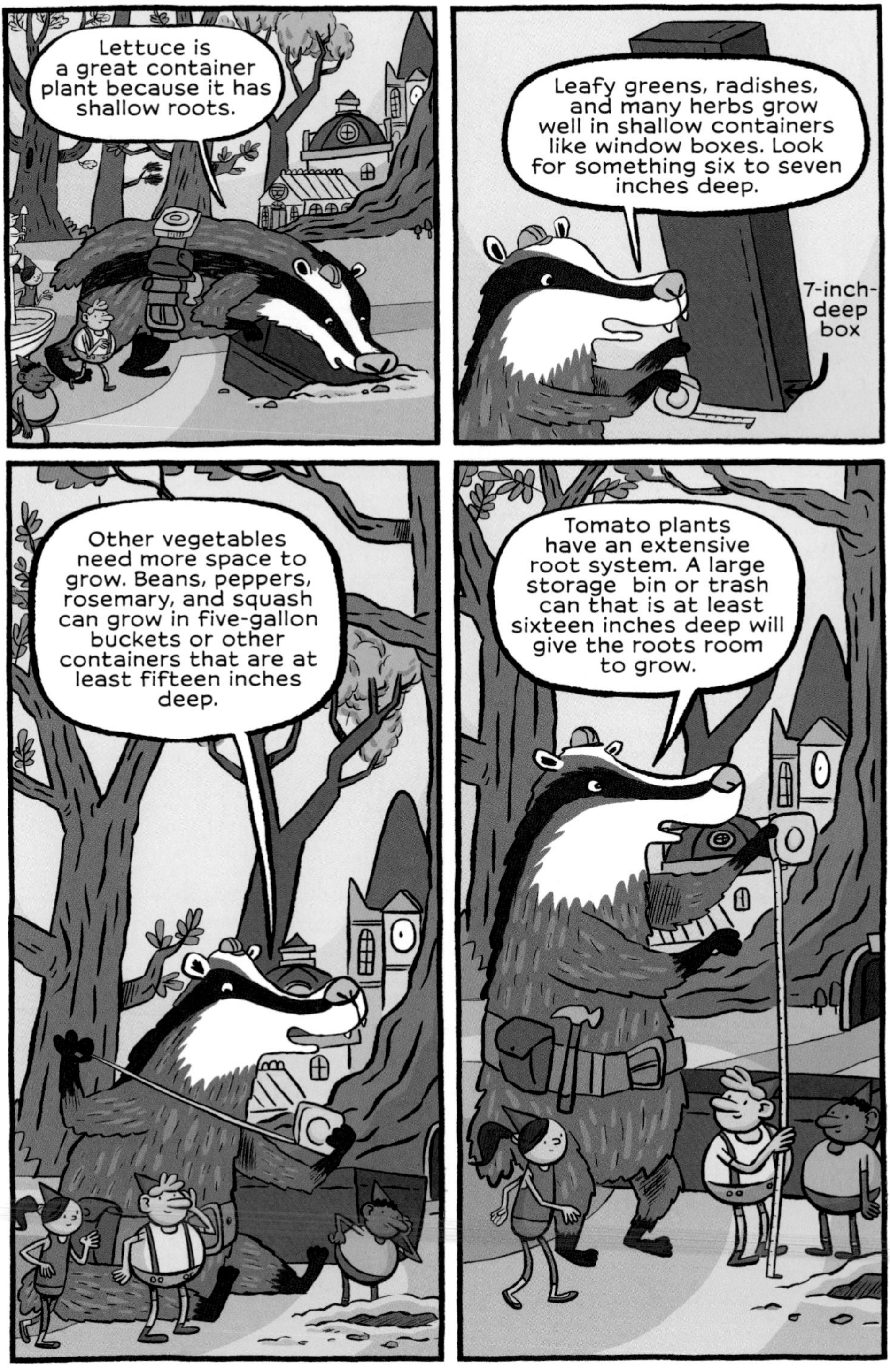
Lettuce is a great container plant because it has shallow roots.
Leafy greens, radishes, and many herbs grow well in shallow containers like window boxes. Look for something six to seven inches deep.
7-inch-deep box
Other vegetables need more space to grow. Beans, peppers, rosemary, and squash can grow in five-gallon buckets or other containers that are at least fifteen inches deep.
Tomato plants have an extensive root system. A large storage bin or trash can that is at least sixteen inches deep will give the roots room to grow.

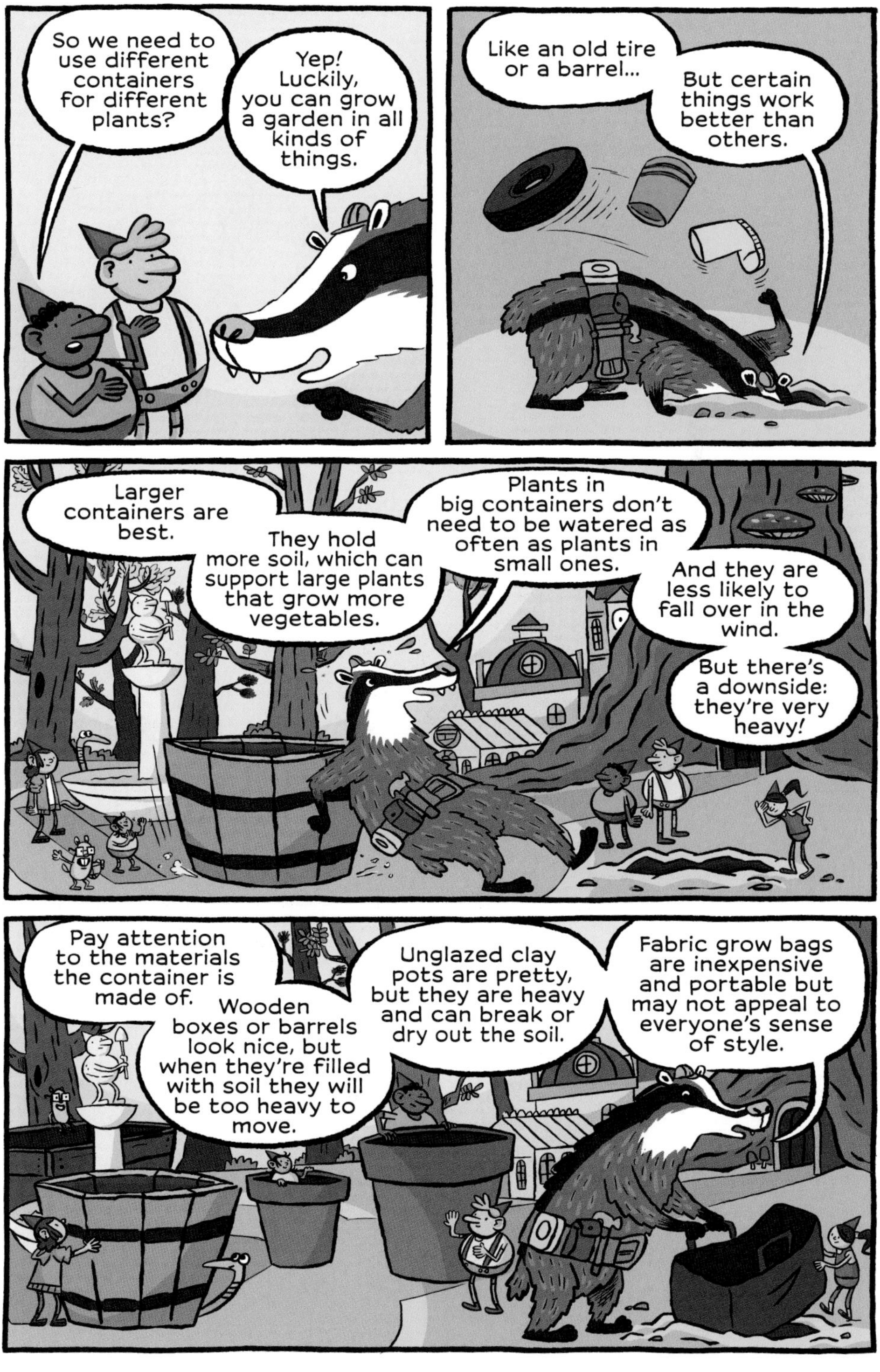
So we need to use different containers for different plants?
Yep! Luckily, you can grow a garden in all kinds of things.
Like an old tire or a barrel...
But certain things work better than others.
Larger containers are best.
They hold more soil, which can support large plants that grow more vegetables.
Plants in big containers don't need to be watered as often as plants in small ones.
And they are less likely to fall over in the wind.
But there's a downside: they're very heavy!
Pay attention to the materials the container is made of.
Wooden boxes or barrels look nice, but when they're filled with soil they will be too heavy to move.
Unglazed clay pots are pretty, but they are heavy and can break or dry out the soil.
Fabric grow bags are inexpensive and portable but may not appeal to everyone's sense of style.

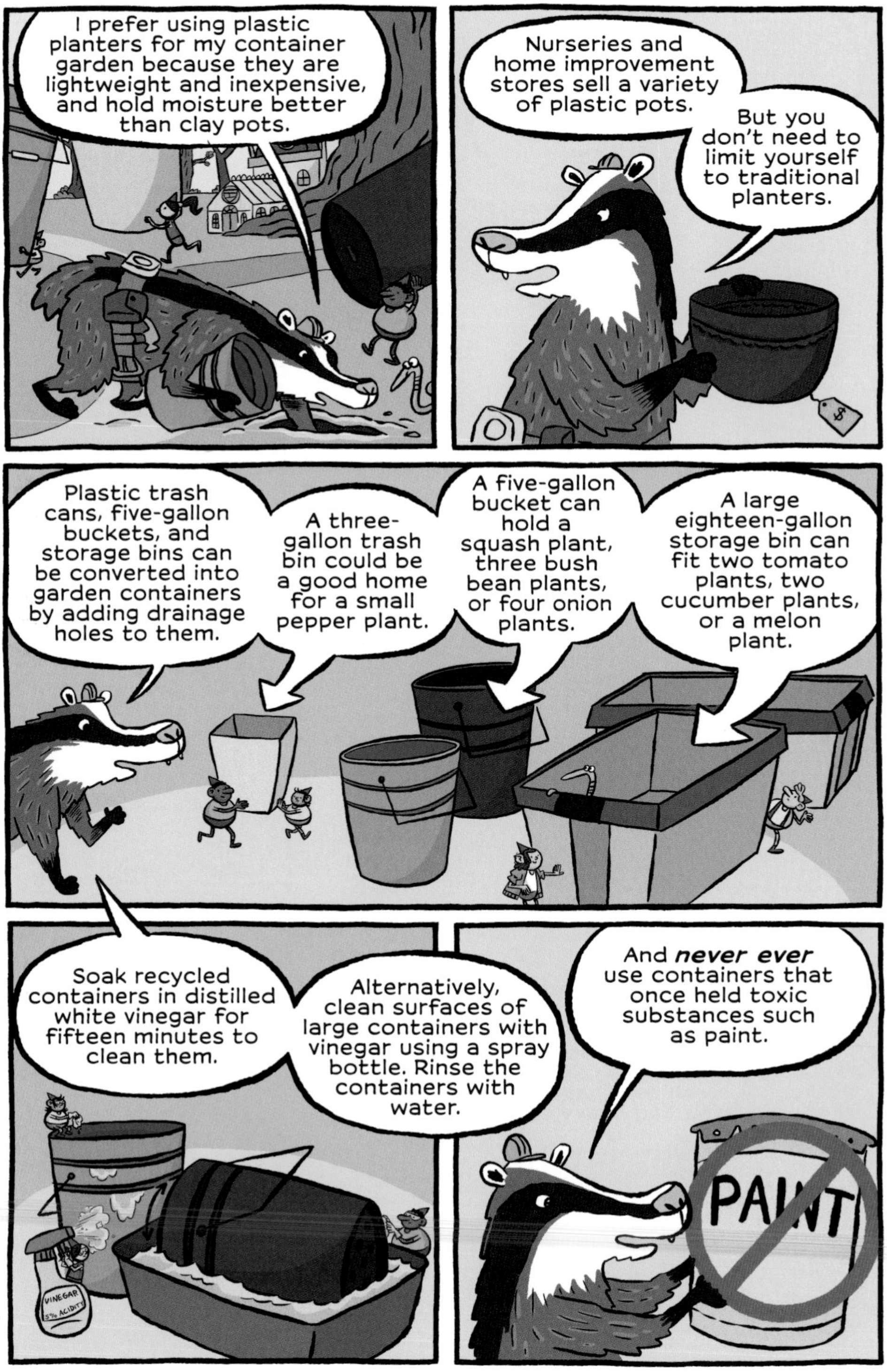
I prefer using plastic planters for my container garden because they are lightweight and inexpensive, and hold moisture better than clay pots.
Nurseries and home improvement stores sell a variety of plastic pots.
But you don't need to limit yourself to traditional planters.
$
Plastic trash cans, five-gallon buckets, and storage bins can be converted into garden containers by adding drainage holes to them.
A three-gallon trash bin could be a good home for a small pepper plant.
A five-gallon bucket can hold a squash plant, three bush bean plants, or four onion plants.
A large eighteen-gallon storage bin can fit two tomato plants, two cucumber plants, or a melon plant.
Soak recycled containers in distilled white vinegar for fifteen minutes to clean them.
Alternatively, clean surfaces of large containers with vinegar using a spray bottle. Rinse the containers with water.
VINEGAR
5% ACIDITY
And ***never ever*** use containers that once held toxic substances such as paint.
PAINT

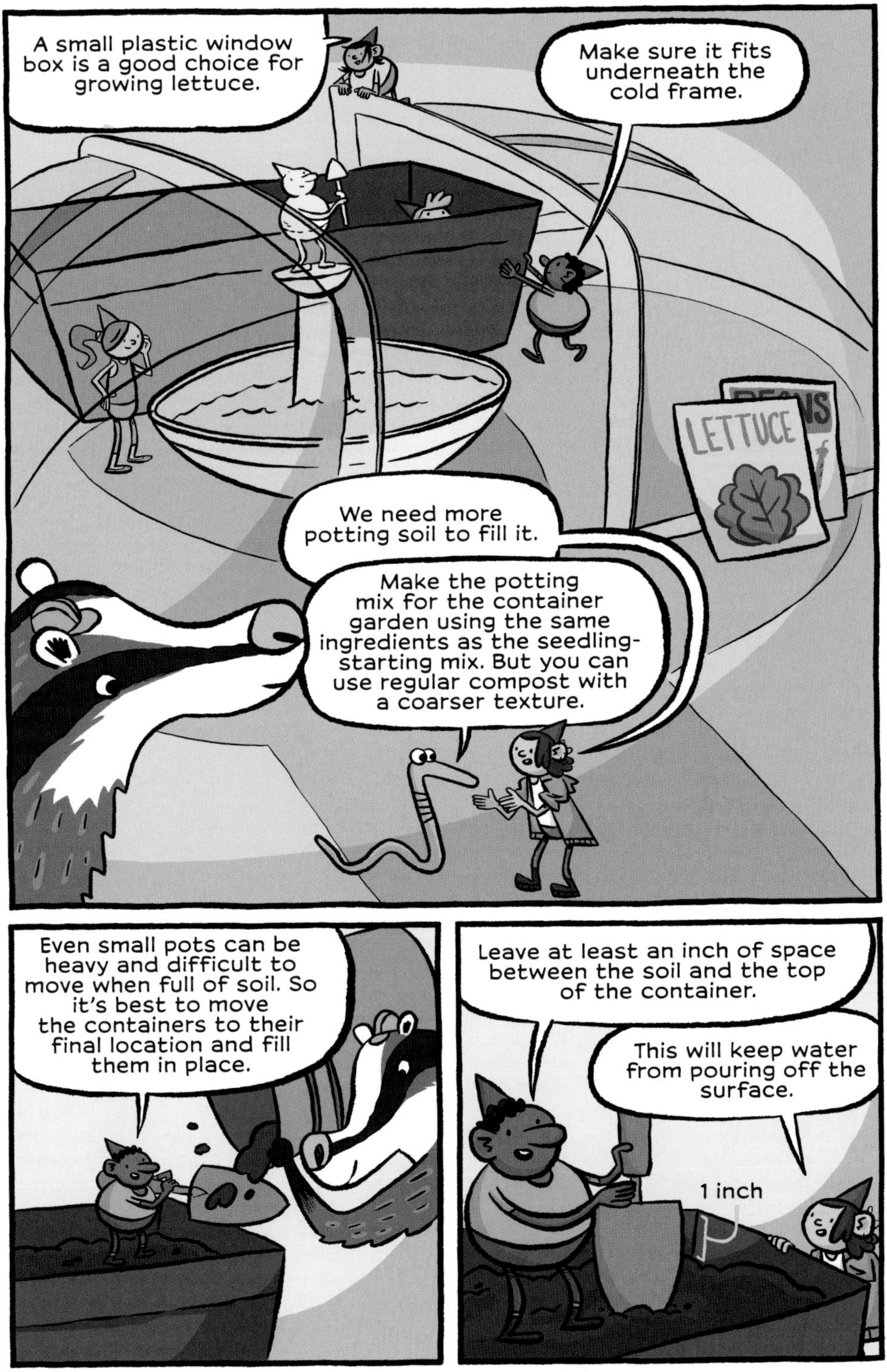
A small plastic window box is a good choice for growing lettuce.
Make sure it fits underneath the cold frame.
LETTUCE
We need more potting soil to fill it.
Make the potting mix for the container garden using the same ingredients as the seedling-starting mix. But you can use regular compost with a coarser texture.
Even small pots can be heavy and difficult to move when full of soil. So it's best to move the containers to their final location and fill them in place.
Leave at least an inch of space between the soil and the top of the container.
This will keep water from pouring off the surface.
1 inch

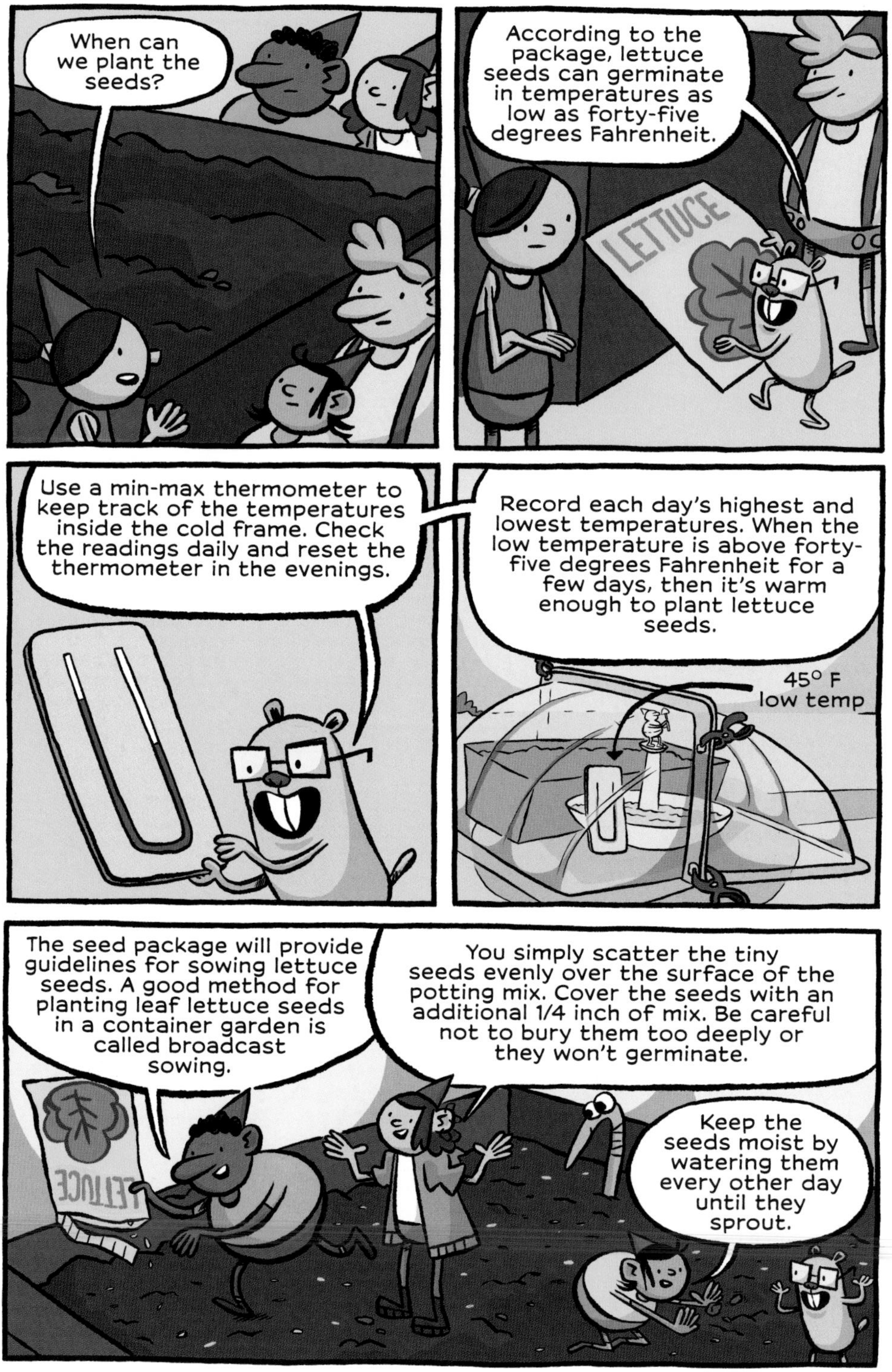
When can we plant the seeds?
According to the package, lettuce seeds can germinate in temperatures as low as forty-five degrees Fahrenheit.
LETTUCE
Use a min-max thermometer to keep track of the temperatures inside the cold frame. Check the readings daily and reset the thermometer in the evenings.
Record each day's highest and lowest temperatures. When the low temperature is above forty-five degrees Fahrenheit for a few days, then it's warm enough to plant lettuce seeds.
45° F low temp
The seed package will provide guidelines for sowing lettuce seeds. A good method for planting leaf lettuce seeds in a container garden is called broadcast sowing.
You simply scatter the tiny seeds evenly over the surface of the potting mix. Cover the seeds with an additional 1/4 inch of mix. Be careful not to bury them too deeply or they won't germinate.
LETTUCE
Keep the seeds moist by watering them every other day until they sprout.

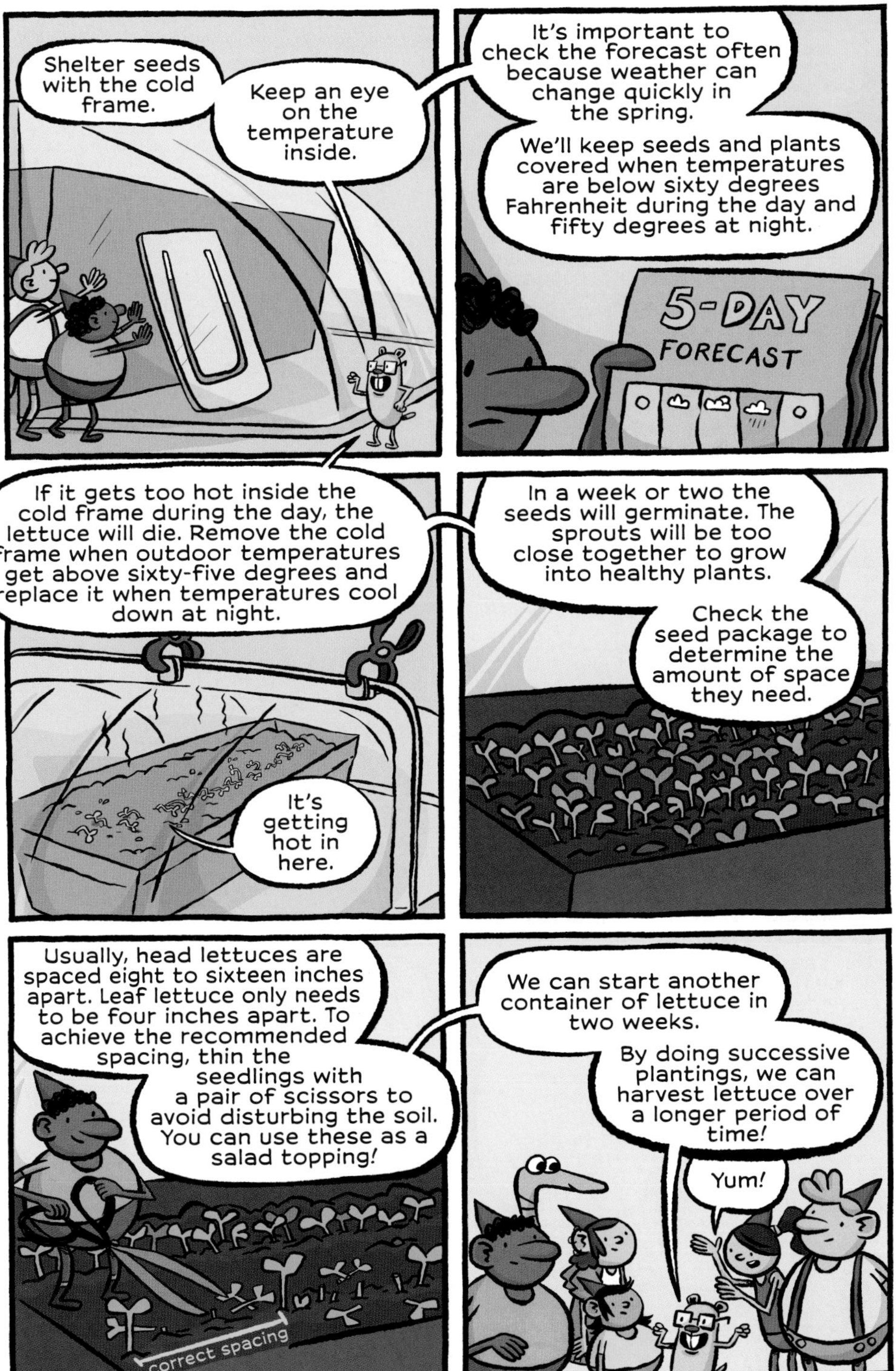
Shelter seeds with the cold frame.
Keep an eye on the temperature inside.
It's important to check the forecast often because weather can change quickly in the spring.
We'll keep seeds and plants covered when temperatures are below sixty degrees Fahrenheit during the day and fifty degrees at night.
5-DAY FORECAST
If it gets too hot inside the cold frame during the day, the lettuce will die. Remove the cold frame when outdoor temperatures get above sixty-five degrees and replace it when temperatures cool down at night.
It's getting hot in here.
In a week or two the seeds will germinate. The sprouts will be too close together to grow into healthy plants.
Check the seed package to determine the amount of space they need.
Usually, head lettuces are spaced eight to sixteen inches apart. Leaf lettuce only needs to be four inches apart. To achieve the recommended spacing, thin the seedlings with a pair of scissors to avoid disturbing the soil. You can use these as a salad topping!
correct spacing
We can start another container of lettuce in two weeks.
By doing successive plantings, we can harvest lettuce over a longer period of time!
Yum!

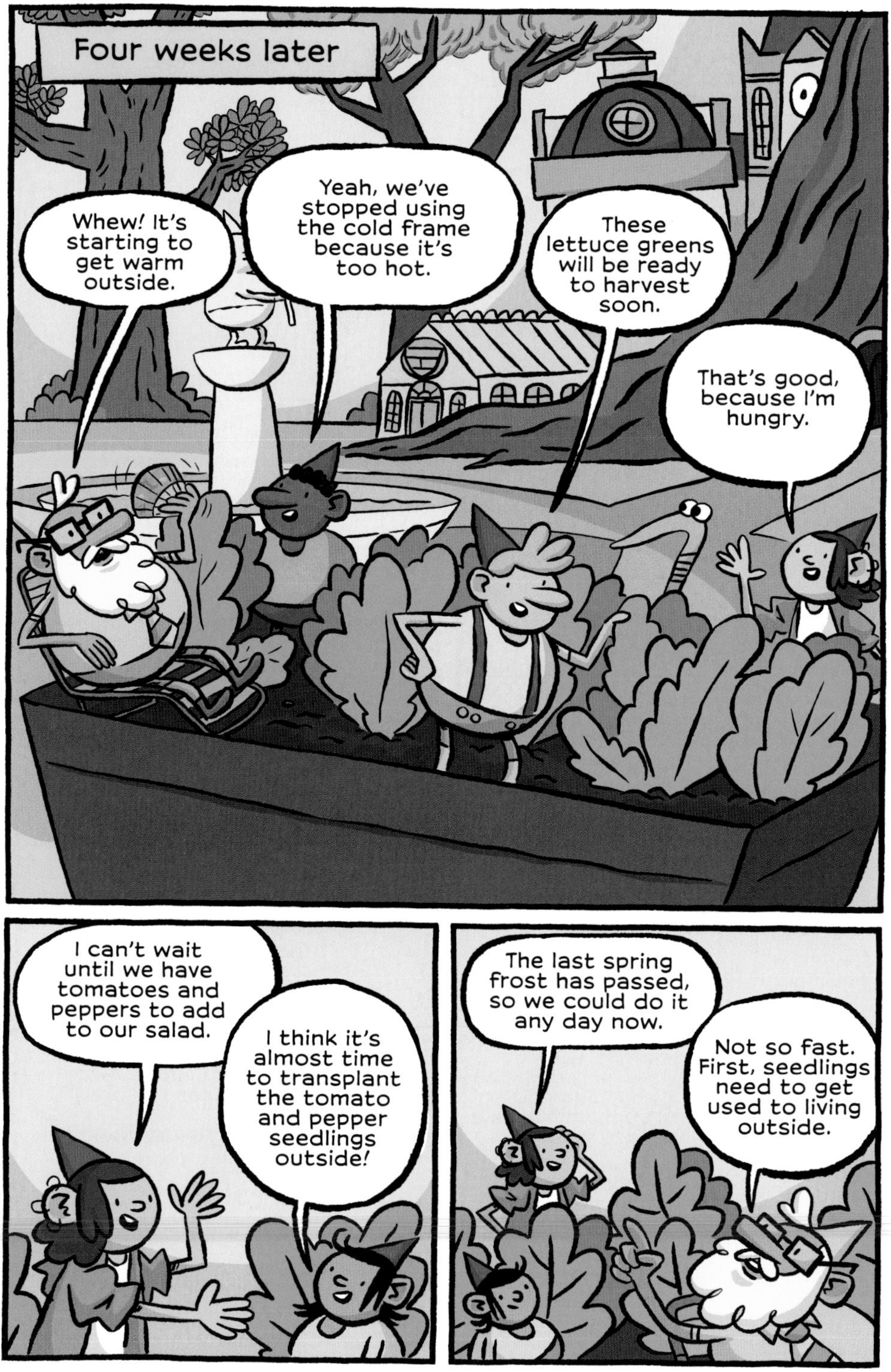
Four weeks later
Whew! It's starting to get warm outside.
Yeah, we've stopped using the cold frame because it's too hot.
These lettuce greens will be ready to harvest soon.
That's good, because I'm hungry.
I can't wait until we have tomatoes and peppers to add to our salad.
I think it's almost time to transplant the tomato and pepper seedlings outside!
The last spring frost has passed, so we could do it any day now.
Not so fast. First, seedlings need to get used to living outside.

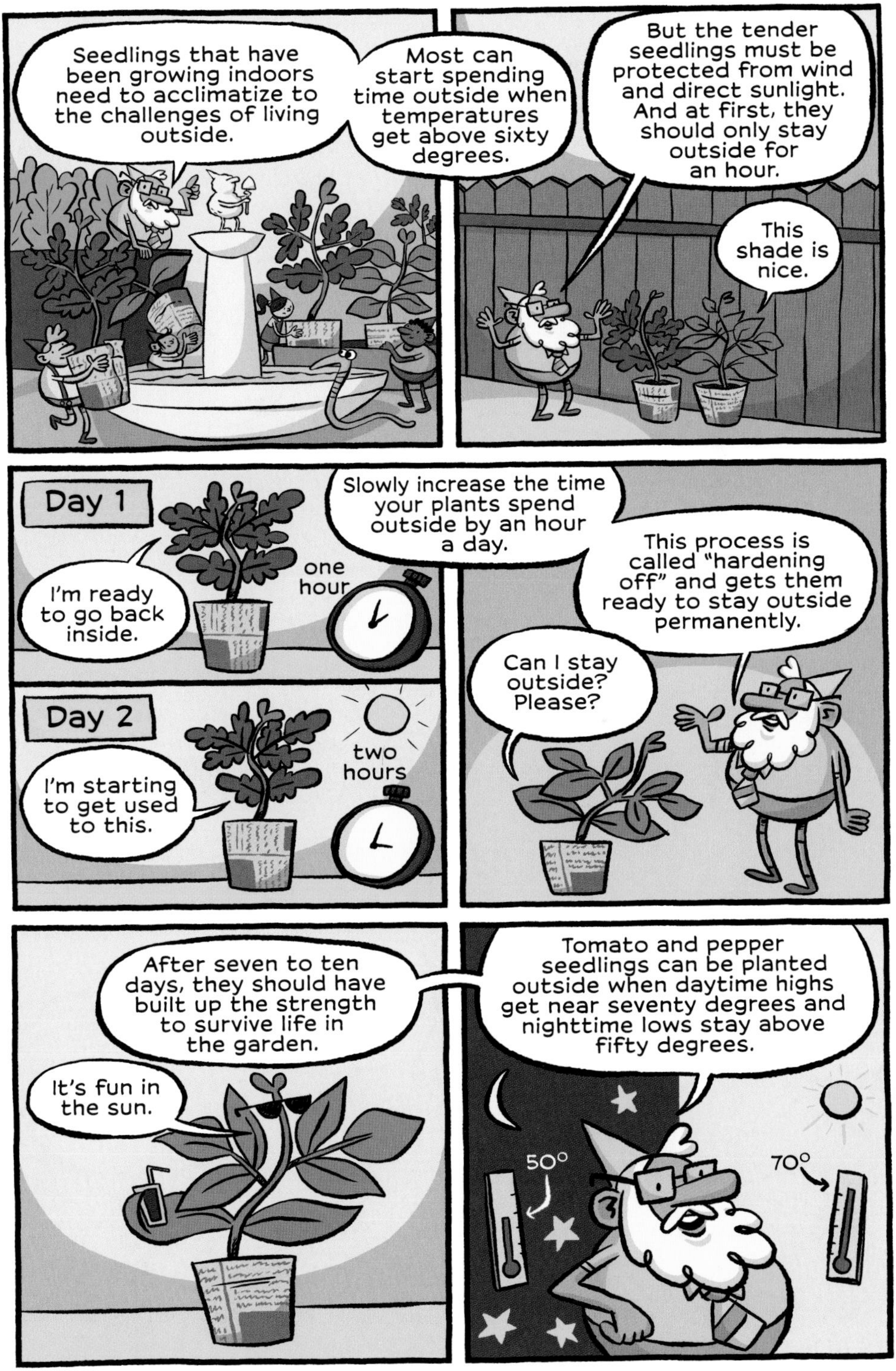

Seedlings that have been growing indoors need to acclimatize to the challenges of living outside.
Most can start spending time outside when temperatures get above sixty degrees.
But the tender seedlings must be protected from wind and direct sunlight. And at first, they should only stay outside for an hour.
This shade is nice.
Day 1
I'm ready to go back inside.
one hour
Day 2
I'm starting to get used to this.
two hours
Slowly increase the time your plants spend outside by an hour a day.
This process is called "hardening off" and gets them ready to stay outside permanently.
Can I stay outside? Please?
After seven to ten days, they should have built up the strength to survive life in the garden.
It's fun in the sun.
Tomato and pepper seedlings can be planted outside when daytime highs get near seventy degrees and nighttime lows stay above fifty degrees.
50°
70°

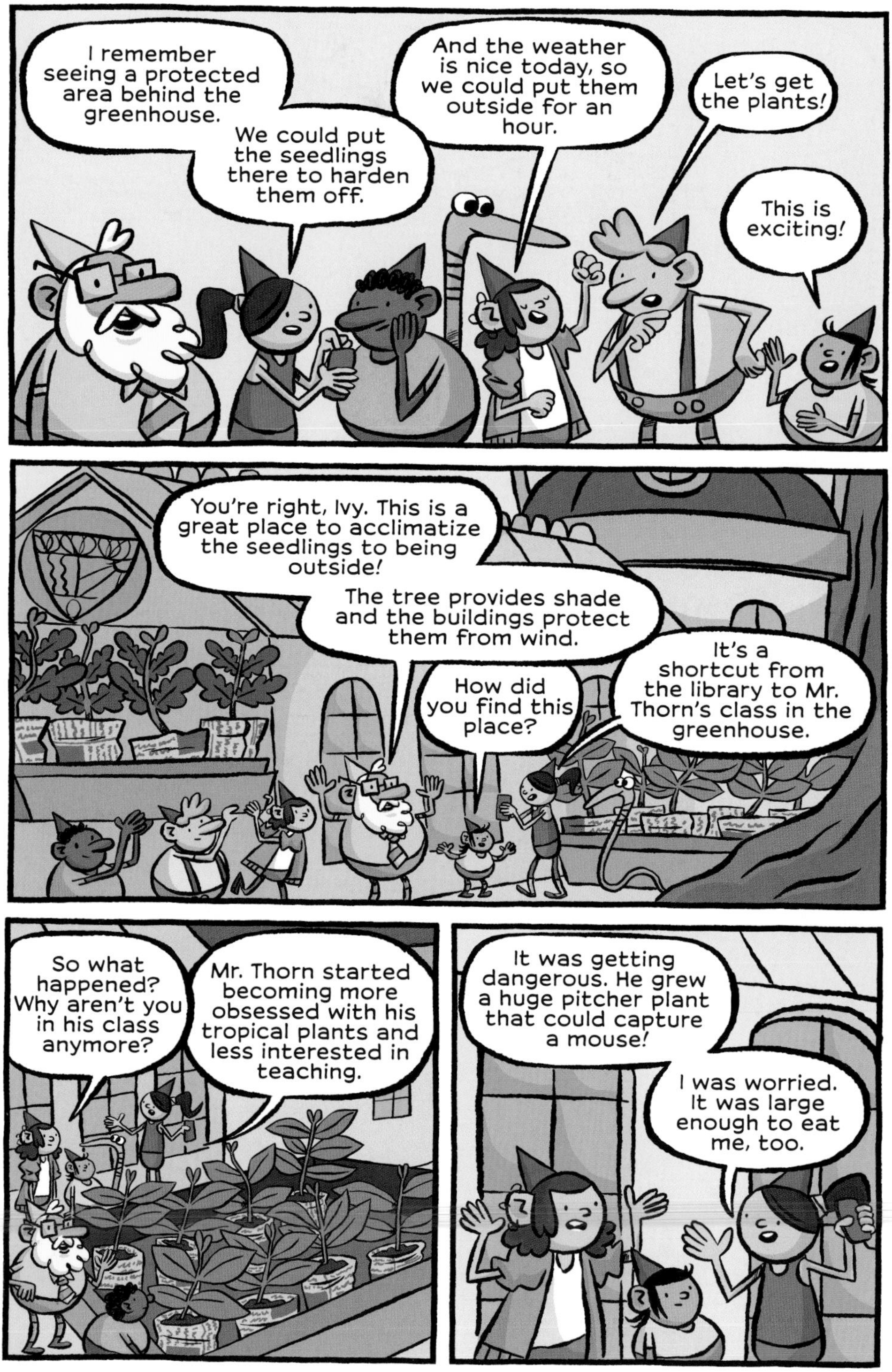
I remember seeing a protected area behind the greenhouse.
We could put the seedlings there to harden them off.
And the weather is nice today, so we could put them outside for an hour.
Let's get the plants!
This is exciting!
You're right, Ivy. This is a great place to acclimatize the seedlings to being outside!
The tree provides shade and the buildings protect them from wind.
How did you find this place?
It's a shortcut from the library to Mr. Thorn's class in the greenhouse.
So what happened? Why aren't you in his class anymore?
Mr. Thorn started becoming more obsessed with his tropical plants and less interested in teaching.
It was getting dangerous. He grew a huge pitcher plant that could capture a mouse!
I was worried. It was large enough to eat me, too.

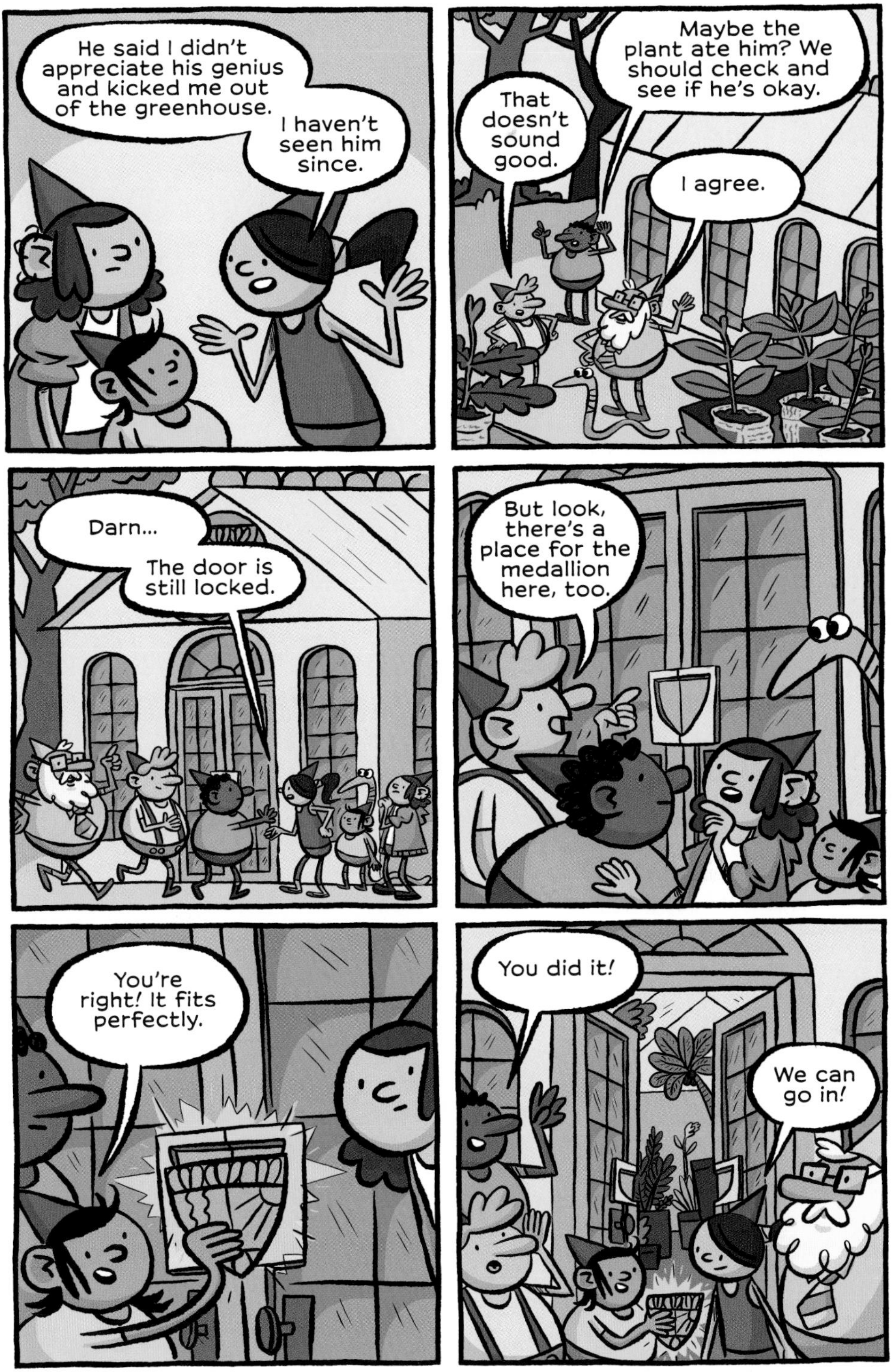
He said I didn't appreciate his genius and kicked me out of the greenhouse.
I haven't seen him since.
Maybe the plant ate him? We should check and see if he's okay.
That doesn't sound good.
I agree.
Darn...
The door is still locked.
But look, there's a place for the medallion here, too.
You're right! It fits perfectly.
You did it!
We can go in!

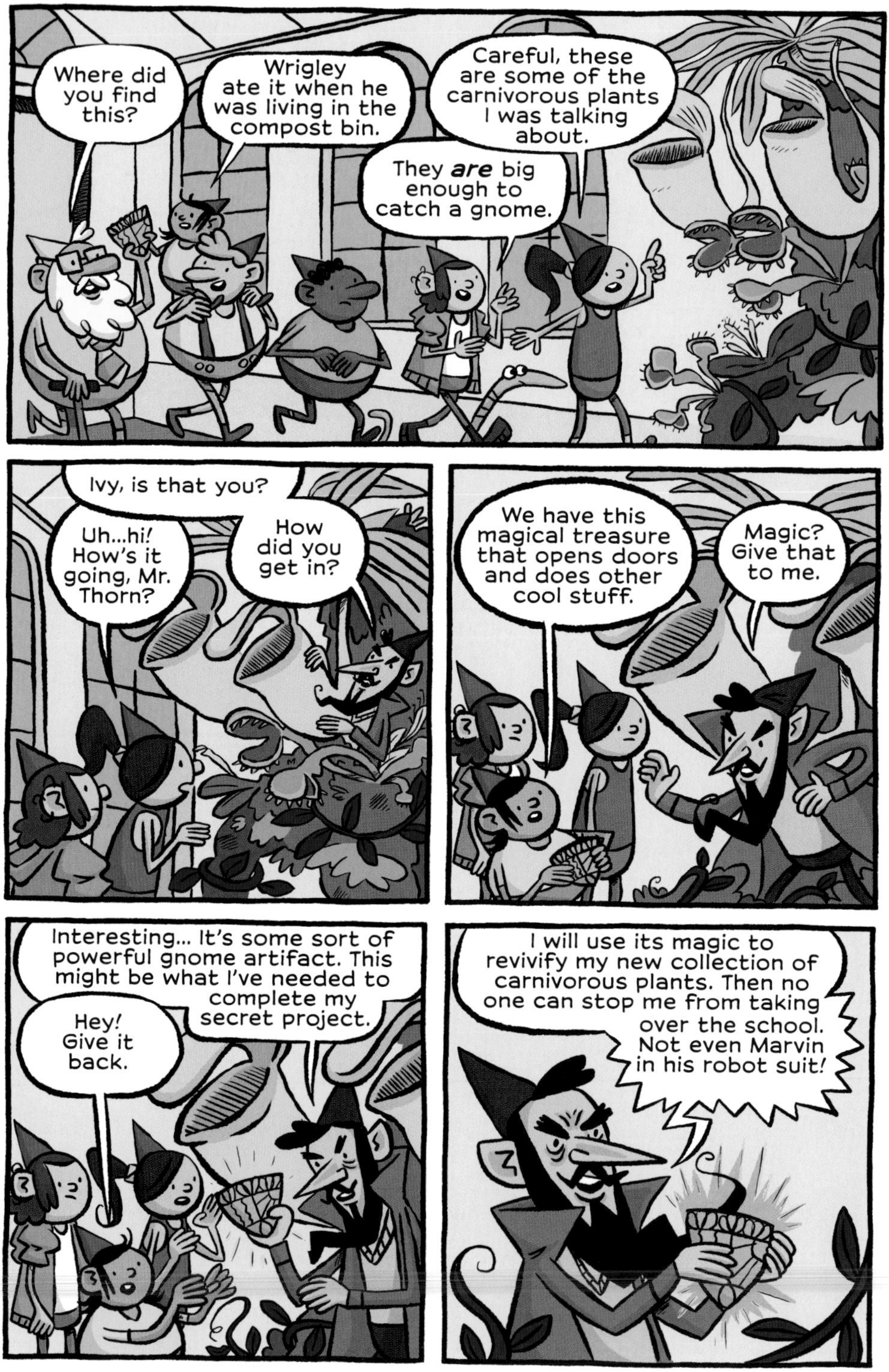

Where did you find this?
Wrigley ate it when he was living in the compost bin.
Careful, these are some of the carnivorous plants I was talking about.
They *are* big enough to catch a gnome.
Ivy, is that you?
Uh...hi! How's it going, Mr. Thorn?
How did you get in?
We have this magical treasure that opens doors and does other cool stuff.
Magic? Give that to me.
Interesting... It's some sort of powerful gnome artifact. This might be what I've needed to complete my secret project.
Hey! Give it back.
I will use its magic to revivify my new collection of carnivorous plants. Then no one can stop me from taking over the school. Not even Marvin in his robot suit!

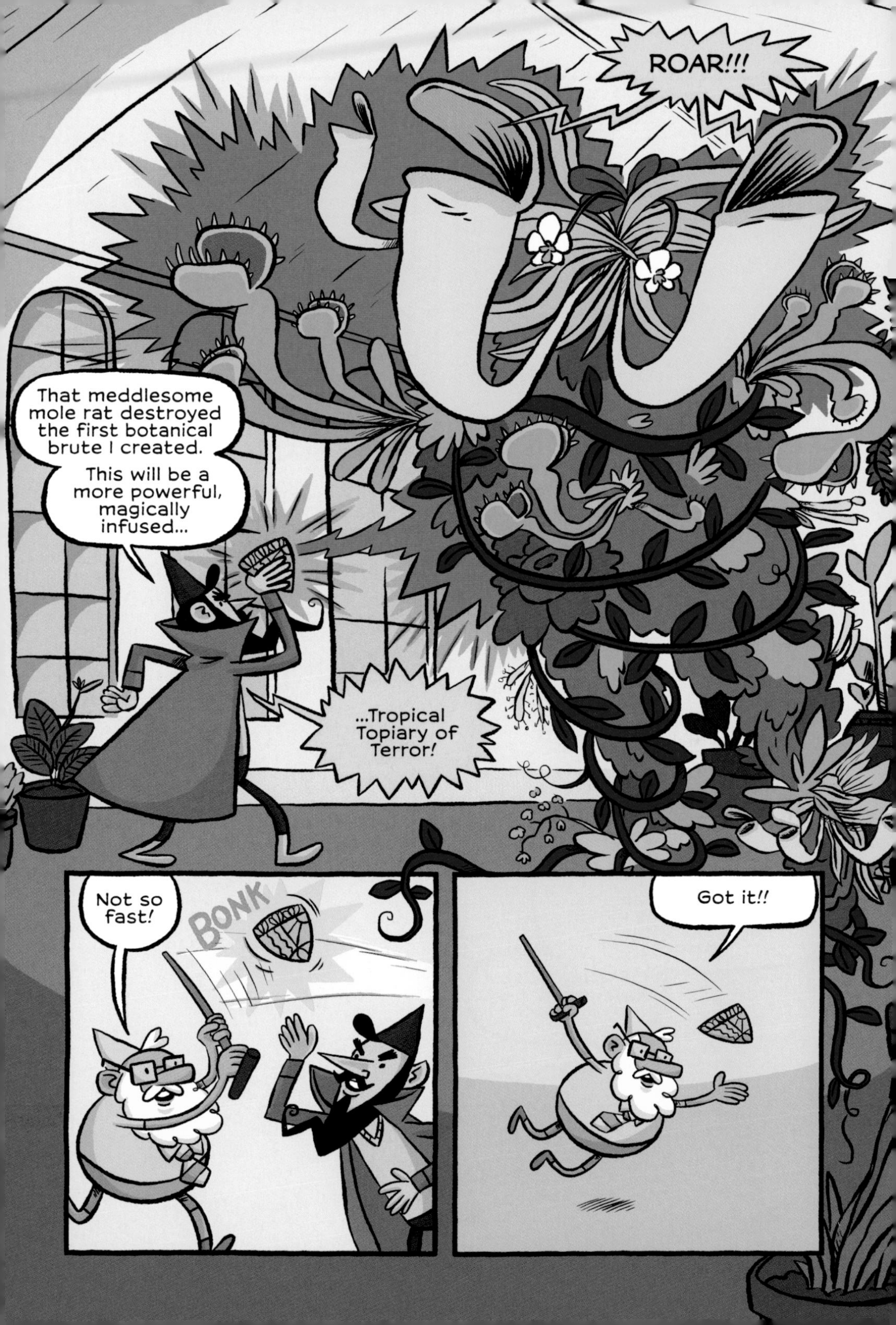
ROAR!!!
That meddlesome mole rat destroyed the first botanical brute I created.
This will be a more powerful, magically infused...
...Tropical Topiary of Terror!
Not so fast!
BONK
Got it!!

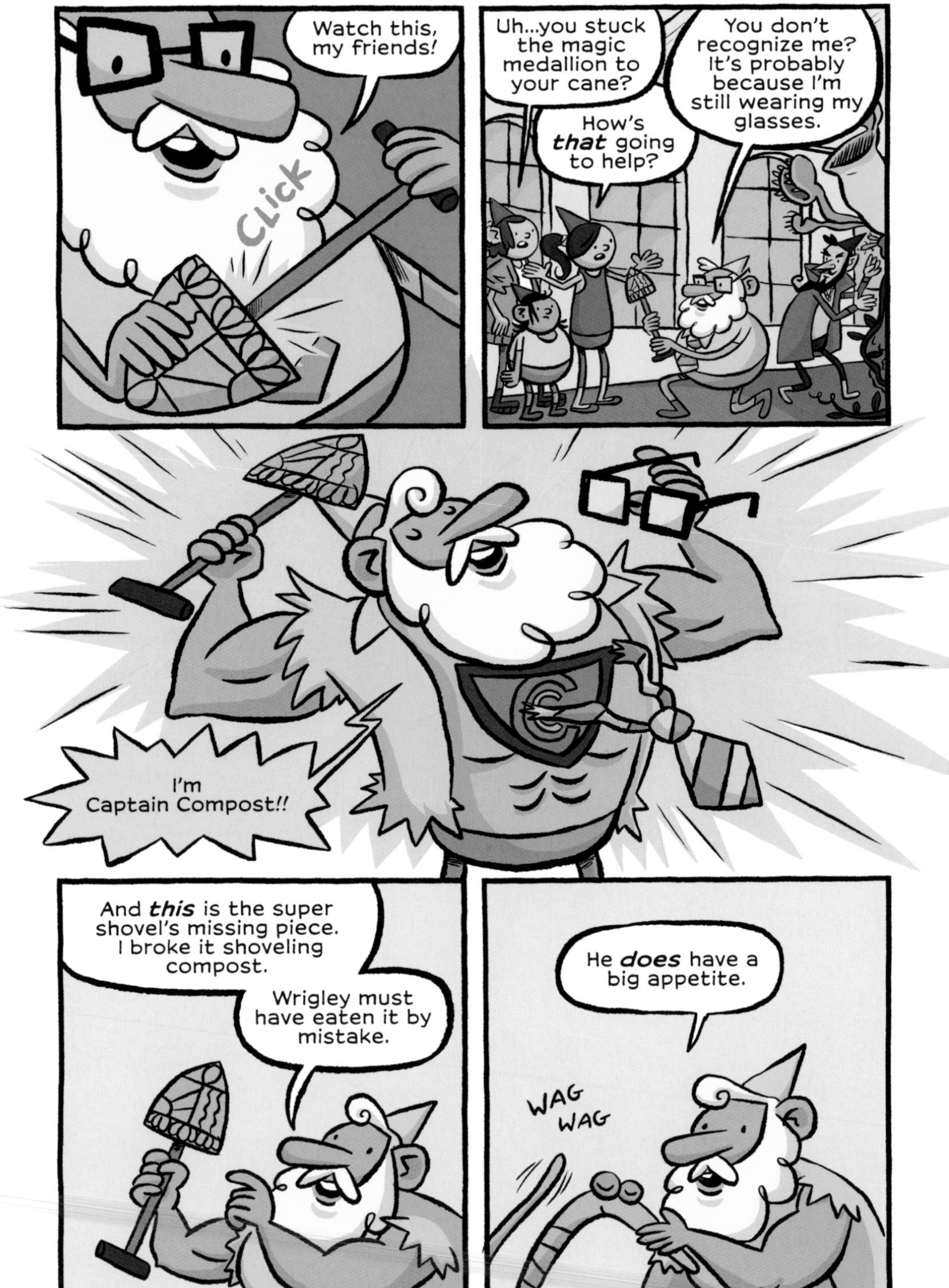

Watch this, my friends!
CLICK
Uh...you stuck the magic medallion to your cane?
How's *that* going to help?
You don't recognize me? It's probably because I'm still wearing my glasses.
I'm Captain Compost!!
And *this* is the super shovel's missing piece. I broke it shoveling compost.
Wrigley must have eaten it by mistake.
WAG WAG
He *does* have a big appetite.

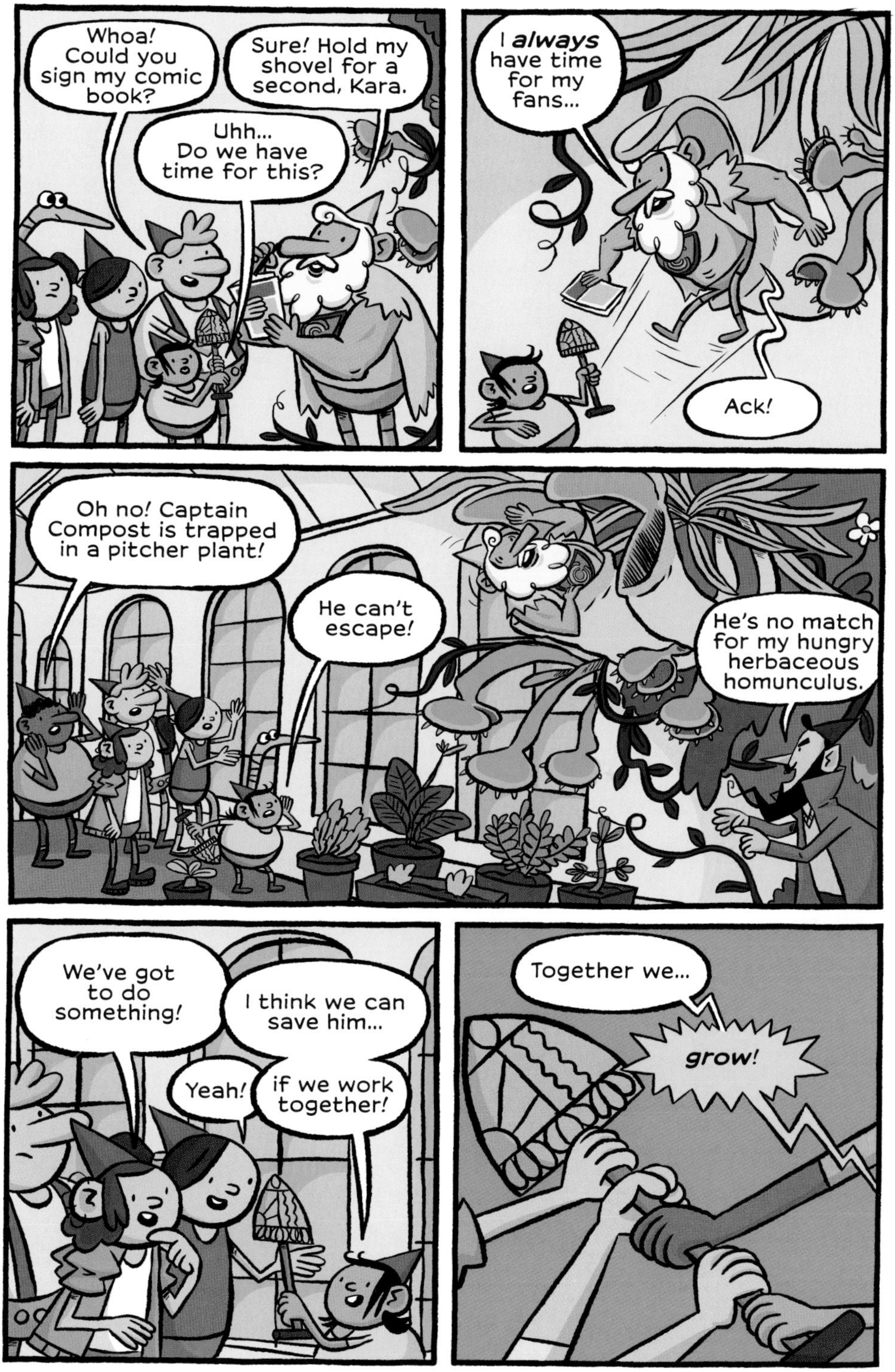
Whoa! Could you sign my comic book?
Sure! Hold my shovel for a second, Kara.
Uhh... Do we have time for this?
I *always* have time for my fans...
Ack!
Oh no! Captain Compost is trapped in a pitcher plant!
He can't escape!
He's no match for my hungry herbaceous homunculus.
We've got to do something!
I think we can save him...
Yeah!
if we work together!
Together we...
grow!

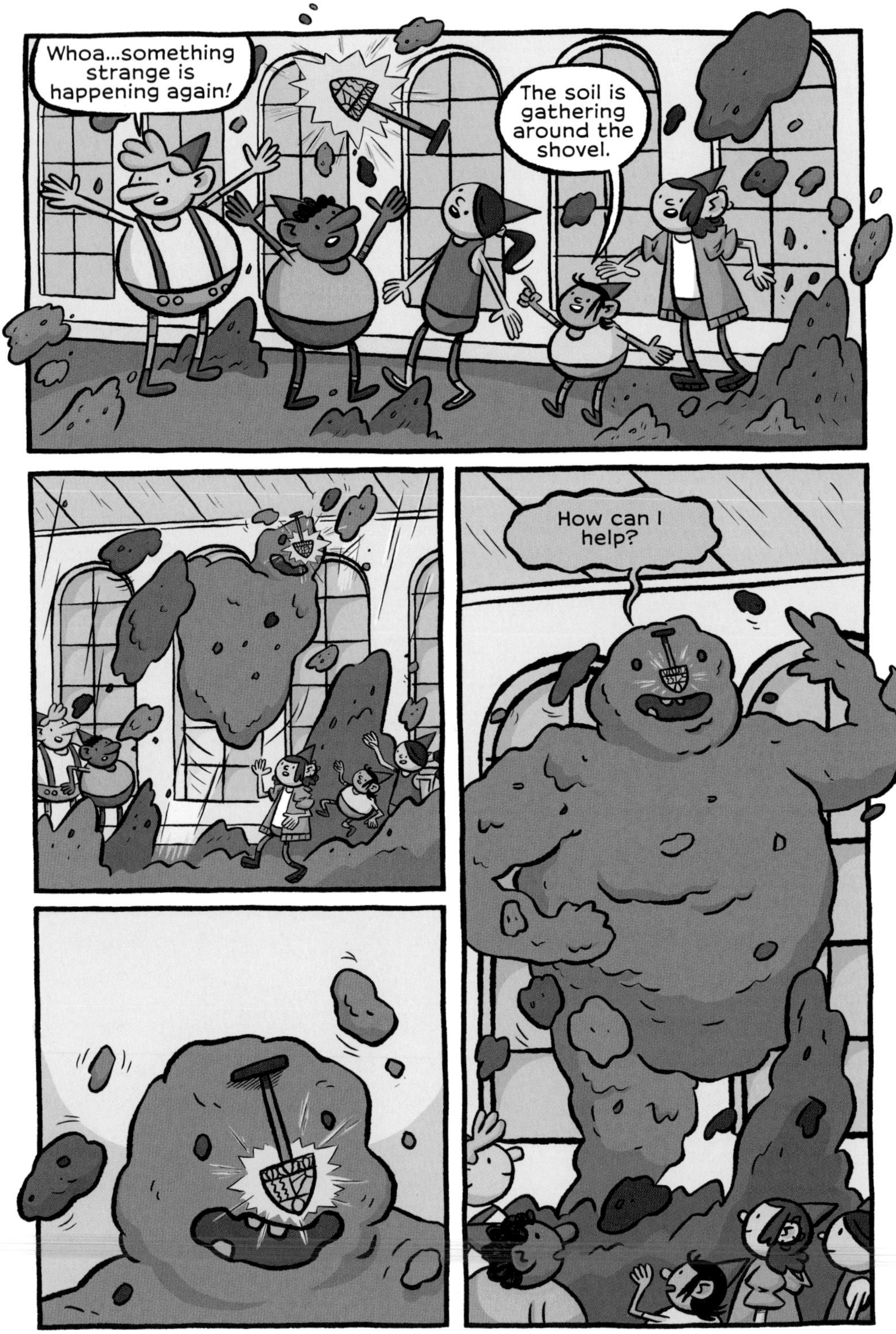
Whoa...something strange is happening again!
The soil is gathering around the shovel.
How can I help?

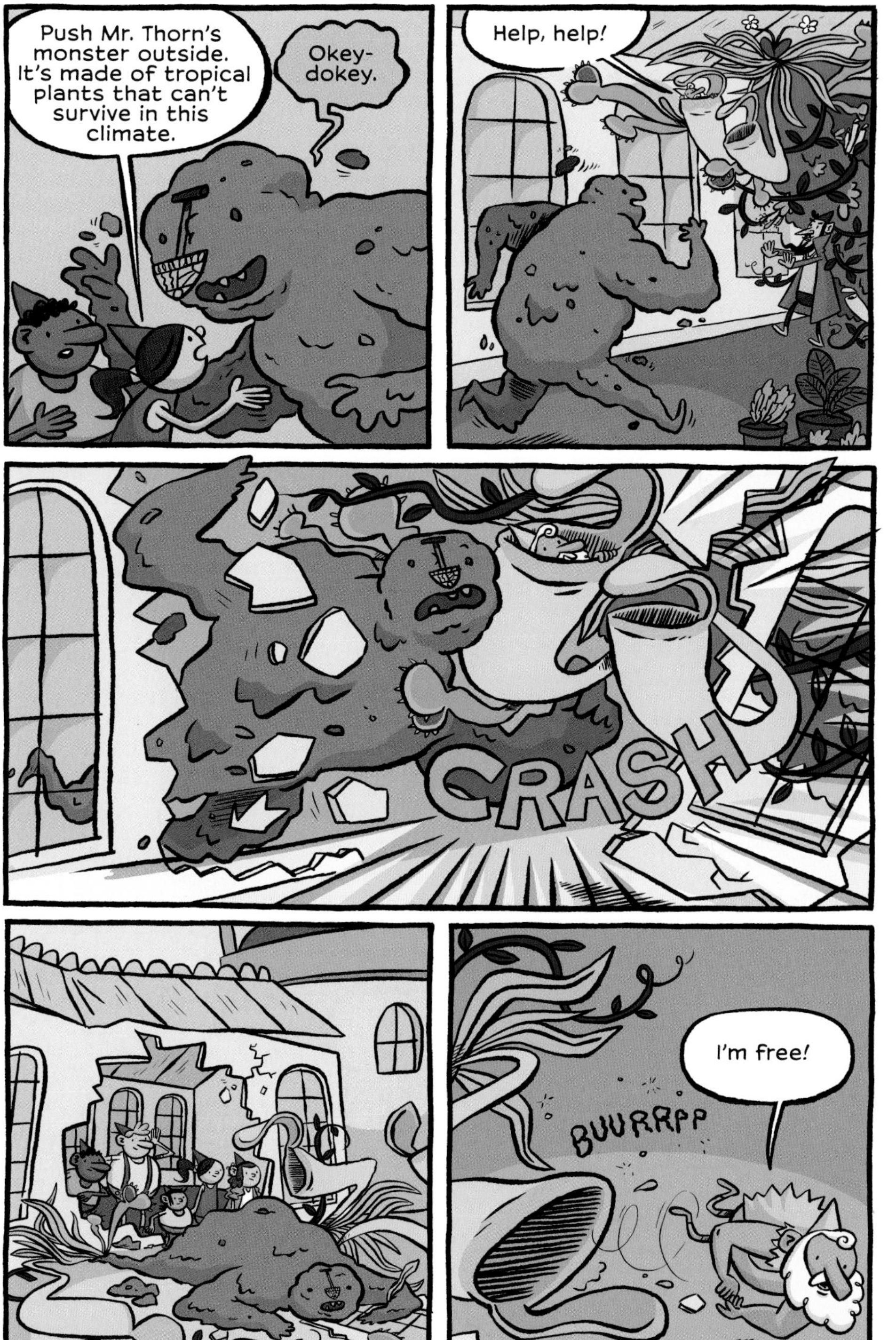
Push Mr. Thorn's monster outside. It's made of tropical plants that can't survive in this climate.
Okey-dokey.
Help, help!
CRASH
I'm free!
BUURRPP

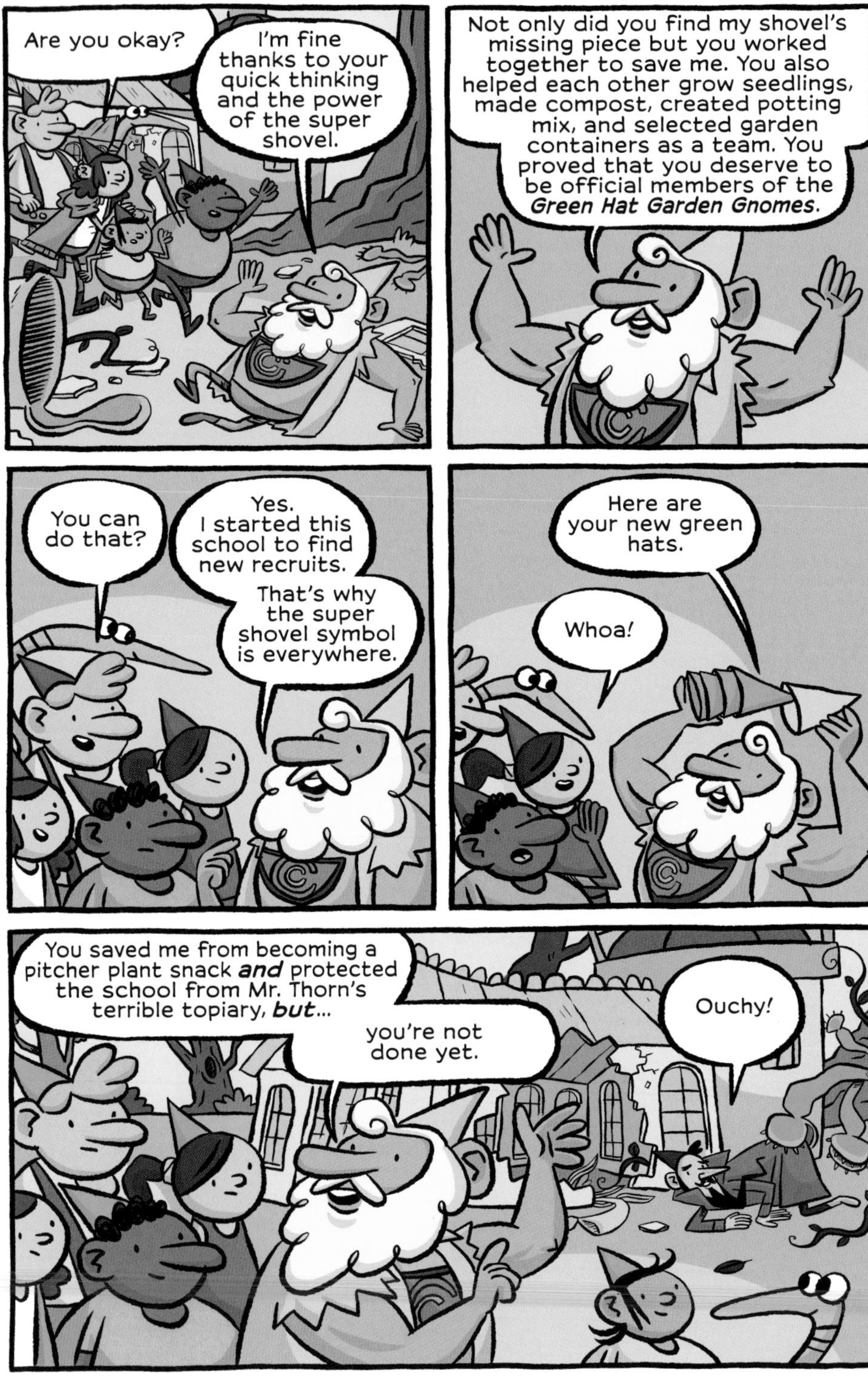
Are you okay?
I'm fine thanks to your quick thinking and the power of the super shovel.
Not only did you find my shovel's missing piece but you worked together to save me. You also helped each other grow seedlings, made compost, created potting mix, and selected garden containers as a team. You proved that you deserve to be official members of the *Green Hat Garden Gnomes*.
You can do that?
Yes. I started this school to find new recruits.
That's why the super shovel symbol is everywhere.
Here are your new green hats.
Whoa!
You saved me from becoming a pitcher plant snack ***and*** protected the school from Mr. Thorn's terrible topiary, ***but***...
you're not done yet.
Ouchy!

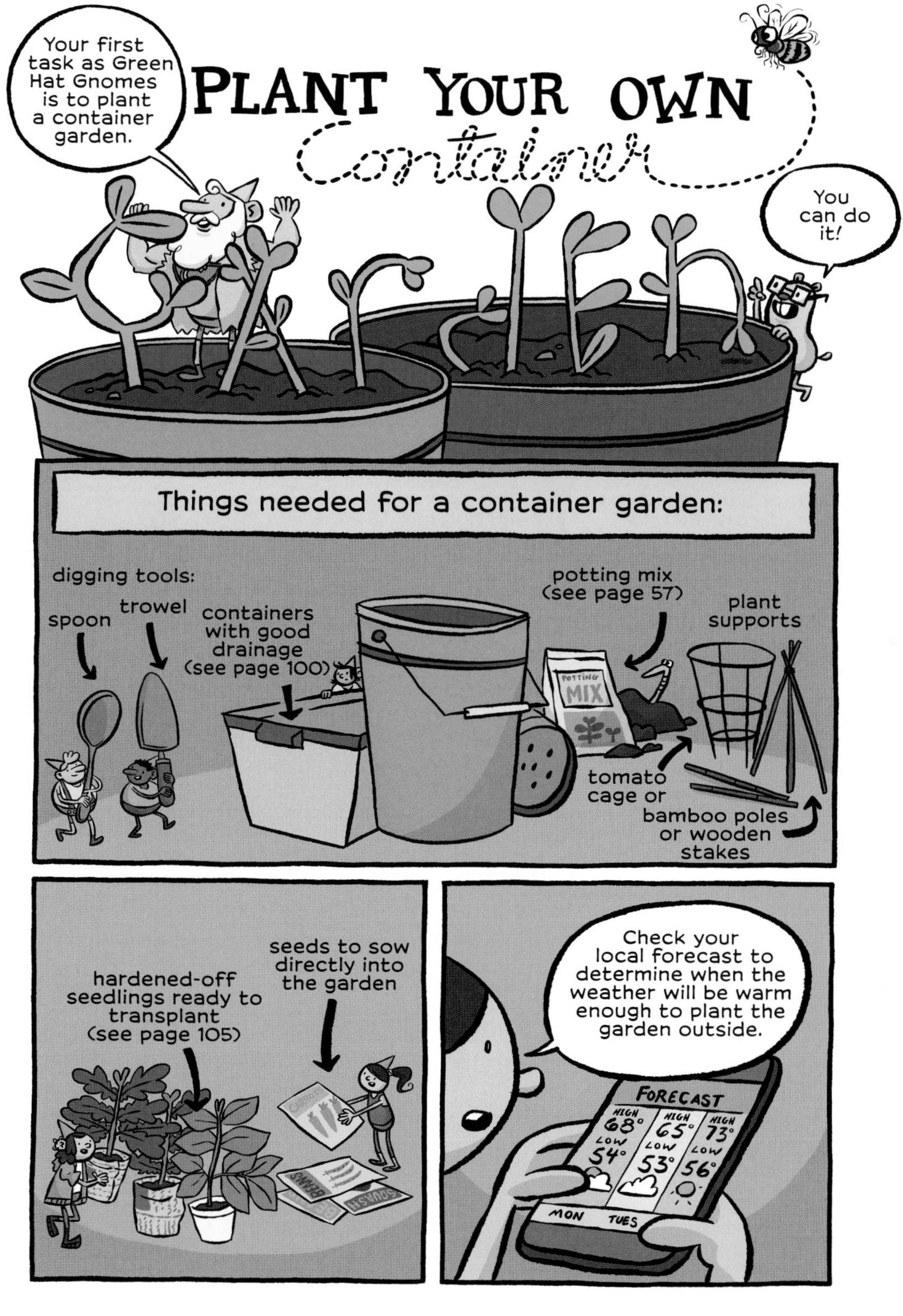

Your first task as Green Hat Gnomes is to plant a container garden.
PLANT YOUR OWN Container
You can do it!
Things needed for a container garden:
digging tools:
spoon
trowel
containers with good drainage (see page 100)
potting mix (see page 57)
POTTING MIX
plant supports
tomato cage or
bamboo poles or wooden stakes
hardened-off seedlings ready to transplant (see page 105)
seeds to sow directly into the garden
CARROTS
BEANS
SQUASH
Check your local forecast to determine when the weather will be warm enough to plant the garden outside.
FORECAST
HIGH 68° LOW 54°
HIGH 65° LOW 53°
HIGH 73° LOW 56°
MON
TUES

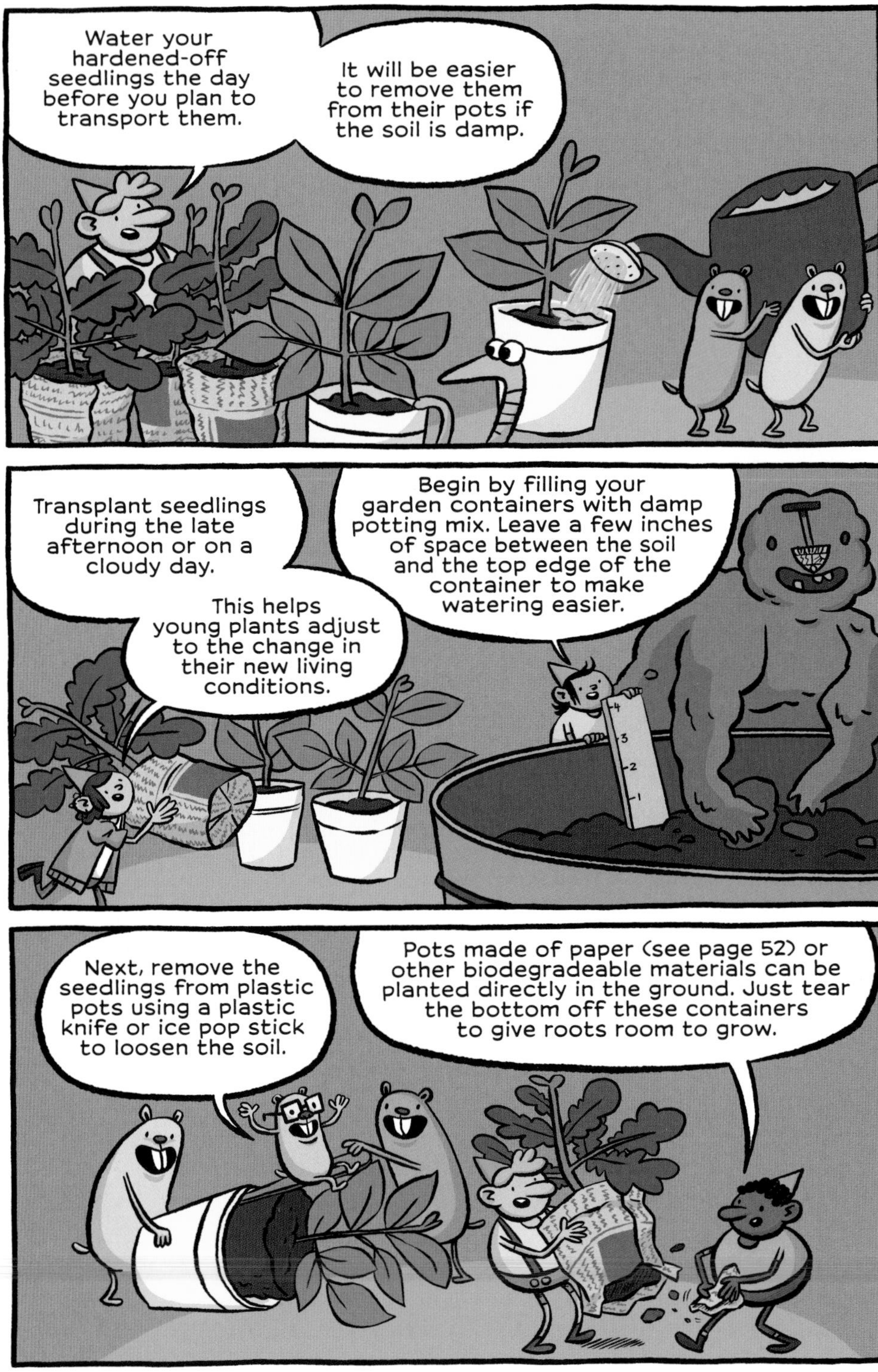
Water your hardened-off seedlings the day before you plan to transport them.
It will be easier to remove them from their pots if the soil is damp.
Transplant seedlings during the late afternoon or on a cloudy day.
This helps young plants adjust to the change in their new living conditions.
Begin by filling your garden containers with damp potting mix. Leave a few inches of space between the soil and the top edge of the container to make watering easier.
Next, remove the seedlings from plastic pots using a plastic knife or ice pop stick to loosen the soil.
Pots made of paper (see page 52) or other biodegradeable materials can be planted directly in the ground. Just tear the bottom off these containers to give roots room to grow.

Dig a hole large enough for the transplant's entire root ball.

Most seedlings should be planted at the same depth as they were in their pots.

But tomato transplants like having some of their stem buried.

remove bottom leaves

bury stem

After planting the seedlings, install supports for tall or climbing plants like tomatoes.

Give newly transplanted sprouts a good watering. Use a gentle shower to avoid disturbing the soil.

Stop watering when liquid starts to leak out from the drainage holes.

Empty any water collecting in trays sitting beneath the containers. Do not let them stand in pools of water.

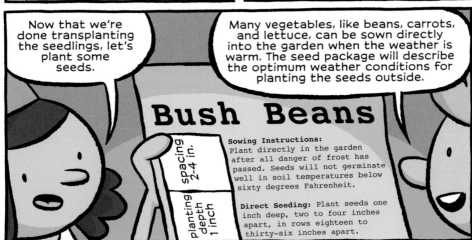

Now that we're done transplanting the seedlings, let's plant some seeds.

Many vegetables, like beans, carrots, and lettuce, can be sown directly into the garden when the weather is warm. The seed package will describe the optimum weather conditions for planting the seeds outside.

Bush Beans

planting depth 1 inch

spacing 2-4 in.

Sowing Instructions:
Plant directly in the garden after all danger of frost has passed. Seeds will not germinate well in soil temperatures below sixty degrees Fahrenheit.

Direct Seeding: Plant seeds one inch deep, two to four inches apart, in rows eighteen to thirty-six inches apart.

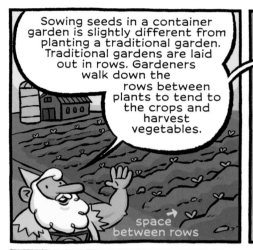

Sowing seeds in a container garden is slightly different from planting a traditional garden. Traditional gardens are laid out in rows. Gardeners walk down the rows between plants to tend to the crops and harvest vegetables.

space between rows

Container plants are accessible from all sides, so there's no need to plant seeds in rows.

easy access for harvesting and plant care

The sowing instructions on seed packages provide measurements for the spacing between plants.

Measure the spacing between the seeds you sow. Keep them the same distance away from the side of the containers, too.

Bush Beans

If you're having difficulty determining seed spacing, here are general measurements to use for a few popular crops:

Bush Beans

Bush Beans:
   2-4 inches apart
Broccoli:
   10 inches apart
Carrots:
   1-2 inches apart
Cucumbers:
   8-10 inches apart
Lettuce:
   4-9 inches apart
Peppers:
   8-10 inches apart
Squash:
   12-20 inches apart
Tomatoes:
   12-20 inches apart

Water seeds after sowing them.

Keep the soil moist (but not soggy) until they sprout.

Don't let the container dry out completely or it will be really difficult to get the potting mix wet again. After a few weeks, when the seedlings are established and have a few true leaves (see page 76), you can water less often.

water when top 1 inch of soil is dry.

During the hottest months of the summer, container gardens dry out quickly and might need water every day.

Try to water them during the morning when it's cooler.

Water in the soil will help plants endure the hot sun during the day.

Thanks for my morning drink.

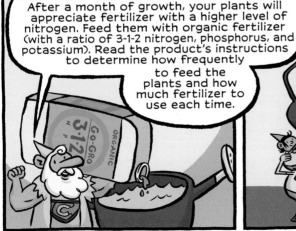

After a month of growth, your plants will appreciate fertilizer with a higher level of nitrogen. Feed them with organic fertilizer (with a ratio of 3-1-2 nitrogen, phosphorus, and potassium). Read the product's instructions to determine how frequently to feed the plants and how much fertilizer to use each time.

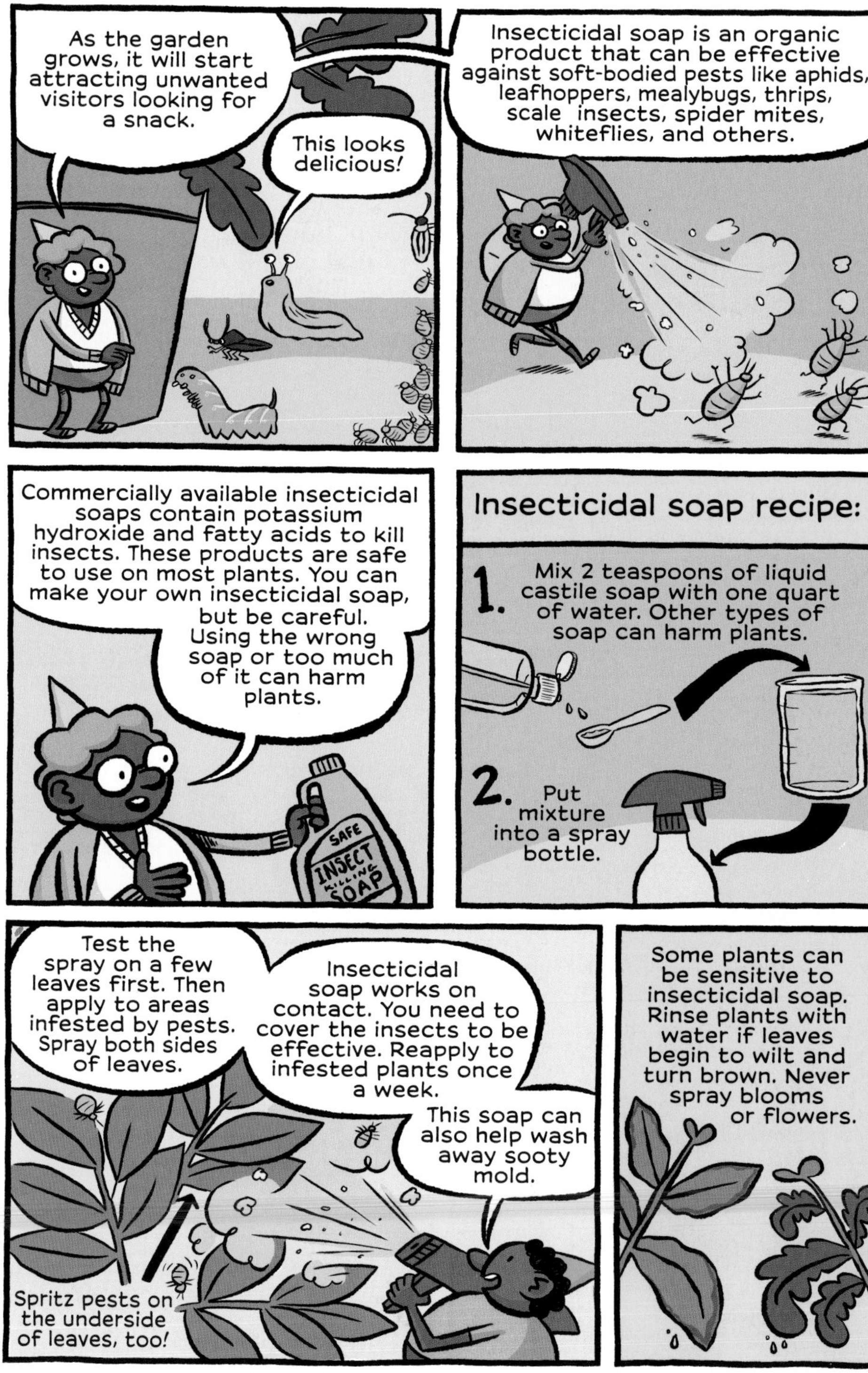

As the garden grows, it will start attracting unwanted visitors looking for a snack.
This looks delicious!
Insecticidal soap is an organic product that can be effective against soft-bodied pests like aphids, leafhoppers, mealybugs, thrips, scale insects, spider mites, whiteflies, and others.
Commercially available insecticidal soaps contain potassium hydroxide and fatty acids to kill insects. These products are safe to use on most plants. You can make your own insecticidal soap, but be careful. Using the wrong soap or too much of it can harm plants.
SAFE INSECT KILLING SOAP
Insecticidal soap recipe:
1. Mix 2 teaspoons of liquid castile soap with one quart of water. Other types of soap can harm plants.
2. Put mixture into a spray bottle.
Test the spray on a few leaves first. Then apply to areas infested by pests. Spray both sides of leaves.
Insecticidal soap works on contact. You need to cover the insects to be effective. Reapply to infested plants once a week.
This soap can also help wash away sooty mold.
Spritz pests on the underside of leaves, too!
Some plants can be sensitive to insecticidal soap. Rinse plants with water if leaves begin to wilt and turn brown. Never spray blooms or flowers.

The spray won't deter all hungry visitors. Sometimes, you just have to remove pests from your garden by hand.

slug

tomato hornworm

If the idea of touching slugs grosses you out, try these other methods to keep them away from the garden.

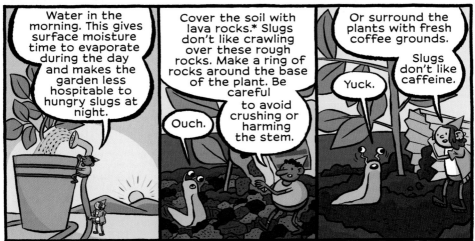

Water in the morning. This gives surface moisture time to evaporate during the day and makes the garden less hospitable to hungry slugs at night.

Cover the soil with lava rocks.* Slugs don't like crawling over these rough rocks. Make a ring of rocks around the base of the plant. Be careful to avoid crushing or harming the stem.

Ouch.

Or surround the plants with fresh coffee grounds.

Slugs don't like caffeine.

Yuck.

Whew, planting a garden is a lot of work.

Even a small gnome-sized one like this.

But all the time and energy we've spent growing strong seedlings, preparing good potting mix, and finding the sunniest spot for the garden will be worth it when we harvest our first crop of vegetables.

*You can buy lava rocks at gardening supply stores.

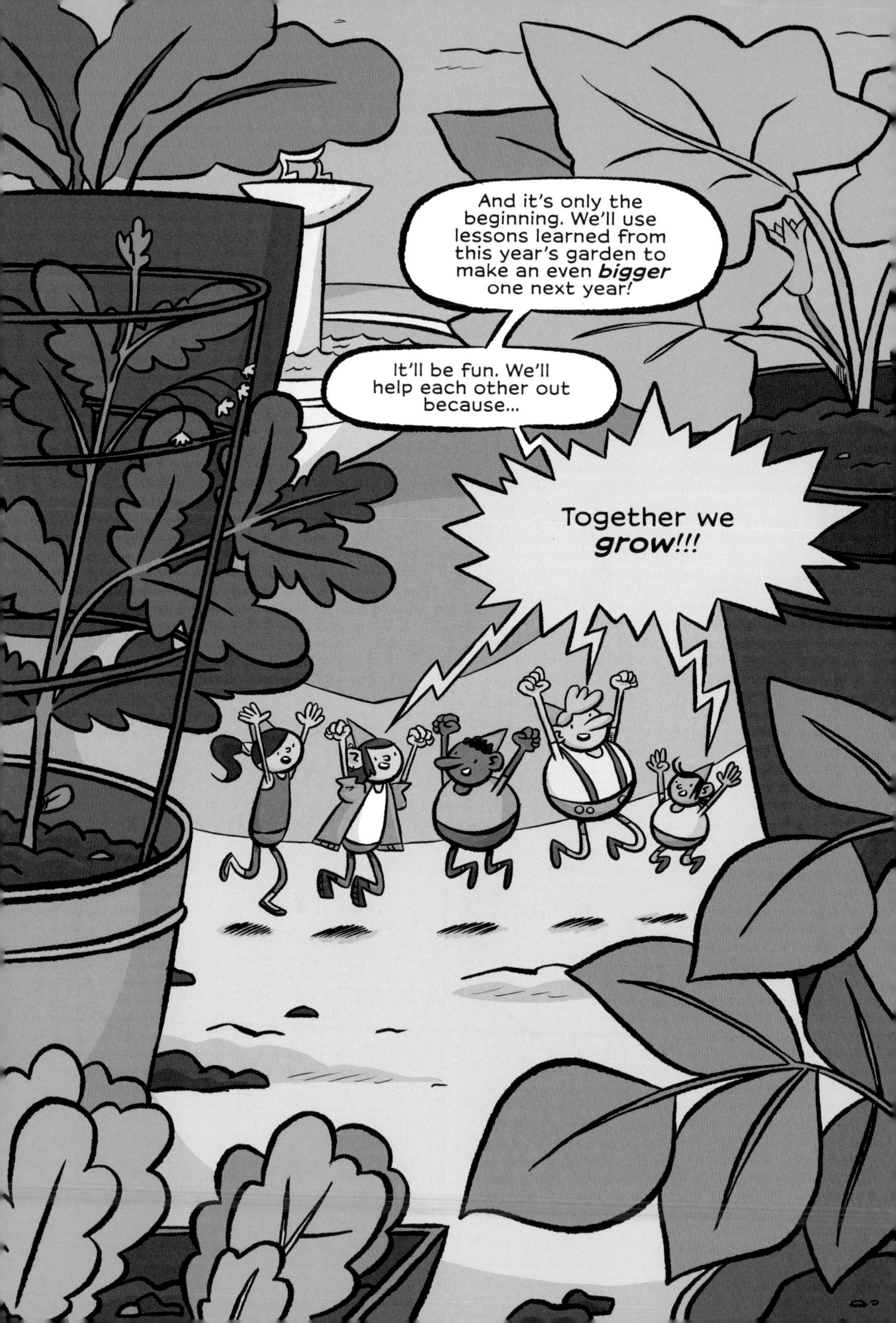
And it's only the beginning. We'll use lessons learned from this year's garden to make an even ***bigger*** one next year!
It'll be fun. We'll help each other out because...
Together we ***grow***!!!

You don't need access to Marvin's secret storage facility. Here are a few highly regarded seed suppliers you can order from.

Fedco Seeds—fedcoseeds.com/seeds
Based in Maine, Fedco is a good source for cold-hardy vegetables well suited for areas with a cooler climate like the Northeast. Their large selection of certified organic and heirloom seeds is available online.

High Mowing Seeds—highmowingseeds.com
High Mowing Seeds is a company with a strong focus on sustainable gardening and is a verified fully organic seed company.

Southern Exposure Seed Exchange—southernexposure.com
Located in Virginia, this company offers many varieties of heirloom and organic vegetable seeds. They emphasize varieties that perform well in the mid-Atlantic and Southeast.

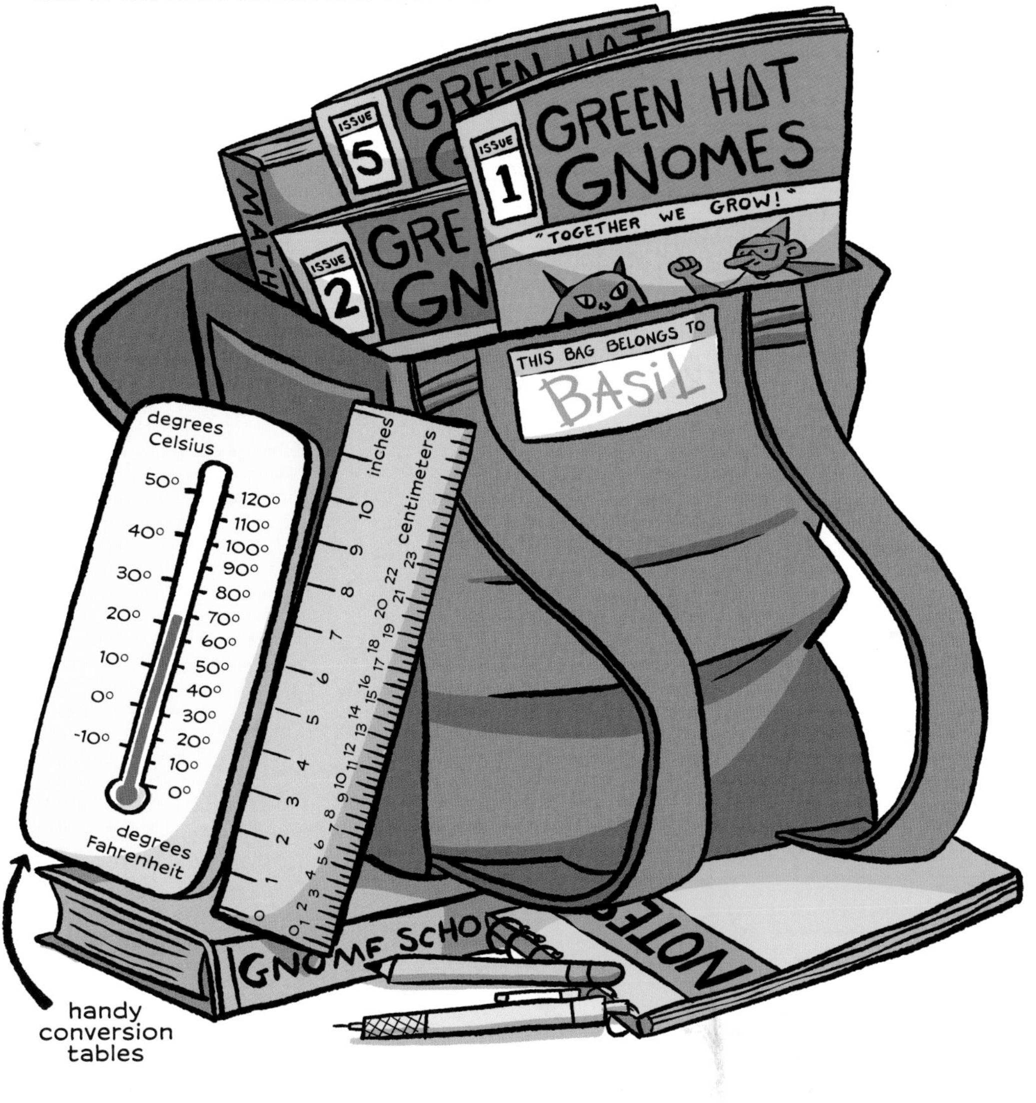
GREEN HAT GNOMES
ISSUE 1
"TOGETHER WE GROW!"
ISSUE 5
ISSUE 2
MATH
THIS BAG BELONGS TO
BASIL
degrees Celsius
degrees Fahrenheit
inches
centimeters
GNOME SCHO
NOTE
handy conversion tables

For K and C
Together we grow!

First Second

All instructions included in this book are provided as a resource for parents and children.
While all due care has been taken, we recommend that an adult supervise children at
all times when following the instructions in this book. The projects in this book are not
recommended for children three years and under due to potential choking hazard. Neither
the authors nor the publisher accept any responsibility for any loss, injury, or damages
sustained by anyone resulting from the instructions contained in this book.

Published by First Second
First Second is an imprint of Roaring Brook Press,
a division of Holtzbrinck Publishing Holdings Limited Partnership
120 Broadway, New York, NY 10271

Don't miss your next favorite book from First Second! For the latest updates go to
firstsecondnewsletter.com and sign up for our enewsletter.

All rights reserved

Library of Congress Control Number: 2019930671

Paperback ISBN: 978-1-250-15214-5
Hardcover ISBN: 978-1-250-15213-8

Our books may be purchased in bulk for promotional, educational, or business use.
Please contact your local bookseller or the Macmillan Corporate and Premium Sales Department
at (800) 221-7945 ext. 5442 or by email at MacmillanSpecialMarkets@macmillan.com.

First edition, 2020
Edited by Robyn Chapman and Bethany Bryan
Expert consultation by Margaret Roach
Cover design by Andrew Arnold
Interior book design by Alexis Frederick-Frost and Rob Steen

Printed in the United States of America by Worzalla, Stevens Point, Wisconsin

Created in Photoshop. Inked digitally using a Wacom Intuos tablet and stylus with flex nib and Kyle Webster's
Classic Cartoonist digital brush. Colored with Kyle Webster's PRO comics inker digital brush.

Paperback: 10 9 8 7 6 5 4 3
Hardcover: 10 9 8 7 6 5 4 3 2 1